M000282262

B is for Bauhaus,
Y is for YouTube
Designing the Modern World, from A to Z

Deyan Sudjic

Rizzoli
ex libris

Published in the United States of
America in 2015
By Rizzoli Ex Libris, an imprint of
Rizzoli International Publications, Inc.
300 Park Avenue South
New York, NY 10010
www.rizzoliusa.com

First published in Great Britain by
Particular Books, an imprint of
Penguin Books Ltd, 2014

2015 2016 2017 2018 / 10 9 8 7 6
5 4 3 2 1

Distributed in the U.S. trade by Random
House, New York
Printed in U.S.A.

ISBN-13: 978-0-8478-4551-4
Library of Congress Catalog Control
Number: 2014944525

Contents

Preface by Deyan Sudjic ix

A is for Authentic 1

B is for Bauhaus 21

B is for *Blueprint* 41

C is for Car 61

C is for Chair 75

C is for Chareau 89

C is for Collecting 97

C is for Critical Design 121

D is for Design 137

D is for Design Art 151

E is for Expo 169

F is for Fashion 179

F is for Film 187

F is for Function 197

G is for *Grand Theft Auto* 211

H is for Habitat 219

I is for Imperfect 229

J is for Jim Nature 239

J is for Jumbo 245

K is for Kaplický 253

K is for Kitchen 259
K is for Krier 267
L is for Logo 281
M is for Manifesto 289
M is for Museum 305
N is for National Identity 319
O is for Ornament 335
P is for Postmodern 347
Q is for QWERTY 363
R is for Rams 377
S is for Slum 387
S is for Sottsass 403
T is for Taste 417
U is for Utzon 427
V is for Vienna 437
W is for War 443
X is for Xerox 447
Y is for YouTube 457
Z is for Zip 463
Acknowledgements 473

Preface

The book is far from dead. The tactile values of ink on paper, of carefully designed covers, of lavish typography and production quality retain their appeal in a world which is still charmed by the analogue, despite the triumph of the digital. But I am not so sure about the dictionary, which does indeed look as if its print format is moribund. Seven years ago, at just about the time I became the director of the Design Museum in London, I signed a contract with my current British publisher to do two books. The first, titled the *Language of Things*, came relatively easily. It gave me the chance to explore the various messages, from gender to politics, that design can express. Book two was more of a problem. The commission was to deliver a massive 250,000-word conventional dictionary of design.

It was daunting, and it took a while to get started – by hiring an assistant to get into the research. But a couple of years later my publisher's managing director called me:

"People have stopped buying dictionaries," he said. "There is this thing called Wikipedia. Of course you can keep the advance, and if you really want to, go ahead and do a dictionary. But really, you might think about something else."

And there it was: the dictionary had become the first victim of the digital explosion in publishing.

B is for Bauhaus, Y is for YouTube is what finally emerged from that hiatus. And it isn't a dictionary. The dictionary once gave the appearance of objectivity; but few dictionaries have been read for pleasure. *B is for Bauhaus . . .* takes the apparently banal format of an alphabetically ordered A-to-Z to structure a series of essays that explores what are, at least for me, some of the essential ideas that underpin the meanings of contemporary design and architecture.

It's also a chance to use my own experiences – reading Reyner Banham for the first time as a schoolboy in West London, starting *Blueprint* magazine with Peter Murray and Simon Esterson – in many of those essays. I remembered the day I saw Wally Olins and Michael Wolff capture the essence of branding when they mocked up a bottle of aspirin in a typographic style associated with whisky, and vice versa. I reflected on my first job at the *Sunday Times,* writing the obituary of my formidably talented predecessor Ian Nairn, and at the fickleness with which critical reputations are treated.

It allowed me to explore the concept of authenticity from the moment I was seduced into buying a vintage Korean War–era US Army parka. Not because it was a chance to revisit the youth that I never had as a Vespa-riding mod, even though I grew up in the same west London suburb as The Who, but because in its apparent rejection of the obvious seductions of consumerism, the parka – with its narrative label in the place of a brand, its impressive brass zip, complete with six-inch fabric cord, designed to be manipulated by hands protected from the cold by gloves – had the charms of authenticity. It is the quality that all designers value and pursue, and through their endless exploration of it, make its very presence impossible. Design's pursuit of authenticity, in fact, makes designers into endlessly inventive fakers.

Proceeding through the alphabet, this book does indeed touch upon "B is for Bauhaus," but as much through an exploration of the significance of a massive exhibition catalogue for the Bauhaus show I saw in London as a schoolboy as through an objective appraisal of the movement. I am equally fascinated by the significance of collection, of the squalor of car interiors, and the impact of a Qwerty keyboard on my approach to writing.

This is a book that reflects my life over the last thirty years as a critic and a curator, and is written from the vantage point of the Design Museum. There is no better place to look at the constantly fluctuating, endlessly fascinating world of design.

is for **AUTHENTIC**

I have a green fishtail parka that I bought in a shop on a backstreet by a canal in Milan. It was hanging on a rack, alongside a couple of elderly flying suits, a selection of brand-new khaki vests, and some second-hand cargo pants. It is the coat – sometimes called the snorkel because it comes with a built-in fur-trimmed hood – that the American army wore to the Korean War. I wanted it because the cuffs are held in place by strips of webbing and slightly chipped green buttons, because it has a detachable rust-coloured quilted nylon lining, and because it has a complicated stock number with a narrative description of the garment, and its function instead of a maker's brand name on the label.

The fact that it had been worn by at least one previous owner, and probably several others, before me did not detract from its charm. It has a heavy brass zip and popper studs, details that are too costly to have been specified by any but a military user free of the usual budget constraints of retailing.

I grew up in the same west London suburb that produced the Who, but I was not a mod. I wear my parka now, not because I feel nostalgic about teenage memories of the mirror-decked Vespa that I never had, but because every time I pull the zip with the six-inch-long green braided cord, designed to be used in conditions that would be unendurably cold without gloves, I have a sense of the thoughtfulness that went into every detail. The parka seems like a garment beyond fashion, yet it is a category that has clearly taken a conspicuous place in the language of fashion. The parka is far removed from its Inuit origins and its subsequent military incarnation, so much so that it now carries multiple mutually contradictory meanings. It is both authentic and self-conscious, the sign of a youthful hipster, and an ageing museum director.

I wear it to the embarrassment of my family, who find it a little unseemly. I wear it because it seems somehow 'real'. But for all I know, the authenticity that attracted me in the first place could have been lovingly and inventively faked.

'Authenticity' is a word that makes no promises about performance. It might not necessarily involve beauty, but it does suggest an irresistible combination of sincerity with authority. In the world of mass-produced objects, these are highly desirable qualities. Even if they are slippery and hard to define, grasping them is essential to an understanding of the nature of design.

Authenticity is a guarantee that an object really is what it purports to be. The more authentic it is, the more secure we can feel about its price, if not its value. But when factories make large numbers of identical objects over long periods of time, a gap opens up between what might be called the original and the authentic. Sometimes authenticity is understood as the degree to which an artefact succeeds in replicating the bloom of the factory-fresh perfection that a mass-produced object has when it is new, but which it quickly loses in use. In other contexts, authenticity is measured by the degree to which the physical remains of an object have survived, no matter how decayed they have become. Along with patina, holy relics acquire a sense of sanctity over time. The decayed remains of an ancient chair are regarded as more authentic than a polished but fake whole. Authenticity can have mutually contradictory definitions. It can be found in the making of a faithful replica of what an object once was, or in the careful maintenance of what that object has become as the result of the passing of time.

The outputs of the Bugatti car factory in the Alsace between 1909 and 1940, or those, slightly later, of Jean Prouvé's furniture workshops in Nancy, are as highly prized as works of art. As a result, they are just as much the target of fakers and forgers.

Ettore Bugatti kept careful records of exactly how many cars he built, month by month. Even so, the price that the real thing now commands has ensured that it is not just Bugatti's wrecks and write-offs that are being 'authentically' restored. Entirely new cars have come into being, many of which are now passed off as originals. Sometimes they have fragments of authentic cars incorporated into them, fragments that might carry an original chassis number. But the body, the seats and most of the mechanical parts are either new or else have been salvaged from another car. In either case, they look just like the cars that were made in Bugatti's day, and have been restored using the same techniques and skills. It's not because they are essentially new that they are fakes in the eyes of the specialists, it is because they are missing that vital chassis number, or because the number has already been used on a car with better provenance.

The argument about the nature of authenticity

applies to buildings too. The issue here is more a reflection of cultural values than it is of price. In Japan, the Ise Grand Shrine is rebuilt plank by plank, at twenty-year intervals, yet is understood as retaining its original spirit, even if every piece of timber that goes into it is new. In Western Europe, authentic restoration has a different meaning. Rather than make old buildings look new, and so diminish the significance of the authentically old, William Morris and the Society for the Protection of Ancient Buildings campaigned for less drastic forms of restoration. They wanted new work to look like what it was, and not to pretend that it was something it was not, which is to say, old.

George Gilbert Scott set about a campaign to rebuild Britain's cathedrals as he thought they ought to have been, rather than repair what they had become. He was pitting one version of authenticity against its mirror opposite. He was ready to demolish genuine Perpendicular additions to Early English structures, and to replace them with his version of what he believed would have been built had the eleventh-century architects ever got around to finishing what they had started.

By the time Scott got to Tewkesbury, his scorched-earth version of authenticity had at last provoked his opponents to set up SPAB to try to stop him. The approach that they proposed has set the ground rules for an intellectually engaged approach to restoration ever since. But it still has to convince some people. When the Design Museum brought one of Jean Prouvé's prefabricated Maisons Tropicales to London, we found that it had been restored so ruthlessly that a bullet hole in one of the doors was the only visible proof that it wasn't a brand-new structure. The house had been acquired by an American collector from a French antique dealer who had tracked it down to Brazzaville. The dealer persuaded the previous owner to sell and cleaned it up with such vigour that there was little sign of what the house had been through.

It is an approach shared by many car collectors who treat restoration as if it were a surgical facelift, preferring the glossy sheen of perfection rather than letting any traces of age show through. They inject the bonnet with the heritage equivalent of Botox.

In the case of the kind of furniture designed by the pioneers of modernism, definitions of authenticity are even harder to pin down. Mies van der Rohe, Le Corbusier and Marcel Breuer all claimed to have been motivated by the democratic potential of mass production and the abolition of handwork. Their designs were made in various factories during their lifetimes, each producing objects that were a little different from earlier versions. The rights to produce 'authentic' versions of their designs were bought and sold, sometimes several times, and in some cases passed out of any control. Faced with multiple versions of an original design, the question of which of them is the most authentic is not easily answered, especially when some of these versions were made in tens or even hundreds of thousands.

An authentic example of a chaise longue attributed to Le Corbusier, Charlotte Perriand and Pierre Jeanneret, for instance, might be understood to be restricted to one of the number made during their lifetimes, under their direct supervision. Alternatively it could be one made today that is licensed by the *Fondation Le Corbusier*, the official guardian of the architect's archive, and the owner of some of his copyrights. But there are also unauthorized versions of his chairs, for which no royalties are paid to the copyright holders, that are more faithful to what they once looked like than are the present-day official versions. The variations between them can be substantial. The cushions are stuffed with foam rather than the original feathers. The standard diameters of steel tube have changed since the 1920s. As a result, manufacturers who produce a version with new steel, with foam cushions and a foot detail that is not the same as the one that was used in the 1920s, can still prosecute those who use authentic materials but do not have the legal right to the design. Authenticity in this context is a guarantee of legitimacy and of price rather than of always following the original intentions of the designer.

And what if the designers were still alive, and had consented to modify a design to take account of contemporary production methods? Would it be their first or second idea that was the more authentic? It's a dilemma that faces a few architects, such as Norman Foster and Richard Rogers, who find that their early work is now officially protected from unauthorized alterations by the listing process. They have to apply for permission from English Heritage to make changes to their own work.

Art asks questions about the nature of authenticity that are no less tortuous. So much so that authenticity itself has become a key subject matter for art. Artists constantly play with appropriating images from mass culture, and then from each other's works that are based on those appropriated images. The Warhol Foundation, established by the artist's executors after his death, acted for many years as a contemporary version of the Spanish Inquisition, setting up an Authentication Board that deliberated on which works purported to be by Warhol were actually to be considered authentic and those which failed the test. Those judged to pass as devout after having been shown the instruments were admitted to the canon. Those that failed were returned to their supplicant owners, stamped with the fatal word 'DENIED'. It was a practice that provoked more than one lawsuit protesting that the foundation was maintaining the value of its own holdings of work by Warhol by limiting supply from other sources. Defending itself against the legal challenges eventually proved so costly that the foundation abandoned its authenticating role. The art critic Richard Dorment published a very damaging attack on the foundation in the *New York Review of Books* in which he demonstrated that the board had authenticated works which it had previously rejected to allow them to be sold as genuine.

For an artist, authenticity is a question about the very nature of things. In Stockholm's Moderna Museet there is a room with a multiple-Marilyn image on one wall, and a stack of Brillo boxes in the opposite corner. Nobody doubts that the Marilyns are Warhol's work. The boxes' authenticity is less clear. The caption says in two languages that they are by Warhol, and were donated by Pontus Hulten, the museum's founding director, but that in itself is enough to raise questions.

Hulten was one of the most influential curators of the second half of the twentieth century, responsible not just for the establishment of the Moderna Museet, but also of the Pompidou Centre in Paris, and the Museum of Contemporary Art in Los Angeles. He gave Warhol his first major European exhibition in 1968, and these Brillo boxes are some of its most highly contested results. Hulten claimed they were first shown in the exhibition that he curated in Sweden, but his detractors say they were made just afterwards. They are not the same Brillo boxes that Warhol had made for the Stable Gallery in New York in 1964, when he copied actual Brillo boxes to make a point about repetition. It would have been too expensive to ship them from America, so according to Hulten the 1968 exhibit featured Swedish-made copies of Warhol's New York copies of real Brillo boxes, authorized by Warhol, alongside 500 cardboard cartons acquired from Brillo as props. But when the exhibition travelled to other venues, Hulten made further Brillo boxes without telling Warhol. It is examples of these versions that appeared on the art market after Hulten's death, causing something of a scandal. Were they authentic fakes of an authentic fake of an authentic fake, or were they fakes of an authentic fake of an authentic fake? What was especially troubling for Hulten's admirers was the possibility that his, at best morally questionable, action had undermined the power of Warhol's original idea, though Hulten had done so much to promote the artist.

Across the corridor from the Brillo boxes is another gallery with four works on the walls. Not only do they look like Warhol's work they were made using the same silk screens that Warhol's assistants used, the same inks, and the same techniques. But in fact they are acknowledged as the work of Elaine Sturtevant, the American artist who has made her entire career out of appropriating the work of other artists.

Sturtevant, by declaring her work as not being by Warhol, is establishing that her work is neither a fake, nor a tribute, but is an assault on the whole quasi-moralistic idea of authenticity, with its connotations of the legitimacy of birth in wedlock. Warhol himself sometimes referred questions about his techniques to Sturtevant, suggesting that she knew as much about them as he did.

With mass production, the point is usually not one of originality, but of what is fake and what is not. There are plenty of stalls in Shanghai or Shenzhen where you can find alleged Rolex wristwatches complete with impressive-looking authenticating holograms that crumble the first time you try the winding mechanism. There are what look something like Apple iPods but which are not produced in the Shenzhen factory that assembles those sold by the company Steve Jobs and Steve Wozniak started in 1976. More worrying for Apple was the way in which Samsung was able to replicate not just the iPhone but also the iPad. Apple claimed that they are copyright infringements, rather than fakes.

For a designer, authenticity has taken on a paradoxical aspect. An authentic design might be understood as a design which is more than merely not a fake. It is also an object which is unselfconscious, one which is not shaped by a desire to please or to seduce. This is a quality which depends on responding with a certain sincerity to the practical questions that are raised by providing a serviceable solution to a technical problem. Yet design is a highly self-conscious business, one that can barely help itself but attempt to manipulate the emotions. The very involvement of a designer in the creation of an object militates against this kind of authenticity. Design cannot but have the most knowing of views of the world. Even to acknowledge that a designer is pursuing the quality of authenticity is to undermine that objective. Striving for authenticity signals its antithesis.

The Bugatti name is in the hands of Volkswagen, a company which uses the brand for exceptionally expensive two-seater sports cars, built in tiny numbers, in sharp distinction to its primary business of making cars in their millions for a mass audience. The associations with elegantly engineered cars from the past give Bugatti's horseshoe-shaped radiator grille and the red-and-white enamel badge a value for Volkswagen. They add distinction to its range, but these are no more 'authentic' Bugattis than the Bentleys which are also made in a factory owned by Volkswagen are 'authentic' Bentleys in the sense that the original company would have understood them in the 1920s.

During the civil strife in the Britain of the 1980s, the Metropolitan Police became concerned enough about

how they were perceived by the public to look to designers for help in presenting themselves in a more sympathetic
way. While the Home Secretary ordered the police to recon-
sider their racial-profiling strategies, one of the more daring
members of New Scotland Yard's senior staff went to Wolff
Olins, the same brand consultancy that had given a building company called Bovis a hummingbird for a logo, and
which had designed the look of petrol stations and budget
airlines, for help. At the time, it was a much more transgressive idea than it is today, now we are all customers rather
than passengers.

The most visible result of their work was to take
the font that the police had used to write their name, and to
recast it in what appeared to be a hand-drawn style. Moving
from the sharply delineated edges of Times Roman, a serif
font with its roots in a stonemason's chisel, cutting travertine, to a vulnerable-looking brushstroke, could certainly be
described as softening the look of the word 'police' painted
on the door of a riot-squad van. By itself it is unlikely to have
made police officers any more sensitive in their approach to
patrolling the streets of Brixton. To critics of the police, it
was a cynical attempt at camouflage, an inauthenticity of
the most blatant kind. Painting squad cars pink might have
done more to change the organization's self-image and the
public's perception of the police that drove them. Putting
police officers on bicycles rather than in patrol cars has gone
much further in changing their interactions with the world
than the identity project achieved.

Designers cannot help themselves. The harder they

try to achieve authenticity, the more they drive it out. But the quality fascinates them. They look for it everywhere, from their collections of supposedly undesigned vernacular objects accumulated on their travels around the globe, to their lust for high-performance sports equipment. They look for it in the way the knobs and dials that Leica devised to control their cameras are shaped, or in the form of the pistol grip of an AK-47. They use these clues as precedents to inform their own work. They obsess like fetishists over the most intricate details of weaponry and the buckles and Velcro fastenings on military uniforms. These are examples of design shorn of the sell factor, as it is sometimes described. When price is no limit, and choices are made not by consumers, but by expert specialists, then objects take on a different character. The equipment adopted by climbers to scale Everest, the materials developed for use in military aircraft and weapons and in medical equipment for surgeons provide an image bank for designers of all kinds. These are objects rich in the kind of visual signals that shape their imaginations. When Sony wanted to give its consumer electronics a hint of the high performance of professional equipment in the 1980s, it adopted a range of visual cues to do the job. There was olive drab moulded plastic with integral carrying handles, and toggle switches that did all that they could to suggest the no-nonsense quality of military equipment. And there was brushed aluminium to create a slightly suaver version of the same idea.

When car designers wanted to produce cars that looked rugged, they explored the off-road signals that denoted Jeeps and early Land Rovers. They styled vehicles to look as if they had not been styled. They made functional mannerisms into a form of decoration. The transformation of the Humvee – once known as the high-mobility multi-purpose wheeled vehicle – into the Hummer was another demonstration of the continuing appeal of the real.

Authenticity for a designer is a quality that comes from attempting to understand how design communicates a sense of sincerity, and then faking it. Nowhere is this more apparent than in the field of graphic design. Gotham is a typeface designed by the American typographer Tobias Frere-Jones, initially in response to a commission from the American edition of *GQ*, the fashion glossy for men, for a font that could give the magazine a sharp new look.

Frere-Jones's former company, Hoefler & Frere-Jones, describes Gotham's origins in its sales catalogue in loving detail which betrays the artifice that lies behind it.

> Every designer has admired the no-nonsense lettering of the American vernacular, those letters of paint, plaster, neon, glass and steel that figure so prominently in the urban landscape. Gotham celebrates the attractive and unassuming lettering of the city. Public spaces are teeming with handmade sans serifs that share the same underlying structure, an engineer's idea of 'basic lettering' that transcends both the characteristics of their materials, and the mannerisms of their craftsmen. These are the cast

bronze numbers outside office buildings that speak with authority, and the engravings on cornerstones whose neutral and equable style defies the passage of time. They're the matter-of-fact neon signs that announce liquor stores and pharmacies, and the proprietors' names painted majestically on the sides of trucks. These letters are straightforward and non-negotiable, yet possessed of great personality, and always expertly made. Gotham is that rarest of designs, the new typeface that somehow feels familiar. Gotham inherited an honest tone that's assertive but never imposing, friendly but never folksy, confident but never aloof.

These are precisely the qualities that Barack Obama's team were looking for when the campaign for his first presidency got underway in 2008. You could see the Gotham font on his banners at the Democratic convention, with their bold-face promises of 'Change We Can Believe In', as a deliberate attempt to convey those qualities.

Obama wanted to appeal to the values of a vanished America. Gotham is the font that reflects what was used by the New Deal when the Hoover Dam was built. It is the font of the New York Parkway system, and the law courts and federal buildings of the 1930s. It is a signal of an America that engaged with the world, and which believed it could make that world better. When the font that inspired Gotham was young, America was actually building dams, high schools and national parks. Obama's programme could not run that far, but his typography gave America a subliminal message about itself. A message that could be understood as reflecting an awkward mismatch between substance and presentation. But at least Obama's use of Gotham had a genuine political agenda. He wanted what he was promising to be real, even if he could not make it so. Idealism is not so clearly a part of the personality of Starbucks, or of Crest toothpaste, who have both put Gotham to work in the wake of Obama's first victory.

When Gotham is used by an inspirational politician with a gift for oratory, the qualities it is understood to reflect are being underpinned and reinforced. When it is adopted by coffee-shop chains, those qualities are undermined and diluted because in the end the qualities of any typeface come from the associations that it triggers, rather than any inherent meaning.

Frere-Jones himself has used the metaphor of clothes for fonts. Perhaps it is true that clothes do need to be suited to the personality of the wearer, but it is also possible that they serve as a form of disguise. Another way to look at fonts would be to consider them in the same way we understand an accent. Some fonts and some accents are associated with authority; others are not.

The uses of the Gotham font went from Obama's vision of hope to the cynical expression of commercial self-interest.

It was not the first time that typography had gone through this kind of transition. In the last years of the Soviet

Union, when Western distilleries had been producing vodka with glossy labels and slick packaging for decades, there was a sudden interest in the commercial uses of authenticity. Instead of the evocations of double-headed eagles that had decked Smirnoff's labels, it became a fad to give vodka manufactured in Warrington and New Jersey the appearance of a more authentically contemporary Russian origin. That meant crude, rather than slick. Colour printing out of register came to be seen as a sign of authenticity, and so of quality, rather than its opposite.

Stolichnaya, once the property of the Soviet state, had its proletarian roots signified by a label that was resolutely un-glossy, not embossed with gold foil, and embellished with nothing more seductive than an image of the factory in which it was made. Pretty soon it became the model for every supermarket own brand, which set out with the utmost artfulness to replicate the artless authenticity of a label untouched by marketing skills and which was just a little imperfect.

This phenomenon is not confined to two-dimensional typography. A carefully contrived version of authenticity is at its most pronounced in the design of the interior world. We live much of our lives on a sequence of stage sets, modelled on dreamlike evocations of the world that we would like to live in rather than the world as it is.

I am sitting in a relatively new restaurant, not far from London's Strand. It is named for a once celebrated, now obscure and long-dead motorcar marque, the Delaunay-Belleville. The automobile backstory is something of a nervous tic for the proprietors, who have previously enjoyed considerable success with another restaurant on Piccadilly named after the Wolseley car showroom that it had once been, and went on to start yet another named – for reasons that can only be whimsical – after the Zedel, one of the few cars manufactured in Switzerland

The Delaunay looks as if it first opened its doors a century ago. With its elderly clock, its black-and-white patterned floor and its felt curtains positioned just inside the entrance doors to protect against a howling central European gale, it is a remarkably faithful recreation of something that never quite existed. For a moment, the illusion that we are in a Viennese coffee house, somewhere just off the Stephansplatz, is complete. It brings the nuanced pleasure of imagining that we have stepped inside from the black-market cold of Harry Lime's Vienna under four-power occupation, if not to the Vienna of the brilliant café conversations of Adolf Loos and Robert Musil. In a London in which table talk is about anything but philosophy, the Delaunay is a chance to play at being intellectuals. It's a theatre in which we can toy with the idea that the rituals of everyday life have more significance than, in truth, we suspect that they really do. It's an infinitely more modest version of the kind of escapist solace that the Indian domes of the Brighton Pavilion gave a Prince Regent without throne or empire.

The Delaunay is a particularly vivid demonstration of what eating out has become: a vicarious experience of how we would like other people's lives to look. Once, all the way back in 1973, it was Midwestern truck stops and dust-bowl diners that inspired the enthusiasm for authentic hamburgers, Rolling Rock and home fries throughout the world. Self-conscious restaurant interiors used to serve as signals of ethnicity; paper lanterns suggested Asian cuisine, zinc tables were associated with steak frites. Now the range of archaeologically precise reconstructions of particular times and places has detached itself from the specifics of food. In New York, and in London, you can find such extreme examples as Balthazar, a lovingly authentic recreation of a Parisian brasserie circa 1924, with its distressed mirrors, its elaborate gilded lettering, its marble-topped counters. Except there is no blue haze of Disque Bleu smoke in either place, and the food is standard North American restaurant fare.

This is several steps beyond the fantasyland Englishness of Ralph Lauren's Rhinelander Mansion store on Madison Avenue, where wooden toys, cricket bats, rowing boats and picture frames were shipped across the Atlantic by the container load to festoon every square inch of the interior. Lauren went on to develop another dreamland, not so much new money masquerading as old but, in the shape of the Double RL brand, new money masquerading as old poor. It's a brand designed to give his customers the feeling that they are salt-of-the-earth ranch hands, wearing garments with every button a clasp, and every seam double-reinforced. They are sold in carefully crafted urban outlets that have been lovingly kitted out with salvage sourced from the backlots of vintage pick-up-truck America.

It is the same hallucinatory quality that you get

sitting in the Café Delaunay where the illusion of authenticity involves more than one of the senses; taste as well as sight. A bite of the Wiener schnitzel, or the bratwurst, is enough to convince those with first-hand experience of Vienna, yet the bubble bursts when it becomes clear that the waiter, though willing enough, has never set foot in Austria, and has not the faintest idea that his surroundings are inviting him to play a part.

The memory of what Vienna's metropolitan culture had once been lingers in the dreams of London restaurateurs. Adolf Loos's American Bar in Vienna, completed in 1908, with its sadomasochistic precision and restraint, has the quality of reality rather than the Delaunay's knowing authenticity. Yet Loos was dreaming of elsewhere too; what else could an American bar at the heart of the Austro-Hungarian empire be but a mirage? It was authentic, but it wasn't necessarily real. It's authentic in its artistic sincerity. Loos designed an original vision that he believed in, rather than a paraphrase of the work of others, and that can be the only measure of real authenticity.

is for

bauhaus

For most of the twentieth century, there was a premier league for modern architects. Membership was limited to just four people: a Swiss-born Frenchman, Le Corbusier, and three Americans (two of whom came originally from Germany): Frank Lloyd Wright, Walter Gropius and Mies van der Rohe. It was a list that reflected a hierarchy created in the 1920s by a self-selected group of historians, propagandists and critics. This particular gang of four did not have much in common. Le Corbusier, the closest that architecture ever came to producing its own Picasso, went from building his personal interpretation of the Arts and Crafts movement in the Swiss watchmaking town in which he was born, to the concrete sculpture of his church at Ronchamp in eastern France. Mies van der Rohe aspired to a steel-and-glass version of classicism in his minimalist towers. Frank Lloyd Wright, in his cape and beret, still trying to finish the Guggenheim Museum well into his nineties, was, as Philip Johnson, the Museum of Modern Art's first curator of architecture, who went on to become the most prolific of postmodernists, acidly put it, 'the greatest American architect of the nineteenth century'. Not surprisingly, the four horsemen of modernity were never entirely comfortable with each other. But they were presented by their champions as being way out in front of the rest of the field, ahead of Alvar Aalto and J J P Oud – drawn respectively from the Finnish and Dutch fringe – who constituted the first division. Assorted Austrians, Italians and Russians, notably Adolf Loos, Otto Wagner, Guiseppe Terragni and Konstantin Melnikov, came some way behind. But at least they were more visible than

Pierre Chareau – responsible for the remarkable Maison de Verre in Paris, finished in 1932, but still radical enough to have inspired Richard Rogers and Renzo Piano's Pompidou Centre four decades later – or Eileen Gray. Chareau and Gray were regarded by the mainstream as no better than decorators or dabblers, or both. It was a dispensation that never made much sense, but it served to define the limits of the conversation about contemporary architecture until modernism began to lose its allure.

Despite their detractors, Le Corbusier, Wright and Mies all produced architecture that half a century later has not lost its power. Walter Gropius's place in the hierarchy is more questionable. His career was based on a series of lucky breaks, not least in the people that he was fortunate enough to work with. He met Adolf Meyer when they were both employed as assistants in Peter Behrens's studio in Berlin and saw how classicism could be modernized to deal with an industrial economy. They watched the birth of the practice of corporate identity, the contemporary version of witchcraft. Behrens designed everything for AEG, from kettles to trademarks and entire factories. It was not only Gropius but also Mies van der Rohe and Le Corbusier who worked for him. Look at the German embassy in St Petersburg that Behrens gave his name to, and which Mies van der Rohe built, and you can see that Mies was wrestling with the problem of how to turn a corner lined with classical columns, which he later returned to with steel I-beams.

Meyer joined his more famous partner when Gropius left Behrens to start up on his own. Between them they had the talent to ensure that the Fagus shoe-last factory that they built just before the First World War would earn Gropius a leading role in the development of the modern movement.

After Gropius fled from Germany in the early 1930s, he created a new career for himself, but floundered without the right help. In its twilight years, the Architects' Collaborative, as Gropius called his American practice, was reduced to designing the London outpost of the Playboy Club in lumpen concrete aggregate. Gropius's most notorious project in Manhattan was the Pan Am tower, erected on top of Grand Central Station, where he was responsible for persuading Emery Roth & Sons, who had retained him as a consultant, to take the urbanistically disastrous decision to align it in such a way as to block the view down Park Avenue. But there was one aspect of his career that was remarkable enough to secure Gropius his reputation as a pioneer of modernism. It was not his architecture, but his role as a teacher. He created the Bauhaus, or, as he and his militantly lower-case typographers preferred to call it, the bauhaus; and made it, thanks in part to an impressive publicity campaign, the most famous art and design school of the twentieth century. As a school, it may not have represented the full creative range of modernism, but it had a prestige unmatched by any other art education institution at the time, or since. After the Bauhaus succumbed to the Gestapo and closed its doors in Berlin, its myth grew and grew, eventually coming to overshadow every conversation about design. It spawned a conveyor belt of exhibitions and books that has continued to gather speed ever since.

I was a schoolboy in 1968 when I saw my first
Bauhaus exhibition at the Royal Academy in London. I could
not afford the 658-page catalogue at the time. I got mine
three years later, and it is still on my bookshelf. It is a kind
of sacred text, rarely opened but always there, decade after
decade, constantly in the background as a silent reminder
of the fundamental place that the movement has played in
shaping the thinking of every contemporary designer.

The catalogue has a massive three-inch-thick spine
that is taken up entirely by a single word rendered all in capitals as BAUHAUS, in three overlapping colours. It looks
like a fading banner proclaiming its cause to the whole room
from the shelf on which it sits. The black-and-white illustrations inside reflect an impossibly exotic-looking avant-
garde landscape populated by mysterious illustrations of
machines, experimental photography, cubist puppets and
textiles with the consistency of porridge.

One image in particular still has the power to
shock. A woman, conventionally dressed for the time, in
kitten-heeled shoes, stockings and a pleated skirt, sits in
a tubular steel Wassily chair, designed by Marcel Breuer.
So far so normal; then you see that where her head should
be is a polished metal egg, into which are cut three gashes
for eyes and mouth. It is a monstrous half-human-half-
machine, which seems to encapsulate the anxieties and
regrets of modernity rather than its optimism. What, I can
remember thinking when I first saw it, had this mask made
by Oskar Schlemmer to do with what my art teacher had
told me about the Bauhaus, as he saw it, being the way into

the modern world? How did this deeply unsettling image of a Kafkaesque hybrid fit in with a world of smooth contemporary architecture and the discreet good taste of Design Council-selected domestic appliances?

Since then, I have seen the Bauhaus portrayed with mind-numbing tedium at the Museum of Modern Art in New York, with rather more concision at the Design Museum in London, and most recently with some style at the Barbican's spatially challenged art gallery, where it was only when I glimpsed Lyonel Feininger's woodcut *The Crystal Cathedral*, which decorated the school's original prospectus, that I knew I had found the starting point of a chronologically organized show.

Every generation needs its own Bauhaus exhibition. But the story always seems to be the same. The credits roll; the Bauhaus is born in 1919, in the midst of the revolutionary traumas that followed the collapse of imperial Germany. Gropius takes on the art school in Weimar, originally established by the Belgian designer Henry van de Velde, and rebrands it with a new name and a new mission. It becomes the focus for all the radical ideas about design that had been crystallizing across Europe in the previous two decades. For fourteen years it is the centre of everything; then the Nazis take over Germany, and shut the school down. But the Bauhaus idea is too strong for them to wipe it out. The Bauhaus ethic spreads everywhere, and reshapes the world in its own image, and everybody lives in tasteful simplicity ever after.

In fact there is rather less to the Bauhaus story than

the myth suggests. Gropius did indeed launch his school in 1919 with a prospectus impressively emblazoned with Feininger's woodcut. It contained a set of declamatory propositions about the unity of all the arts. But, while it suggested a coherent ideology on paper, in practice the Bauhaus really never had a single clear position. The school saw continual shifts of emphasis and accommodated different, and often conflicting, creative currents. The school's programme was presented as the embodiment of the modern movement, but Gropius himself cited William Morris as an influence. And Morris had no love for the machine age. The school was structured much like a medieval guild, with masters, journeymen and apprentices. And that Feininger woodcut suggested more of a commitment to expressionism than to functional rationalism.

Gropius believed that the Bauhaus could erase the hierarchy between the various forms of visual culture and claimed that there was no difference between what was politely called 'applied art' and 'fine art'. Less politely, in the Anglo-Saxon world, applied art was known as 'commercial art', in order to distinguish it from the real thing.

The Bauhaus was remarkably effective at self-promotion. It had to be to bring in the bright students, on whom any school depends for success. It had famous faculty members and an international reputation. If it was to survive in a hostile climate – and it was not only card-carrying Nazis who called it un-German – it needed to make the most of its friends, who included Albert Einstein, Marc

Chagall and Oskar Kokoschka. There was also friction with potential allies, such as Theo van Doesburg, who implied that he had been invited to teach in Weimar. The Bauhaus suggested that he had invited himself and then set up off-campus with an alternative programme of his own.

Within five years of opening, the school was looking for a new home; not because it needed more space, but because it had become too uncomfortable a presence for its hosts when the local elections brought the Right to power. Several cities were interested in taking the school on. Frankfurt, with its progressive social-housing policies, might have been the most obvious place to go. But Dessau, not far from Berlin, made what Gropius saw as the most attractive offer. It had an ambitious mayor, ready to pay for a striking new Bauhaus building, designed by Gropius.

Gropius's choice of Dessau has been interpreted by at least one architectural historian, Francesco Dal Co, as evidence of an innate conservatism that ran counter to the professed radicalism of Bauhaus cultural politics. If he had really wanted to involve the school in the transformation of society, argues Dal Co, Gropius would have moved to Frankfurt, a city that was already building a vision of the modern city on an impressive scale. Instead he was content to preserve the Bauhaus's autonomy and stay on the sidelines in Dessau.

Gropius's buildings for the school's second home in Dessau, with their tautly stretched plaster skins, looked as if they had been extruded from a mould, even though they were actually made painstakingly by hand. They were a kind of billboard, an austere monochrome advertisement for the world that Bauhaus graduates would create, if only they were given the chance. And, of course, they were given that chance. For half a century, the products manufactured by every advanced industrial economy in the world looked the way that they did because of what had happened at the Bauhaus. Even America, with its addiction to a diet of market-driven built-in obsolescence, and the overripe sensuality of Elvis Presley seasoned by the Buick-and-Coke-bottle school of styling, could not escape its influence. Textiles, typography, furniture, architecture and ceramics were all indelibly marked by the Bauhaus and its chilly neutrality. It was a movement that seemed to have the prestige of historical inevitability on its side.

There is a photograph of a group of Bauhaus masters in Dessau, taken on the school's roof shortly after it opened in 1926. Gropius stands in the centre. Like most of the men in the photograph, he is wearing a bow tie, but it is defiantly modern, cut down to a minimalist rectangle. He has a homburg and a long jacket that look conservative enough for him to pass as a businessman, but his stance (one hand in pocket, cigarette in the other), more extrovert than the pose adopted by László Moholy-Nagy, suggests something more culturally ambitious. The artist, in rimless glasses and proletarian cloth cap, is two sidesteps from the director, partly obscuring Herbert Bayer, who is wearing plus fours, not the first garment that one expects to see adopted by a radical typographer. Wassily Kandinsky and Paul Klee (wielding a cigar) are to the right of Gropius, and look even more conservative. Faculty members Josef

Albers, Lyonel Feininger and Oskar Schlemmer are all there too. A bomb detonated under this group would have left the course of visual culture in the twentieth century looking entirely different. Between them they touched everything from photography and theatre to painting and architecture.

From this image, it is hard to conceive of the Bauhaus as a living, breathing art school but, judging by the personalities involved, it must have felt quite a lot like the kind of campus life portrayed by Richard Burton and Elizabeth Taylor in the film *Who's Afraid of Virginia Wolf?*. The Bauhaus was a hothouse of squabbling exhibitionists, philanderers and egotists struggling for position, a place in which Johannes Itten, who initiated the notorious Bauhaus foundation course, the forerunner of the British art school foundation year system, sported a variety of eccentric haircuts. On one occasion he had a star cropped into the fuzz on the back of his skull. He wore clothes of equal eccentricity, and pursued a strict macrobiotic diet. Itten belonged to a mystical cult, inspired by Zoroastrianism. To the dismay of those with more orthodox views, he recruited converts from his classes. The other masters seduced their students, and intrigued against each other. The students got drunk, went on strike and complained about the school. The townsfolk, as townsfolk always are, were appalled.

Gropius had clear views about design as he thought it should be practised in the machine age, but he was prepared to accept a wide variety of voices among his faculty. He put talent well ahead of adherence to any specific party line. And he was ready to make the most of the gifts of his ideological opponents. He appointed a Marxist, the Swiss architect Hannes Meyer, as his successor, and when the time came for Meyer to be sacrificed to the political realities of an increasingly polarized Germany, Gropius was ready to nominate Mies van der Rohe as the director, despite their lifelong rivalry. Even after they had both moved to America, Mies never warmed to Gropius and what he regarded as his aristocratic condescension. While he, Mies van der Rohe, the son of a mason who specialized in carving tombstones, was banished from Berlin to provincial Chicago to run the school of architecture at the Illinois Institute of Technology, Gropius, the son of one architect, the great-nephew of another, and the deceived husband of Gustav Mahler's widow, Alma, was able to lord it at Harvard.

Gropius's successor had had a promising start. Meyer was asked to design social housing for Dessau. He secured a royalty for the school on the commercial output of its workshops. The bestseller was a wallpaper pattern that even Albert Speer wanted to use when he redecorated the Berlin headquarters of the National Socialists, creating a sleek backdrop for Hitler's activists in the run-up to his seizure of power. In Meyer's hands, the Bauhaus version of modernism became increasingly austere and materialistic. If Gropius had managed to maintain its cultural roots, it was Meyer who pushed functionalism to its logical conclusion.

In 1929 Meyer suggested that:

> In every creative design appropriate to living,
> we recognize an organized form of existence;

given proper embodiment. Every creative design appropriate to living is a reflection of contemporary society – building and design are for us one and the same, and they are a social process, as a 'university of design'. The Dessau Bauhaus is not an artistic, but a social phenomenon. As creative designers, our activities are determined by society, and the scope of our tasks is set by society. Does not our present society in Germany call for thousands of people's schools, people's parks, people's houses? Hundreds of thousands of people's flats? Millions of pieces of people's furniture? What are the connoisseurs' gibberings worth when set against these after the cubistic cubes of Bauhaus objectivity? Thus we take the structure and the vital needs of our community as given.

We seek to achieve the widest possible survey of the people's life. The deepest possible insight into the people's soul, the broadest possible knowledge of this community. As creative designers, we are the servants of this community. Our work is a service to the people. All life is an urge to harmony. Growing means striving after the harmonious enjoyment of oxygen + carbon + sugar + starch + protein. Work means our search for the harmonious form of existence. We are not seeking a Bauhaus style, or a Bauhaus fashion. No modishly flat plane-surface ornamentation divided horizontally and vertically and all done up in neoplastic style. We are not seeking geometric or stereometric constructions, alien to life and inimical to function. We are not in Timbuctoo: ritual and hierarchy are not dictators of our creative designing. We despise every form which is prostituted into a formula.

It's an approach which had its attractions, but it is far removed from the reality of production even at the time that it was first being formulated and when it was still possible to explore the mechanical moving parts of a duplicator, for example, or a bicycle, and use them as the basis for making a formal composition. Meyer's successor, Mies van der Rohe, was brutally dismissive. Carbon + sugar + starch? 'It stinks.'

Dessau's funding for the Bauhaus building, the civic commissions and the financial subsidies it provided the school (even if it took money away from other cultural projects cherished by some influential local figures) made sense for a small city trying to put itself on the map. It was importing a high-profile educational institution that it hoped could boost its factories, and attract visitors too. But as the political climate in Germany degenerated into totalitarianism, Meyer's beliefs triggered a crisis. A group of Communist students organized a party cell inside the school. Meyer refused to expel them, and, in so doing, threatened the survival of the Bauhaus. Gropius was consulted by the city, and recommended Mies van der Rohe to take over the running of the school. A new director was not enough to allow the Bauhaus to stay in Dessau much longer. An attempt by the

National Socialists to evict the Bauhaus immediately and demolish the building was unsuccessful, but the mayor of Dessau did try to stop the Bauhaus from spelling its name without an upper-case B. In the Germany of that period, such a blatant subversion of formality was clearly understood as a calculated sign of defiance. Its provincial context had allowed the Bauhaus to flourish, but it was also what finally killed it when bigotry overcame opportunism.

In 1932, the local newspaper, the *Anhalter Tagezeitung*, demanded that the city should 'tear down the oriental glass palace of the Bauhaus'. The Nazi newspaper, the *Völkischer Beobachter*, was even more brutally crazed: 'The Bauhaus that was the cathedral of Marxism, a cathedral, however, which dammed well looked like a synagogue.'

The school came to be seen as the embodiment of progressive political values. In a grotesque oversimplification, flat roofs and tubular steel furniture became the sign of radical politics while classical columns were closely associated with fascism. It was no more than a fable. While Gropius certainly left Germany as a refugee, many of his assistants stayed on. They quickly found work on the Nazi building programme; Hitler loved classical architecture but the Luftwaffe's airbases looked like typical architectural products of the Bauhaus. Ernst Sagebiel, who built Göring's air ministry, had been the distinguished modernist Erich Mendelsohn's chief assistant. Mies expelled the school's Communist students and found an escape route for the survivors to Berlin from Dessau and its politicians. But even in the capital, he could not keep the Bauhaus going for long. He arrived at the school in its new home one morning to find armed guards posted at the doors and staff and students locked out by the Gestapo.

The Bauhaus did not last long enough to turn formulaic, nor was it forced to face up to the need to re-examine its founding assumptions when the course of events challenged them. Repression in Nazi Germany helped to secure the Bauhaus's worldwide impact. After Hitler consolidated his grip in 1933, those who refused to compromise with his views realized they had little choice but to leave the country or be silent. The final closure of the Bauhaus triggered a creative diaspora; the message of the school, its working methods and its radical approach spread in all directions, to England, to Turkey, the United States, Latin America, Japan and Israel. Certainly the Bauhaus had a sympathetic hearing in America, or at least a certain reading of the Bauhaus did. Philip Johnson, who seemed to have had something of a crush on Mies van der Rohe, sent his mother a postcard of a photograph of Gropius's Dessau building, telling her that she had to see it. On the other side of the card, he wrote that under Meyer's leadership the Bauhaus no longer had anything much of interest to offer.

Mies van der Rohe, whose relationship with the Nazis was more nuanced than that of his predecessors as Bauhaus directors, stayed in Germany until 1937, when he finally left for Chicago. The city was also the home of the short-lived New Bauhaus, established by László Moholy-Nagy in 1938. The Bauhaus's most direct post-war successor was the Hochschule für Gestaltung in Ulm, the design school established by Max Bill, the graphic designer Otl Aicher and Inge Aicher-Scholl, as a memorial to Aicher-Scholl's martyred siblings, Sophie and Hans, who started the anti-Nazi White Rose movement.

Long after Mies disbanded the Bauhaus, its legacy continued to shape the idea of design education, even if it eventually came to be seen as a model to react against rather than follow. For the Bauhaus pioneers, design, art and architecture were all part of a unified approach to culture, as demonstrated by the foundation year that every student shared before choosing a specialism. Yet art and design have drifted further and further apart. During Meyer's time as director, the artists felt threatened. The Bauhaus, especially under Gropius and Meyer's leadership, maintained a strong sense of social commitment. But once the survivors reached America, they began to fall out with each other. Annie Albers gossiped about Mies van der Rohe's willingness to collaborate with the totalitarians. In Europe, the Ulm school was dissolved after bitter internal disagreements between the Aichers, who saw art as a part of its activities, and the irascible Max Bill who rejected it as an attempt to dilute its rational principles with an element of subjectivity. In America, Gropius continued to teach architecture at Harvard, where he inspired a generation of modernists, and provoked the young Charles Jencks to start formulating the ideas that would one day lead him to declare modernism dead.

Perhaps the most remarkable of the many remarkable things about the Bauhaus in its Dessau years was how it was able to achieve so much from so provincial a setting. Even the apparently bucolic Cranbrook Academy, with Eliel Saarinen as president and Charles Eames on the staff, was actually on the edge of Detroit. Dessau is just another small town in Germany with no more than 80,000 people. As a creative centre, it hardly registers in the German context, let alone on an international scale. Yet in the 1920s and 1930s, Dessau briefly had a convincing claim to being regarded as the epicentre of the design world, rather than a peripheral outpost. There wasn't much in Dessau's past to suggest this outcome. Hugo Junkers started his famous aircraft-building business there, and the town saw the test launch of the world's first liquid-fuelled rocket. Kurt Weil was born in Dessau, but by comparison with Weimar, which was home to Schiller and Goethe, and which retains a certain intellectual aura, Dessau's creative achievements had always been more limited. Set against Frankfurt, or Stuttgart, there was little evidence of the new spirit in architecture beyond the Bauhaus's own buildings.

The residue of the refurbished Bauhaus building, emerging from its successive incarnations as a school for Nazi officials and an aircraft factory, and from Communist antipathy followed by neglect, is a key asset for the city today. The building, which was designated as a World Heritage Site by UNESCO in 1999, and which is now again occupied by a school of design, is Dessau's best hope for the future. The kind of metropolitan culture on which creative centres depend works best when populations are numbered in their millions. The ambitious and the talented congregate in fewer and fewer places that need to be larger and larger to compete. No less metropolitan a city than Berlin has had to work very hard at re-establishing itself as a place that can genuinely claim to be an international cultural leader.

Perhaps the most difficult question that the Bauhaus poses is why no subsequent art school has been able to match its impact. Many schools have managed to produce a generation of students with something to say. In London, Goldsmiths can be seen as a school which triggered off a very particular strand of British art in the 1980s, just as the Royal Academy of Arts in Antwerp created a generation of Belgian fashion designers led by Martin Margiela and Dries van Noten. The Eindhoven Design Academy redefined the nature of Dutch design. The Royal College of Art in London has a remarkable range of achievement in many fields, with students from Mary Quant to David Hockney, James Dyson to Jasper Morrison. Its design and automotive schools in particular attract gifted students from all over the world, year after year, but there is no RCA style or manifesto. This might be seen as being more helpful for the students than it is for the professors.

But what the Bauhaus had that no other school has had before or since is the combination of successive leadership from three of the leading designers of their time, a building that embodied the philosophy of its founder in a single unmistakable image, and an unshakable place at the heart of modernism, the dominant movement of twentieth-century culture. Other schools have had strong leaders who have themselves been leading practitioners, though there are fewer now than there were. A few schools have been associated with movements in design – such as the Domus Academy in Milan, which in the 1980s was closely identified with postmodernism. And there are schools with architecturally distinguished buildings – from Glasgow's Charles Rennie Mackintosh landmark to the Art Center in Pasadena. But the Bauhaus had all three: a landmark building, a student body drawn from around the world, and a celebrated faculty which, as Tom Wolfe memorably put it, were treated like 'Silver Princes' by an awestruck America when they moved en masse across the Atlantic at the end of the 1930s.

B

is for
BLUEPRINT

Trapped halfway down the stack of ancient magazines sitting on the floor of my study is a yellowing copy of *Blueprint*, the monthly started in London in 1983 by Peter Murray, with a group of journalists, photographers, writers and designers. We thought we were going to turn the world of design and architecture upside down. As is usually the case, this took the form of doing all that we could to trash the reputations of a previous generation of designers, architects, and so, by implication, of a previous generation of critics too. We were championing a new group of names, drawn from our contemporaries, to help them in their struggle to supplant their predecessors.

And of course, as they floated apparently effortlessly to the top of the professional tree, so would we. Now we wait with more or less resignation for another generation to dispatch us, in electronic haikus, 140 characters at a time. Or, if we are quick enough, we contemplate knifing our own discoveries and finding a fresh set of designers and architects to champion, if necessary, repeating the same trick once more in a few years' time.

Fashion cycles are the natural means for one generation to be edged out of the way to make room for another, but they don't always make for the most reliable of critical judgements. When I began writing about architecture for newspapers in the 1980s, the politely provincial British architectural world of the time was evidently running out of steam. A thrusting fifty-year-old Norman Foster had just ushered in the gleaming aluminium-skinned face of the future with the Sainsbury Centre at the University of East Anglia, which looked more like an aircraft hangar than a museum. But there wasn't much else of interest being built, and that meant it was a free-fire zone on almost everybody else. *Blueprint* set out to be iconoclastic, disposable, and tried to root architecture, design, graphics, fashion and the visual world in the popular culture of the time.

There was an undeniable frisson to be enjoyed from the slaughter of so many sacred cows. Poor Sir Hugh Casson, architect by royal appointment, was a particular target. Now it's not just Norman Foster who is in the cross hairs of another generation of critics. It is Zaha Hadid, who was described as a safe choice just six years after her Cardiff Bay Opera House was said to be unbuildable. David Chipperfield and Will Alsop are also taking the heat. For those who are looking to supplant them, they are establishment figures and fair game.

It is part of the natural order of things for one generation to turn on the last. Critics face the same process. The opportunity for architectural critics to overturn conventional wisdom doesn't come that often. But very occasionally a few of them get to tell us that something we had accustomed ourselves to seeing as irretrievably awful is in fact an unacknowledged masterpiece, and, having told us so, they manage to persuade us to believe them. In the 1950s, it was John Betjeman who took most of the credit for opening our eyes to the qualities of Victorian architecture – though John Summerson probably did more of the spadework and

Nikolaus Pevsner also played his part. After their efforts, what had been seen as at best an amusing embarrassment became priceless heritage.

Iain Nairn, the maverick RAF pilot-turned-critic, made us look at what we thought of as the commonplace and understand it for what it really was. He explored Essex suburbs, provincial factories, bypass architecture and industrial estates. He had a gift for the kind of turn of phrase that stays with you. 'Doomed, and grimly magnificent,' is how he once described Hawksmoor's great Christ Church in Spitalfields, words that still go through my mind every time I see the building.

Succeeding generations play off each other. We are inspired by our predecessors, but we also threaten them, just as we are threatened by our successors. My first job at the *Sunday Times* was to write Ian Nairn's obituary. Three decades later, I was reviewing Owen Hatherley's book *A Guide to the New Ruins of Great Britain*. I found myself reading the words of somebody from a generation younger than mine, who was also looking back to Nairn, and attempting, like him, to make us look at what we take to be the ordinary elements of the world around us, and to make us understand them as anything but ordinary. In Hatherley's case it is a plea for the brutalism of the English provinces. But, of course, reviewing the work of a member of a generation that is upstaging yours is not the most objective of processes.

Hatherley's history reads something like Tom Stoppard's *Rosencrantz and Guildenstern are Dead*, with the action of Hamlet seen through the eyes of two minor characters. His account of the past thirty years of British architecture reduces Norman Foster, James Stirling, Alison and Peter Smithson and Denys Lasdun to walk-on parts; the greater part of the action is focused on such figures as Owen Luder, Rodney Gordon and Robert Lister, responsible for provincial shopping-centre megastructures, bush-hammered concrete car parks and trade union offices.

Blueprint's tabloid format, powerfully designed by Simon Esterson, was borrowed from *Skyline*, a short-lived New York magazine art directed by Massimo Vignelli that set a worrying precedent by going under just before our first issue came out. The range of subject matter, from fashion to car design by way of architecture, came from *Domus*, the Milanese magazine established by Giò Ponti. *Blueprint*'s main aim was to be everything that the once crucial *Architectural Review*, by that stage, was not. When the *Review* had Betjeman, Pevsner and Reyner Banham on its staff, it set the pace in its approach to layout and the ambition of its ideas. But by the time *Blueprint* emerged, the *AR* had faded into timid irrelevance. It found anywhere more remote than Finland alarmingly foreign.

Blueprint offered a chance to ask questions and to look at places that seemed interesting. We began to explore exotic new centres of design that were making an impact. Tokyo suddenly came into focus as the first fax machines started up, with their curious electronic whine bringing news of mysterious commissions in the small hours from various locations around the planet.

The particular issue of *Blueprint* on my study floor is a quarter of a century old, and the cover features the portrait of an angelic-looking David Chipperfield, posed in the foreground of the shop that he had just completed for Issey Miyake in London. Behind David is Ken Armstrong, his business partner at the time, once an equally promising young architect, now somewhat off the radar. Chipperfield, with offices in Berlin, Milan and Shanghai as well as London, is still working and has built in China, Korea, America, Japan, Italy, Spain and Germany. He has been knighted, collected the Royal Gold Medal for Architecture and lost some hair.

Our attempt at making design and architecture accessible beyond the professional ghetto involved putting photographs of our designer heroes (and, regrettably, not nearly enough heroines) on the cover. The idea was to give a face to the abstractions of architecture, even to offer a design magazine that could make eye contact with you from the newsstands. But there were never that many buyers, and in the end we were simply making our own small contribution to the dismal celebrity cult that has threatened to overwhelm architecture and design. Pretty soon we found that there was some sort of curse overshadowing the operation. Partnerships that had appeared on *Blueprint* covers had an uncomfortable habit of splitting up shortly afterwards, just like the celebrity weddings pictured on the cover of *Hello!* magazine that end in divorce. Armstrong disappeared to Paris soon after the issue with his picture on the cover came out, to build the Maison de la Culture du Japon on his own. I knew something was wrong when he called me after the photograph was taken to complain that the nature of his partnership with Chipperfield had been misrepresented. He was standing, while David was seated, and in front of him.

Chipperfield took longer to get a project to match the visibility of Armstrong's first solo work, which, for a brief moment, looked as if it would be the next Institut du Monde Arabe, Jean Nouvel's breakthrough building on the banks of the Seine. The introduction to Miyake, through the shop, was enough to get Chipperfield to Japan, where he was one of the earliest Western architects to build in the Tokyo of the Bubble Economy.

London in 1985, as depicted by *Blueprint*, was an unimaginably different place from the London presided over by Boris Johnson. As unlike the present incarnation of the magazine to the one written on typewriters and prepared for press by pasting down photographs and columns of type on layout boards with Cow Gum glue. In fact, the very first issues used an ancient technology, Letraset, the dry-transfer lettering system, for headlines.

Chipperfield had an office in the same semi-derelict building as *Blueprint*. Unlike architectural practices starting out today, who can't afford Hoxton and end up banished to the outer limits of the city, we were able to rent space in the West End, just off Marylebone High Street, in Cramer Street. Chipperfield had room to spare and turned the basement of the building into the 9H architecture gallery, with space for its associated magazine of the same name. Unlike

Blueprint, *9H* was serious, scholarly and intellectually committed. Named after the hardest of hard lead pencils, *9H*'s editorial board (Chipperfield, Ricky Burdett, Yehuda Safran and Wilfried Wang) were determined to bring the unsentimental ethos of what were then seen as obscure Swiss firms, such as Herzog & de Meuron, and assorted Austrians to the blinkered attention of the Anglo-Saxon world. Later *9H* turned into the Architecture Foundation, an outfit dedicated to getting the subject of contemporary architecture taken seriously in Britain. The Architecture Foundation regarded the Royal Institute of British Architects as dismayingly provincial, and incapable of taking the intellectual fight to the Prince of Wales, whose petulant crusade against anything that he did not like the look of was just getting underway.

If *Blueprint* was an attempt to transform magazines, *9H*, and subsequently the foundation, wanted to do the same for architectural institutions. Ricky Burdett, its first director, shrewdly signed up Nicholas Serota, Alan Yentob, Doris Saatchi and Andreas Whittam Smith as board members, ensuring that its message percolated out of the professional ghetto.

For the London of those days, whose self-regarding insularity led to an unjustified faith in its own pre-eminence as an architectural centre, the astringency of *9H* was something of a departure. Indeed, *9H*'s policy was to have some unintended consequences. Herzog & de Meuron were selected to rebuild the derelict Bankside Power Station for the Tate, not Chipperfield. He had put everything that he could into his competition design, including a last-minute plan to castrate the building by removing the landmark chimney, but it wasn't enough for him to win.

No less than three directors of the Venice Architecture Biennale emerged from Cramer Street. I did the job in 2002, followed by Ricky Burdett in 2008, and ten years later by David Chipperfield.

Look closely at the Miyake shop portrayed on that *Blueprint* cover, Chipperfield's first substantial project, and you see veined white marble, wide timber floorboards, and an intricate palette for the supporting cast of materials. A little rich for the Chipperfield of today, perhaps, but a sophisticated exercise in place-making that, in its intentions and ambitions, is not so far from what he is doing now. Even then he was ready to say that it was important not to do too much; all that a shop might need could simply be to install a very beautiful floor.

Early on in his career there were a couple of bruising encounters with the militantly philistine nature of the British way of doing things. When Chipperfield designed a sober house for the photographer Nick Knight, in an undistinguished suburb west of London, the neighbours, unabashed by the pebble-dash banality of their street, did all they could to prevent what they saw as an intrusion from being built. Chipperfield had an equally hard time with his own offices in a mews in Camden. The *Evening Standard* gleefully egged on opponents of what it called his 'aggressively modernist, and out of scale design'. Chipperfield realized that to have any chance of building, or indeed surviving, he would have to look beyond Britain, to mainland Europe. Here he could see himself as part of a group of architects who brought a seriousness and a certain intellectual ambition to their work that went further than stylistic mannerisms. Chipperfield, who is in so many ways quintessentially English, has become the most European of British architects.

It is a complex position in which to find himself, especially for an architect who believes in rooting his work in place, memory and material qualities. When you have joined the international flying circus, how do you resist the tendency it encourages towards the showy gesture and the quick fix?

Chipperfield's work can be seen as conservative in the best sense. He is looking for architecture that lasts that resists the culture of spectacle. I remember seeing him present his design for a new BBC headquarters in Glasgow to a competition jury that included an enthusiastic Greg Dyke, then the BBC's director general, who got down on his hands and knees for a closer look at the model. The site was on the edge of a derelict dock on the fringes of the city, surrounded by a howling void of anonymous business parks and apartment towers.

Chipperfield described his task as trying to find a way to give some sense of permanence and place to an environment that looked, as he put it, as if it might blow away with the first gust of wind. The other contenders included Richard Rogers, who was not having a good day, Wilkinson Eyre, who could not find the right words to meet the occasion, and Mecanoo, the Dutch practice who came up with a

Hawaiian shirt: a design that might look fine on the day of the presentation, but would have been pretty embarrassing for the day-to-day operations of the BBC ten years later.

Given the restrictions of the budget and the brutal simple-mindedness of a procurement procedure that saw the BBC outsourcing the project to a finance house, there were not too many options for Chipperfield. But he came up with a project that made the most of its interior. As though preparing an Adolf Loos *Raumplan* – and Loos was a particular hero of the 9H group – Chipperfield took the fixed elements of the brief (the studios) and placed them on the floor of the building like giant steps. He put the social spaces on top of them in a cascading sequence of volumes that rise up through the height of the interior. In the process, he made somewhere out of nowhere and, despite a near-terminal falling-out with the executive architects for the project, succeeded in producing a handsome building.

His most complex and hard-to-categorize work is the Berlin Neues Museum. Almost twelve years in the making, it stands as his most impressive achievement to date, and is perhaps also the building in which he has taken the biggest conceptual risks. His solutions are traditional, in that they refer back to the restoration strategies advocated by William Morris when he set up the Society for the Protection of Ancient Buildings in the nineteenth century, and yet have an entirely contemporary astringency.

The Neues Museum, with its painstaking approach to preserving every flake of paint from a building mutilated by war and dissolving after decades of post-war neglect, represents a new departure in its attitude to history. It is a museum in which the container has itself become content. It was a shell-shattered ruin for half a century, destroyed during the closing stages of the Second World War. Before that, its history closely reflected the genesis of the modern museum. When the building first opened in 1850, Prussia had little in the way of actual archaeological artefacts. Instead the museum was a kind of interpretation centre, full of evocations and simulations, rather than authentic objects. The walls were painted to represent Egyptian temples, the Athenian acropolis and the Roman pantheon. After teams of German archaeologists started bringing home the real thing, the original interior became an embarrassment, and quickly vanished underneath an all-enveloping blanket of Bauhaus-inspired restraint that provided the setting for the booty from excavations throughout the Middle East.

The impact of bombing during the war unevenly peeled away fragments from every layer, to leave a new kind of reality. The brickwork, the cast-iron underlying struc-ture that had never been meant to be visible, the fragments of old plaster, the patches of flaking murals, the traces of dropped ceilings that had been used to hide the original layers, they were all in themselves part of the history of the building. Chipperfield spent more than a decade stitching together the shattered remains of a dead building, bringing it back to warm life, not by what is conventionally under-stood as a restoration, but by finding a new quality in the layered traces of the past.

This approach is only one strand in his work. The

building he did for Valencia's waterfront when it hosted the America's Cup is a reminder of his interest in the relationship between architecture and urbanism, and his concern for the social aspects of a building. Chipperfield gently subverted what was intended to be a viewing platform for an elite group of sponsors for the yacht-racing season by connecting it with the city and making it partly permeable to the public.

Equally original, in its own way, is the emergence of a group of buildings that began with Germany's Museum of Literature in Marbach. With a clifftop setting, alongside a classical neighbour, Chipperfield broke the greatest post-war taboo of German architecture. He ignored the authoritarian taint associated with classicism, and introduced what can only be understood as a modernized classical building, with a colonnade, though no entablature or capitals on its columns.

In a period when much architectural production has been overtaken by a mania for promiscuous shape-making, these are all designs that have a certain sobriety that are immersed in the traditional architectural concerns. For Chipperfield, the impact of sunshine on a white wall, the sense of enclosure and release that moving through a sequence of rooms can offer, are important issues. He has a sophisticated understanding of the imperative for an architect to find meaning in a project, rather than blithely build more space. For Chipperfield, a master plan is more than the disposition of blocks on a map, or a kind of large-scale architecture, but is a means of articulating a shared vision about what a university might be like, or how a cultural centre can be part of the life of a city. He is a pragmatist, of course. Anybody with a large office to maintain has to be. He is ready to make silk purses out of the sow's-ear scheme; bringing a certain dignity to an affordable mass-housing programme on the edge of Madrid, for example. But he has stuck to his belief in an architecture of substance.

The first time I went to Barcelona was in 1980, to look at the architectural hippy commune that Ricardo Bofill had established in a derelict cement factory at Sant Just Desvern. There were cypress trees planted on the roof, tables designed by Antoni Gaudí at the foot of soaring concrete silos, and a resident poet. In those days, Bofill had yet to embark on his relentless precast-concrete classicism that purported to offer the masses social housing that looked as palatial as Versailles but had the usual shoebox plans behind the pretentious façades. His intricate and colourful early buildings were attracting a lot of attention. Nothing could be more different from Chipperfield's huge and sober law court complex in the city.

Most of Barcelona in those days looked as if it were living off its ample supply of memories from better times. The Gothic core of the city was half derelict, the business district had a clump of would-be skyscrapers, and its ramshackle suburbs spilled out over the dusty hills beyond the city's boundaries.

I went back to Barcelona to work on a *Blueprint* special issue on the city on a warm November night, in an attempt to find out what it was that had made it come to life in the intervening years. The differences were startling.

Two hours after midnight and things were only just getting started at Otto Zutz. It was a raw concrete and black-painted steel playground, embellished by gritty murals in muted grey and a network of catwalks, threaded over the vertiginous, cavern-like void above the dance floor. The pace quickened after the neighbouring bars started to close. Customers came in from Bar 33 (cava served in a mirror-and-Perspex environment), from the Universal (the ambience of a Lower East Side loft) and from the Bar Snooker (proud owner of a shiny new billiard table).

It was a hedonistic Spain, far from the stereotype as a Third World outpost that many Brits cherished then, in which public kissing let alone topless bathing landed people in jail. Its bar life managed to make Barcelona look sophisticated, even if it was still building SEAT cars from time-expired Fiat designs.

Javier Mariscal put his finger on what was behind the sense of discovery outsiders experienced when they went to Barcelona in those days. 'Unlike Paris, Hollywood had never created a sense of what Barcelona looked like; we had to make our own image of it,' Mariscal told *The New York Times*. And of course that is exactly what his BAR/CEL/ONA poster did, as surely and effectively as Milton Glaser's I ♥ NY.

Mariscal was a key figure in Barcelona's re-emergence; he worked with others, cross-fertilizing and collaborating. He went beyond illustration and cartoons to design furniture, interiors and objects. Mariscal had the connections to get drafted in as the Spanish member of

Ettore Sottsass's Memphis Group in Milan, which changed the design landscape in the 1980s. But we missed a trick at *Blueprint*. When we got back to London with the portraits our photographer, David Banks, had taken for us, we didn't put the image we had of a boyish Mariscal, in his John Lennon glasses, looking a lot like Harry Potter, in Pep Cortes's metal workshop, on our cover. Instead we had Cristian Cirici, his arm wrapped protectively around a steel I-beam holding up the roof of his reconstruction of Mies van der Rohe's Barcelona Pavilion, which he had just finished. That remarkable project, bringing back the memory of the brief but intense flowering of the luxurious modernism of 1929, was a reminder that Barcelona in the 1980s was still a city of many conflicted aesthetic attitudes.

Barcelona at that time was still in the first flush of enthusiasm for design. By the 1990s, it had become more confident. No longer seeing itself as an echo of Milan, it had stopped trying to replicate the smooth, tasteful polish of the Italian approach to design and was ready to take a more flamboyant path. Barcelona was remaking itself, investing in the city infrastructure, preparing for staging the Olympics in 1992, and it was trying ever harder to recapture the optimism it had experienced when it first seemed possible to make a new city after Franco's death.

Despite having been born in Valencia and remaining sceptical about the Catalans, Mariscal had a very visible part in this process. He worked with Fernando Amat, the proprietor of Vinçon, Barcelona's first design store. Mariscal and Alfredo Arribas designed the most baroque of all

Barcelona's nightclubs, the Torres de Avila, a project which the ever-more-grumpy Robert Hughes was quite spectacularly dyspeptic about when he went to gather material for his book on Barcelona. For Hughes, Barcelona was a place which 'moved into the 1990s obsessed with design, designers are to it, what the cigar-chomping art stars were to New York in the 1980s'. Hughes claimed that 'it was the sheer awfulness of Torres de Avila and its PoMo clichés that might make it worth preserving'. It is a view that has more to do with Hughes's self-absorption than anything else.

There was nothing quite like Barcelona's design at its most playful and exuberant. It never acquired the intellectual baggage of the Memphis group. Rather it was spectacular and hedonistic. It was identified so strongly with the new Spain that Mariscal moved effortlessly from the underground at the fringes of society to the mainstream. For the Olympic Games of 1992, it was Mariscal who designed Cobi, the mascot that became its official embodiment. He was able to change the tone of voice with which a country could present itself to the world.

Barcelona, while it did a remarkable job investing in infrastructure, new roads and mass-transit systems, new airports and civic buildings, has started to flounder. As Herzog & de Meuron's Forum project, shuttered and empty just a few years after it was completed, has demonstrated, the city has an alarming tendency to build things first and work out what to do with them afterwards. And this was even before the debt crisis engulfed Spain.

In the same issue of *Blueprint* we published a piece about Michael Graves's skyscraper for the Humana Building in Louisville – the high-water mark of the post-modern tide in the form of an astonishingly monumental pastel-coloured temple. It looks like a museum piece now. It was a commission won in a competition against Norman Foster and it would be difficult to imagine two more polarized designs. In fact, Graves went so far as to suggest that he would rather practise law than build high-tech architecture. For a moment Graves was being described by Charles Jencks as the greatest American architect since Frank Lloyd Wright, and he acquired much the same aura that Frank Gehry attained a quarter of a century later when he completed the Guggenheim in Bilbao. Since then, Graves has declined into the construction of a sequence of exhibitionistic holiday resorts on a huge scale.

There is a melancholy feel to looking at those ancient copies of *Blueprint* now. Why would anybody set out to start a new magazine once Amazon had sold more Kindle downloads than physical hardback books for the first time? It is a format that has perhaps reached the end of the line, displaced at one end by newer, cheaper media, and at the other by the physical, shared experience of the exhibition. And yet still the new magazines keep coming, still relishing the scent of fresh ink and the tactility of paper. And they continue to have the energy and the optimism that *Blueprint* once had.

One of the most striking differences I found in making the transition from editing architecture and design magazines to directing a museum was discovering the impact of seeing the audience face to face. To edit a magazine is to find yourself putting messages in bottles and floating them out to sea. Occasionally there is some feedback: an angry letter to my Italian publisher at *Domus*, from Mario Botta, an architect claiming to have been victimized by the Anglo-Saxon mercenaries that I had hired to attack his evisceration of La Scala in Milan; or threats of legal action. The most common form of enquiry, however, is a request for more detail from a technical library about the precise grade of concrete used in Zaha Hadid's Zaragoza Bridge Pavilion.

Running a museum is more like running a theatre. There is a visible response to the programme. If people like what the museum is doing they come and spend time there. You can see when they enjoy what they find. You hear them talking to each other about it. You see them taking photographs of the captions on their mobile phones. Of course, if they don't like it, you can see that too. They don't come.

The numbers are very different. Architectural exhibitions can very occasionally attract a hundred thousand paying customers or more. No issue of any architecture or design magazine in the world sells anything like that number. This is not to make any qualitative judgements about the value of one medium against another. But it is clear that there is something about an exhibition that, when it works, will persuade many more people to pay for the experience than would invest the same amount in a book or a magazine. It is too easy a commonplace to repeat the threadbare observation that an architectural exhibition cannot replicate the primary experience of architecture; that what is on show is in some way second best when compared, for example, with the primary experience of confronting an autonomous artwork. An engaging physical exhibition on architecture does indeed offer a richer, more immersive, experience that speaks to more people than any depiction in a book or magazine. In the same way that live performances continue to flourish even as sales of recorded music have been decimated, so the primary shared physical experience that an exhibition offers has a future. The magazine, at the moment, does not look so promising, unless as a place to offer an antidote to the savagery of what debate on the web has become.

IS FOR CAR

In a paraphrase of an idea first formulated by Roland Barthes, the mercurial British critic Stephen Bayley once claimed that if Michelangelo were alive today he would not be wasting his time in Rome carving marble tomb sculptures for the Vatican. He would be in Detroit working in brown modelling clay on the modern world's true art form, the design of the motor car. Barthes had already gone three centuries further back. He suggested that the anonymous masons of Chartres would by now be putting their creativity to good use on a Citroën production line.

Bayley was writing in the 1980s, when the future of the car industry seemed a lot more secure than it does now. It was before car making's centre of gravity had shifted decisively east, and long before parametric digital modelling had supplanted clay. What lay behind Bayley's words was the idea that contemporary art had lost the power to reach an audience beyond the walls of the gallery. He was trying to suggest just how remarkable an object a car, made in its millions, really is. Perhaps more than any other consumer object, cars have shaped the texture and shape of modern life. They are the distillation of both the blessings and the curses of mass production. A car can be beautiful. It emotionally engages us, and it demonstrates the extent of human ingenuity and resourcefulness. A car offers a sense of personal freedom. At the same time, cars tear our cities apart in their unquenchable thirst for tarmac; their exhaust emissions threaten the future of life on this planet. They are a lethal threat to pedestrians, cyclists and other road users.

The ubiquity of the car has tended to innoculate

us to its significance, but we do not have to consider a car as a piece of art to understand the huge impact it has had on the world. It is, for better or worse, the peak of the industrial culture that gave birth to the practice of modern design. Yet its power is waning. The Ford Motor Company, founded by Henry Ford, who was no more comfortable a personality than Steve Jobs, used to be the model of the modern corporation, with its company towns, its own orchestra, its own company uniform. Apple and Google have supplanted Ford and IBM as the model corporations that others seek to emulate. And while there are now companies around the globe who have managed to make cars more profitably, and more effectively, than Ford, they are essentially in the business of refining a mature product that may have a limited future.

Bayley's proposition would have been more convincing but for one of the more unexpected developments of the post-millennial museum-building explosion: the creation of a mass public for contemporary art. As demonstrated by audiences of more than four million a year for Tate Modern, art did indeed turn out to be the real art form of the twenty-first century. And there is evidence that when artists do turn their attention to car design they do not make much of a fist of it. The Russian-born sculptor Naum Gabo, for example, worked with the very British consultancy the Design Research Unit when it asked him to take on the styling of a car. Somewhat improbably, it was a project for the Jowett Motor Manufacturing Company, a Yorkshire-based factory that went through a short-lived burst of inventiveness in the early 1950s before it imploded, setting an example studiously followed by almost every other British car company. Despite Gabo's training as an engineer, his bulbous car body looked less than convincing by comparison with his revolutionary work as a young artist.

Barthes had been dazzled by the beauty of the Citroën DS. It was a car that looked so modern when it was launched in 1955 that he suggested that it seemed as if it had dropped from the sky as a visitation from another planet. This was the kind of car that you could believe an artist of Gabo's calibre might indeed have produced. But cars are the product of many people, none of whom can operate effectively if they see themselves as artists. In his most feverish passage in *Mythologies*, Barthes suggested that the DS was the exact equivalent of the great Gothic cathedrals, a car that in its smoothness seemed to suggest the kind of perfection that is not easily achieved by human hands alone. The extraordinarily long-drawn-out process that the DS went through certainly suggests an enterprise on the epic scale of building a cathedral. It took eighteen years, from when it was initiated in 1937 by Pierre Boulanger, the man who took over the running of the company from André Citroën, for the completed car to drive down the Champs-Élysées for the first time in 1955. Boulanger wanted to make what he called the world's best, most beautiful, most comfortable and most advanced car, a masterpiece to show the world, and the Americans in particular, what France could do. He did not live long enough to see it happen.

André Lefèbvre was the engineer who made

Boulanger's brief technically possible, along with the teams who worked on the engine, the suspension system and the brakes. Each element was in itself an extraordinarily creative piece of work. The look of the car was the responsibility of Flaminio Bertoni, an Italian, who, although he could certainly draw and had an interest in sculpture, had begun his working life as an apprentice carpenter in a coach-building workshop. If Gabo did not make much of a car designer, Bertoni, brilliant though he was as a car designer, was equally not much of a sculptor. And in that dissonance is the essence of the problem for those who see the car as the ultimate contemporary art form. Real cars are designed by people who do not look like artists, who do not sound like artists, and who are motivated by an entirely different set of aims and ambitions from those of the world of art.

Cars are a highly specialized form of design. They encourage a different mindset from other branches of design, not just for those who design them, but for the people who think about them. I find cars endlessly fascinating, but driving them is not a pleasure for me. Rather than keys to mobility and independence, the cars I have owned became extensions of my kitchen table, filling up with debris: apple cores going brown, orange peel, torn envelopes, stacks of books, old newspapers, bags of washing destined for the laundry, and those self-adhesive clear-plastic envelopes that parking tickets come in. For me, this mobile tip is the most immediate physical experience of a car rather than the sculptural refinement of the bodywork.

By and large, there is little serious crossover between

automotive design and product design, furniture, fashion or architecture, other than at the most trivially superficial level of a paint scheme specified by Victoria Beckham. This is despite the historically celebrated exceptions. The limousine that Walter Gropius helped to style for Adler in 1930 was impressive – even if it did not look much like his architecture – but compared with the technical innovation of Citroën or Volkswagen it was a historical anomaly. Le Corbusier's ambitious attempt to persuade the French car industry to put his design for a low-cost lightweight forerunner of the Citroën 2CV into production ended in failure.

The project that Mario Bellini put forward in 1972 for the New York Museum of Modern Art show on Italian design, 'Italy: The New Domestic Landscape', the Kar-a-Sutra, was more promising. Part funded by Citroën, it might really have helped provoke the change in thinking at Renault that eventually led to the introduction of the people carrier, a fundamental reconfiguration of the basic elements of the conventional format of the European car in the 1980s, taking it from three compartments – engine, passenger and boot – to a single volume.

But otherwise, these noises-off have had very little impact on the approach of mainstream car designers. Cars, on the other hand, have fascinated designers. Architects in particular have struggled to replicate the speed and precision of a car production line on construction sites, without much success. What makes Barthes's words so arresting is that they are so unusual. Cars are a universal part of the landscape, yet outside the claustrophobically narrow view of the automobile-obsessed, they are intellectually invisible. Barthes was looking at a car from the perspective of a wider view of culture, not from behind the wheel. He was interested in meaning rather than acceleration and horsepower.

Pontus Hulten, the founding director of the Pompidou Centre and a man who did more than anybody to shape the contemporary practice of museum-keeping, had a similarly broad view. Hulten curated a show at the Museum of Modern Art in New York in 1968. With remarkable foresight, it was titled 'The Machine as Seen at the End of the Mechanical Age'. Long before digitalization had overturned the analogue order, the transistor was regarded with just as much excitement. Alongside Umberto Boccioni's *Dynamism of a Speeding Horse + Houses* (1915) and Jacques-Henri Lartigue's hauntingly beautiful photographs of the racing cars of the 1912 French Grand Prix, one of Hulten's most provocative exhibits was a car designed and built for the Indianapolis 500 circuit that year. Driven by Graham Hill in pre-race tests, it achieved a record for the circuit of just over 171 mph. Hulten was fascinated by the car's shape, and wrote that

> the modern racing car is a very remarkable object on the border between technology and art. Although it has no practical use it is extremely functional. No one who constructs a racing car would dream of modifying it for the sake of aesthetics. Yet many of

> the cars must be regarded as extremely beautiful.
> The racing car is the apotheosis of the great dream
> of the 1920s as the beauty of the functional pushes
> the possible as close to the impossible as one
> can come.

If nothing else, Hulten's words are a reflection on the meaning of the word 'functional'. But they also slide over the surface of a remarkable story. Hulten singled out one of the five cars made for Andy Granatelli by Colin Chapman, the engineering genius of the British motor-racing circuit and the founder of the Lotus car marque. Granatelli had gone to Chapman with the idea of a turbine-engine-driven car, rather than the previously universal piston drive. Working with a Pratt & Whitney turbine engine originally developed for use in helicopters, Chapman's design team produced the distinctive wedge-shaped car that attracted Hulten's attention. In its day, it was the fastest car that America had ever seen. But this was not the end of Chapman's contribution to the evolution of the motor car. He recycled the lessons he learned from the race track into road cars.

When I was growing up in the 1960s, the coolest thing by far to watch on the still black-and-white 405-line cathode ray television sets of the period was an endlessly knowing drama series called *The Avengers*. In its far from subtle way, beneath the glitter of a continual and stylishly entertaining struggle between good and evil, as represented by the fearlessly nonchalant agents of a slightly off-piste Whitehall department and assorted megalomaniac diamond-collared-kitten-stroking villains, it was trying to tell us something about the changing nature of contemporary British life. Each week Diana Rigg, as Emma Peel, inevitably dressed in a black leather catsuit, would join Patrick McGee's John Steed, kitted out in bowler from Locke and pinstripes tailored by Huntsman, with a carnation in the buttonhole, to take on assorted enemies of the state.

The point made by their contrasting wardrobes was put even more forcefully by the cars that they drove. Steed had a vintage Bentley the size of a haystack, with aerodynamics to match. Peel got around in a svelte and glossy new Lotus Elan. This was the product of Chapman turning his attention away from the almost useless usefulness of the Formula One track, crossing the barrier from pure engineering, if such a thing exists, and into the semantics of motoring. At the touch of a button, its sporty, swivelling headlamps would pop up to emerge from the dune-like moulded contours of the body when required, and duck back out of sight when not needed. The gesture implied a promise to reduce drag coefficients but actually was just for the hell of it.

The Avengers was inviting us to explore a raffish, new Britain, a country in which class barriers were breaking down, and where tradition and pedigree had acquired something of a bad name. It was a place in which making a big splash, without necessarily having the means to pay for it, had become not just socially acceptable, but an essential goal. It was the moment that pop culture arrived. And, of course, that is what ensured that the ingeniously showy Lotus brand always carried with it a certain question mark.

The company was born in austerity Britain at the end of the 1940s, and in its first incarnation was the outcome of trying to have fun during the depths of the make-do-and-mend ethos of rationing. Everything from fresh fruit to fuel, clothing and furniture was in short supply, and baths were limited to three inches of hot water in order to save coal. Lotus cars were shaped by adversity and economy.

Where the Bentley had a Mulliner coachbuilt body in aluminium, the Elan was moulded from fibreglass. Where Bentley had built its engines itself before it was acquired by Rolls-Royce, Lotus bought in an engine block from the Ford Classic, and a steering rack from a Triumph Herald.

With its bold front hiding humble underpinnings, the Elan was a mercilessly accurate reflection of the new Britain. But the car had engineering brilliance as well as style. Lotus was able to draw on all that it had learned from building cars for the Grand Prix circuits of the world over thirty years. As a result, they were able to give the Elan the performance of an E-Type Jaguar.

The original Elan body was styled by Ron Hickman, a self-taught South African who went on to make a fortune from the patents to the Black & Decker Workbench that he designed after he left Lotus. He arrived in Britain with nothing more in the way of experience than his school-boy sketchbooks. He worked for two years for Ford, where he quickly graduated from the clay-modelling studio to working on the new Anglia. He joined the team for Lotus's first street car, which never managed to make money for the company. Then came the Elan project. John Frayling worked with Chapman and Hickman to get the car into production, and they were able to produce a car that was beautiful, practical, reliable and buildable. One thing was still missing: image. As a brand, Lotus simply didn't cost enough. At just £1,200, or £25,000 in today's money, it was within reach of the aspiring. Worse still, from the image point of view, it was available in kit form for the enthusiast. So though the finished car might from a distance look as exotic as a Cisitalia, with its semi-monocoque body, actually it was closer to the ducking-and-diving world of the DIY caravan. The Pininfarina-designed Cisitalia made it into the permanent collection of the Museum of Modern Art in New York, and the Elan did not. Since the Elan has more relevance to the development of the car in the second half of the twentieth century than the Cisitalia, beautiful though the latter is, the omission tells us more about MoMA's design collection than it does about automobiles. The Cisitalia was hammered out of metal, the Elan pioneered the use of fibreglass in the car industry.

Ducking and diving is precisely the world from which Antony Colin Bruce Chapman, the Imperial College-trained engineer who established the Lotus Car Company in 1952, never quite managed to escape despite all his material success. Looking like a louche lounge lizard in his dark glasses, his Leslie Phillips toothbrush moustache and his luxuriant sideburns, Chapman built his first car – a modified Austin 7 – in a north London garage in 1948, and raced it himself. Why he called his marque 'Lotus' he never spelled out. But Lotus Blossom had apparently been Chapman's pet name for the girlfriend who later became his wife. The initials inscribed on the Lotus badge, like some cricket club school blazer, are Chapman's. The racing cars were designated with numbers – albeit skipping the less auspicious ones. There was, for example, no Lotus 13. To distance them from the circuit, Lotus's street cars had names, all of them beginning with E, from Esprit to Eclat, by way of Elise and Europa.

From the unlikely piece of customization that was the Mark 1, Chapman went on to develop the Lotus 7, the quintessential British sports car. He sold the rights to Caterham Cars, who still manufacture its descendants to this day.

What made the Lotus project work was Chapman's ability to think his way around the production and performance issues on which every new car depends. He wasn't the first engineer to come up with the idea of using a space frame to make a stiff but lightweight car. Buckminster Fuller had done that decades earlier when he built his Dymaxion car back in the 1930s. While Fuller was far-sighted enough to see the potential of the approach, a fatal crash at its launch blighted the Dymaxion's future and it was Chapman who was able to make it work in the marketplace. And the brilliant Hans Ledwinka at the Czech car company Tatra – from which FA Porsche took much of the expertise for the Volkswagen – had also worked on the idea of a 'backbone' chassis that shaped Lotus's approach to finding a simple and economical way to stiffen his lightweight fibreglass bodies.

It takes a Nissan or a Ford or a Fiat to achieve the economies of scale, and the investment, that can alone build a plausible industrial car. In the last decades, the only real alternative to mass-produced cars has been the couture approach. The relationship between the runway fashion of an Yves Saint Laurent or a Christopher Bailey, and the shopping-mall Banana Republic version, is not much more distant than between a Lamborghini and a Ford. When car prices reach into seven figures, almost anything is possible. They can have specially designed, and specially made, door handles, wing mirrors and dashboards, as well as vast engines, and bodies with the qualities of sculpture. Chapman's road-car business tried to do something else. From a starting point in the kit-building enthusiasts' end of the spectrum, making things cheap and cheerful, he knew where to find parts that could be put to work in new and unfamiliar ways to achieve the performance that he was looking for. You might find yourself looking at an instrument gauge that recognizably came from somewhere else, or a door handle without quite the same Lotus pedigree, but it worked.

And in the end, it is this that shows why making and designing a car is not the same as making a work of art. The car designer has to work with what is available. The artist works with ideas. A close study of a car says so much about the way we live, about the way we make things, and about ourselves. It is not art, but it is the highest achievement of design, an artefact that has a greater concentration of design talent per square inch than anything else.

C is for Chair

Few objects have attracted so much attention from so many designers as the chair. Perhaps only the bicycle and the corkscrew have gone through such questionable variations, modifications and reinventions in ever-more excitable attempts to make a new and distinctive solution for a problem that has already been solved so often.

It's not hard to see why designing a successful chair would appeal to a designer. To have a chair with your name attached to it confers a certain professional longevity, in a way that so few categories of design make possible. To work on the design of a smart phone or a laptop is to see your efforts fade into irrelevance heartbreakingly quickly. Chairs last, both as physical objects and as designs. They continue in production for much longer than almost any other kind of industrially made artefact. Or at least, they used to. A version of the bentwood café chair that Michael Thonet first made in 1859 is still in production today, many millions of examples later. The Eames Lounge chair, first commercially manufactured in 1956, is still made by Herman Miller in America, and by Vitra in Europe, with scores of unauthorized pirated versions in China. At the end of the 1950s, Ettore Sottsass suggested that Eames had designed not so much a chair as a way of sitting. It looks as modern now as it did then. That is not something that can be claimed for two other once equally charismatic designs from the same year, the Cadillac Coupe de Ville, with its flick-up chopped tail fins, or a Raytheon 405-line black-and-white television sitting on spindly legs. But there is evidence that the way in which we see the chair is changing too. It is being forced closer to the fashion cycle by the relentless search for novelty that has overtaken the way that design is consumed.

Peter Smithson, one of the few architects of the 1960s with a sophisticated understanding of design, believed that the continuing charm of the chair for people who are not designers came down to its cute, anthropomorphic looks. 'People rarely collect cupboards or dressing tables, or stools, but to collect chairs is common. It is probable that we see them as domestic pets; they have legs, feet, arms, and backs. They are symmetrical in one direction, like animals, or like ourselves.' I had never seen them quite like that. Some chairs you want to own because you want to sit in them. Others, the Rietveld red blue chair, for example, or at least the version I have, made by Cassina in Italy, who acquired the licence to manufacture it after Rietveld died, are better to look at from the other side of the room than to sit in. And the Ron Arad Rover chair in my study is a reminder of a particular moment at the beginning of the 1980s when Arad's career was just getting started on the basis of creative salvage and I got to know him.

According to Smithson, 'the act of marking territory starts with our clothes, with their style, with our gestures and postures when we wear them. With a chair we extend our sense of territory beyond our skin. With a chair we first impose ourselves on blind space.' In an echo of Ernesto Rogers's endlessly quoted editorial in *Domus* magazine from 1946 that described architecture as extending 'from the city to the spoon', Smithson went on to suggest that 'It could be said that when we design a chair we make a society and a city in miniature. Certainly this has never been more obvious than in this century. One has a perfectly clear notion of the sort of city and the sort of society envisaged by Mies van der Rohe.'

Smithson and his partner, Alison, best known for their monumental blocks of workers' housing in London's East End, made several attempts to design distinctly un-proletarian chairs. They came up with a sequence of curious objects, including the Pogo chair, with flat, transparent Perspex sheets lashed to a metal frame, the Saddle chair, which had Barbarella-style nylon fur, and, perhaps more convincingly, the Trundling Turk, which had some of the colour sense and spatial qualities of Gerrit Rietveld's red blue chair. Rather than Rietveld's weightless, wafer-thin planes floating in mid-air, the Trundling Turk was a stack of massive foam blocks mounted on wheels. The Smithsons tried, but none of their chairs managed to define a historical moment in the way that the Thonet factories did. In the end, they were perhaps better at architecture than they were at design.

The chair has to be understood as a utilitarian object, and yet, because it has such a long history, one that is so closely associated with so many purposes that go far beyond utility, it has also acquired cultural significance. It has come to embody power and status. The chair has also become a research test bed, putting new materials to work, from bentwood to tubular steel, fibreglass to carbon fibre, and for the shifting manufacturing techniques that they depend on. The impact of technological and aesthetic innovation leaves its traces clearly inscribed in the form of the chair.

It's no wonder then that the history of modern design is so often told as a sequence of chairs rather than of cars, or handguns, or typefaces, all of which could be plausible candidates for the role.

Furniture takes its aesthetic language from the spaces in which it is used, and for which it was originally designed. So a chair can be understood as the distillation of an architectural ideology. In the heroic period of modernism, architects designed a few key pieces of furniture, the cantilevered tubular steel chair, for example, mostly as a substitute for architecture, when they had no chance of realizing anything larger. Such objects were able to act as a kind of surrogate for an architectural approach to design and materials. When Charles Rennie Mackintosh or Rietveld designed chairs, they were encapsulating many of the qualities of their buildings.

Those designers who have managed to produce furniture of distinction have, with surprising frequency, aspired to a more exalted role in designing full-blown architecture. But there are significant differences, not least of scale, which make it a challenging transition.

Those chair designers who are not architects have produced pieces that have often lacked the visibility of the architect-designed canon. The exception to this, and to the dominance of a succession of architect chair designers, was Charles Eames, a man who, though he had trained as an architect and built one remarkable house and studio for himself, made his reputation with a series of chairs. That house, constructed in Santa Monica, embodied all that Eames and his wife, Ray Kaiser, believed in. Made mainly from off-the-shelf industrially produced glass and steel components, it was assembled rapidly like a kit of parts rather than built like a conventional house. Yet its delicate structure and spare proportions seemed to suggest some of the grace of a traditional Japanese house. It was the argument for an approach to design that embraced the modern world with economy of means.

In the summer of 1958, two years after the Eames Lounge first went on sale, Eames's attorneys, Price & Heneveld, lodged his patent application for the side-flexing shock mounts that make the lounge chair so comfortable. The drawings have the deadpan authenticity of a specification for a scientific instrument. They seem to render the design as emotionless and objective rather than seductive or expressive. Every bolt and screw is carefully delineated in bold ink lines, and painstakingly cross-hatched. They show all thirteen screws, washers and bolts, on plan and in section, and in three dimensions. The drawings, lettered Figs 1 to 6, give a hint of the plywood curves on which the chair depends. And Eames's name is charmingly added to the drawings in block italic capitals, beneath the word 'inventor'. These patent drawings, though they are accurate and comprehensive depictions of the design, seem hardly to belong to the same century as the chair that they describe.

The last patent to protect the design was finally granted in 1961 – by which time Eames and his studio of not-always-acknowledged collaborators had been working on the project for the better part of two decades. The Lounge has its roots in a three-piece moulded-ply chair that goes all the way back to 1949. Charles Eames called it 'appealingly ugly'. Its original Brazilian rosewood shells – an endangered timber species – were treading water in terms of technical innovation. His fibreglass shells had already made more of a new material. The cast aluminium he worked with later produced designs of extreme refinement. The Lounge chair turned its back on Eames's ideas about affordability and democratic design that were embodied in his house. At a 2012 price of £5,000 with the stool, it is undeniably expensive. Manufacturing it is not easy, and involves a considerable amount of handwork. But despite all that, the Lounge is one of the handful of pieces of furniture that have served to define design in the twentieth century, suggesting that Eames did not always need to be consistent in his aims.

Design may have become something else since Eames produced his Lounge chair, but without getting the measure of what he did with furniture, it's hard to get to grips with the direction that design has taken. It is the chair that has done more to penetrate the consciousness of the world beyond the design ghetto than any other object. It is the chair that seems most convincingly to suggest the idea of luxury and comfort in a contemporary way. And that was Eames's intention. He wanted to create a chair that spoke of the creased, well-worn ease of a patrician East Coast club chair, with the lived-in appeal of a used soft leather baseball glove. Its buttoned leather upholstery shows off the tactile qualities of a material that ages with grace. Its cushions, which in the original version were filled with goose feathers, allowed for a pleasing degree of wear with time as they took on the imprint of those who sat on them.

The shape of the back of the chair, and its arms, depended on the development of the same moulded plywood, techniques that he had used elsewhere. But the Lounge was larger, heavier and considerably more complex. It took many attempts and many designers to refine the components into one seamless and poised whole.

Its launch by the Herman Miller company, with whom Eames worked for most of his career, was underpinned by one or two carefully polished myths. It is perfectly true that the Hollywood film director Billy Wilder owned one, and that he was photographed sitting in it. But it is not the case that it was designed specifically for him, as used to be claimed, and was occasionally hinted at by Eames himself. Wilder had been interested in Wiener Werkstätte furniture long before he became a film director. His apartment in Berlin had been designed by a Bauhaus graduate, and was furnished with Mies van der Rohe pieces. He knew Eames, but the chair was born long before they met.

While the human race's headlong rush towards universal obesity may eventually lead to a reassessment of the proportions of the Eames Lounge, the act of sitting is unlikely to go the same way as listening to vinyl records, or buying newsprint. The chair as a category will still be relevant even into the distant future.

Chairs take us through a series of key technological

episodes in the evolution of design. After carving, turning and joining wood no longer defined the parameters of chair design, the pace changed dramatically in the nineteenth century, when the Thonet family transformed furniture into a fully industrial process. Michael Thonet deskilled furniture-making by investing in machinery and inventing new techniques that could produce complex shapes without craft skills. He did for furniture what McDonald's did for catering, though with more culturally nourishing results.

After bentwood, chair designers worked with another newly invented material, tubular steel, which became emblematic of the machine age. At the start of the 1920s, Marcel Breuer, Mart Stam and Mies van der Rohe, three of the modern movement's key figures, all developed their own versions of the cantilevered chair using tubular steel within months of each other. In chair-design terms, it had the impact of electricity on lighting. Tubular steel could be bent into tight, springy curves, supplanting the conventional one-leg-at-each-corner format for the chair. There had been technically similar chairs before, devised by anonymous American engineers. But Breuer (one of the former Bauhaus students to become a master at the school), Stam and Mies were doing something else. They wanted to remake familiar domestic objects in radically new forms to make a point about the modern world. They might not be able actually to build utopia, but Stam could at least pay a plumber to knock up something that hinted at what a utopian machine age might one day look like, with the aid of nothing much more than a few feet of gas pipe.

Marcel Breuer made a much more polished chair for use at the Bauhaus, while Mies transformed the cantilever into a languid streak of glittering steel, pursuing a long arc across his travertine-and-glass version of classicism. Eileen Gray celebrated the poetry of mechanisms in her sparely elegant adjustable chairs, lights, tables and mirrors.

Charles Eames's work spanned three of the technologies that transformed furniture in the twentieth century. He took moulded plywood into complex multiple-curved directions that went further than anything that Alvar Aalto had done with glued birch ply in the 1930s. Eames was also one of the first to use moulded fibreglass to create shell seats that were lighter and easier to form than plywood. And he worked with cast aluminium for the structure of his aluminium group seats.

After tubular steel and aluminium casting, chairs came to depend on a wide range of synthetic plastics and glass-reinforced fibre, rotational moulding and carbon fibre. The legend has it that Marcel Breuer was inspired by the handlebars of the Adler bicycle that he rode around the streets of Dessau, when he was at the Bauhaus, to use tubular steel for furniture. Plastics provided no such hints to the designer, and it required a more abstract form of intuition to see their potential. The plastics first used in making chairs were patented by Otto Haas in 1933 under the name Plexiglass. Haas's company went looking for customers for a material that was tougher than glass, but equally transparent, wherever they could find them. Jean Prouvé used a single piece of Plexiglass as the seat and back for a perforated steel-frame armchair. Rohm & Haas made transparent body panels for a special version of a Pontiac shown at the New York World's Fair in 1939.

Robin Day was able to use polypropylene for the shell of a cheap and robust stacking chair that was one of the most successful designs ever produced by a British designer. But both Eames and Day could use plastics only in a limited way, for the seat and back, not for structural legs or arms of a chair. Using a single material for an entire chair would transform the process of manufacturing, and create a truly mass-produced chair, with no handwork of any kind. That did not happen until the 1960s, with the use of injection-moulded plastics.

It was not just the technical problems that had to be addressed before plastics could be used to make anything but the most basic domestic furniture. Designers had to find a way to change the way that people understood and valued objects made from plastics. Plastic was seen as an ersatz substitute for a 'real' material. Its glossy surface revealed none of the signs of skilled workmanship or the preciousness of a material, which had become the conventional measures of the value of an object

Making the tool from which an extruded-plastic chair is formed is expensive and demands a high degree of skill, but that skill is not immediately obvious in the apparently effortlessly finished product. Making the chair itself is neither expensive nor skilled. The raw material is not obviously precious, and the extrusion process leaves no trace of the human hand.

If plastic was to become accepted as a material to make furniture with, ambitions that went beyond the narrowly utilitarian demanded the creation of a new aesthetic. It had to be an aesthetic based on a rejection of the traditions of handwork and conventional ideas of what constituted quality. It was an aesthetic that celebrated high-gloss finishes, and the magical quality of mysterious, enigmatic objects made instantly by a machine.

It is arguable that the Danish designer Verner Panton achieved the summation of all that was possible in the use of plastics as a material for making furniture in his most famous chair, first produced in 1968 in moulded fibreglass-reinforced polyester. It was a single fluid form combining back, seat and support, which was dramatically sculptural, and did away with all fixings. But it was not a commercial or a technical success until it was re-engineered by Vitra twenty years later. Italian designers and manufacturers did better. Joe Colombo's 4867 chair for Kartell, designed in 1967, the first full-size stackable chair to be injected in a single mould, was more practical. It was followed by Vico Magistretti's Selene chair for Artemide from 1968. These were designs that went further than Thonet's bentwood and tubular steel in transforming the way that chairs were made.

Trying to record the evolution of contemporary design as a sequence of chairs now is like seeing history only through a close study of dynasties. There is still a lot to learn about design as a formal, technological and social issue from looking at certain chairs. But if design remained circumscribed by the chair, it would be fading into gentle irrelevance along with such other once vital, but now purely ornamental, skills as bookbinding or iron-forging. What makes design so endlessly fascinating is that it keeps shifting parameters and preoccupations. Design can be about inventing new shapes, but it doesn't have to be. It can be about objects, but it doesn't have to be. It can be about chairs, but it doesn't have to be.

C IS FOR CHAREAU

I had a tour of the Schröder house in Utrecht twenty-five years ago, just a few months before I finally got to see the inside of the Maison de Verre in Paris. The two houses, designed respectively in 1924 and 1928, say a lot about the heroic period of European modernism. The Schröder house, designed by Gerrit Rietveld and Truus Schröder, is spatially explosive, but it is realized with Dutch bluntness. One sheet of timber overlaps another. Nothing is politely hidden away. Its still impressive to see in the flesh, but its clear that some of the perceived spatial complexity of Rietveld's design comes from the fact it was photographed with every window open at ninety degrees. The Maison de Verre is an exquisitely crafted and luxurious celebration of machinery and mechanisms. I know which one I would rather live in, and it's not just because the Maison de Verre is on a turning off the Boulevard Saint-Michel, close by the Café de Flore, and the Schröder house confronts the elevated motorway that skirts Utrecht.

In theory, the architecture of the twentieth century was driven by mass culture and social housing. In practice, it's possible to tell most of the history of modernism through a careful selection of individual houses very few of which score well for affordability. The Maison de Verre and the Rietveld house certainly qualify as architectural landmarks. They also provide a reflection on what happens to remarkable houses once the people who first lived in them have gone.

Rietveld and his client Truus Schröder were both married to other people when they first met. They spent their last years together in the house, which is in the care of

Utrecht's Centraal Museum now. Every trace of the personality of the extraordinary individuals who made it have gone. Visitors are admitted in carefully controlled groups and, at least when I visited, expected to wear paper overshoes. It makes the place feel not like a house but like a laboratory, clean, secure, but stripped of so much of its meaning.

The Maison de Verre is different. Dr Jean Dalsace, the gynaecologist who had commissioned Pierre Chareau to build it, had died some years before I saw the house. His consulting room and surgery were no longer in use, but the place was still owned by the Dalsace family. It was open to the public only haphazardly. While it was still clearly a house, it was not the home that it had once been – a salon for progressive French intellectuals in the 1930s. Its qualities were fading, the rubber floor had turned brittle, the volumes on the bookshelves were unloved and unread.

Since then, the house has been acquired by Robert Rubin, an American former commodity trader and enthusiast for the work of both Jean Prouvé and Pierre Chareau, who is working on a careful restoration, as patient and organized as his approach to the vintage cars that were an earlier passion for him.

The relationship between houses and the people who make them is fragile. John Soane turned his house in London into a museum, and that is what gives it a robustness that withstands the presence of so many visitors.

To visit the house that Alvar Aalto built outside Paris in 1959 for the art dealer Louis Carré shortly after it was acquired by a foundation was a privilege, because you could still feel the presence of its owner. It was there in the Chanel suits hanging in his wife Olga's wardrobe, and in the copy of *Vers une architecture* inscribed by Le Corbusier to Carré – they used to live in the same building. I was able to experience this because there were so few of us there on the day. A house fully open to the public can't have that quality.

Pierre Chareau was a small, dapper man with a weakness for double-breasted suits and silk handkerchiefs. To look at his picture, you would never think he could have been responsible, with the Dutch architect Bernard Bijvoet, for designing one of the most extraordinary houses of the twentieth century. Legally, Chareau was not entitled to call himself an architect. He studied painting at the École des Beaux-Arts in Paris, then took up music before finally becoming apprenticed to a furniture maker. When he set up on his own, he designed interiors, one-off furniture for a few loyal clients, and the occasional film set.

For Chareau, however, the point of life was not to indulge in novelty for the sake of novelty, but the pursuit of perfection. And the Maison de Verre, the house that he built at 31 rue Saint-Guillaume, has been designed in every detail, from the soaring spaces of the living room to the soap dish in the bathroom, to be perfect. Even the coat hangers are specially made.

The façade is the house's most striking, but also most beautiful, feature. Square dimpled glass bricks, held in black-painted steel frames that have the delicacy of Japanese paper screens, create an all-glass wall three floors high. It floods the interior with light, but is patterned in such a way as to stop passers-by from seeing in. The interiors, planned around a double-height studio space, are equally radical.

The idea of using perforated aluminium sheets on the walls instead of wallpaper, leaving huge steel girders, rivets bulging like those at the lower reaches of the Eiffel Tower, exposed in the living room, and putting studded rubber on the floor in a comfortable bourgeois home simply hadn't occurred to anybody before. 'I recall a lady who just could not bring herself to go up the stairs in the Maison de Verre as there was neither a rail, nor stair risers,' wrote one contemporary friend of the owners. Instead of conventional opening windows, there were ventilation hoppers, controlled by specially made flywheels, like something out of a power station. Le Corbusier was said to have been spotted hanging around the site, lost in wonder at the remarkable stream of objects that he saw going in.

The Maison de Verre is one of the handful of buildings that have the energy and the imagination to be able to change everything that follows them. Charles Eames's house in Los Angeles was equally influential. Frank Gehry's own house from the 1980s in Santa Monica or Rem Koolhaas's house outside Bordeaux are probably the most recent examples of this exceptional breed. They depend on an individual designer, like Chareau, who is bursting with ideas, unwilling to take anything on trust, and determined to rethink literally every detail,

The project did not succeed in rescuing Chareau, who was notoriously bad at business, from his financial difficulties. He had to sell off the remarkable collection of art that he had acquired in his more prosperous days after the First World War. The Braque and the Picasso that used to hang on the walls of his apartment, the Mondrian from his office, all had to go. The Modigliani sculpture that he kept in his garden belongs to New York's Museum of Modern Art now. When the Nazis invaded France, Chareau fled to America, where he struggled to make a living. His only major work in the US, where he died in 1950, was a studio in the Hamptons for the American painter Robert Motherwell, which involved recycling a war surplus prefabricated army hut, and combining it with a greenhouse. But even that has been demolished now, as has the hotel that Chareau built in Tours, leaving not much more than a collection of exquisite specially designed furniture that survives from Chareau's period as a decorator, and the Maison de Verre itself.

The Dalsace family were long-standing friends of Chareau and his English-born wife, Louise Dyte. Chareau had already designed an apartment for them. But building the Maison de Verre took four difficult years, in part because the sitting tenant on the second floor of the property that the Dalsace family had acquired with an eye to demolition refused to budge. So Chareau worked out how to jack up her floor, demolish the rest of the building from underneath her, leaving just an access staircase, and insert his house into the gap. There were few working drawings, just some careful sketches, and a lot of improvisation on site. That was how Chareau liked to work. 'The inventiveness of the builder should be respected and encouraged in architecture as in furniture. The craftsman will hit upon ideas that the designer or planner would never have dreamed of,' Chareau said. At the Maison de Verre, Chareau did exactly that, relying on his loyal metal fabricator, Louis Dalbert, who was left exhausted and ruined by the process.

The front of the house is made up of a double-height living room on the two floors above the surgery. Bedrooms are on the top floor, while dining and more private spaces are at the back of the house, overlooking the garden. The bathroom cupboards swing out on carefully balanced pivots to reveal a drawer and a rack for every conceivable need that he or his clients could ever have envisaged. To make sure that electricians would never need to damage walls and floors to get at the wiring, Chareau put all the cables in free-standing metal tubes six inches clear of the walls. And to help his clients find their way in the dark, the light switches were pre-programmed to guide you through the house. One switch at the front door would see you all the way up into the bedroom.

Chareau's inventiveness and elegance are there in every detail. The sadness is that he did not live long enough to build more.

is for collecting

The collecting impulse is universal, and it goes to the roots of what it is to be human. It pre-dates mass production and design, but it reveals the essential nature of our relationship with our possessions, how they communicate with us, and the various ways in which we value them. Understanding the nature of collecting tells us something about ourselves as well as about the nature of things.

We collect possessions to comfort ourselves, from addiction, and to measure out the passing of our lives – from wedding rings to birthday presents. We collect because we are drawn to the glitter of shiny metal, or its more recent matt-black equivalent, and to the subtler pleasure of nostalgia for the recent past, and the memory of far-distant history. We collect objects to learn more about the world, and the people who shaped it. We collect to improve ourselves, to demonstrate our taste, to inject a sense of order, discipline and control into our lives, and sometimes to signal our distress and console ourselves in our inability to deal with the world. These are the motivations that designers need to understand, and the qualities which they manipulate when they create objects, whatever their nominal function.

To collect any kind of ostensibly utilitarian object betrays the anything-but-utilitarian nature of the significance that they have for us. When we collect an object, from a chair to a banknote, we have cancelled out its nominal purpose. We have traded in the original meaning and are looking for something else from them.

Given that it is perfectly possible to use a laptop or smartphone to listen to just about any radio station on earth, perhaps nobody needs to own a radio at all. But putting that to one side, one radio per household member should more than suffice for all practical purposes. How then can I justify the fact that I have four radios in my study, only one of which I have switched on in the past eight years, three more in my bedroom, one in my bathroom and yet another three in my kitchen? An art dealer of my acquaintance has more than 300 radio sets, the most recent of them manufactured in 1961, and some dating back as far as 1924. Clearly it is not their signal and sound quality that explains why we want to have them. They are reminders of a time when a wireless set was a piece of furniture that occupied a position at the centre of the home as important as the hearth. Twist a knob, and a distant announcer's voice would come flooding into sharp focus, bringing news of disaster and deliverance. Tuning Wells Coates's circular set for Ecko, designed in 1932, lights up the name of one long-gone ghost station after another, but it is the voices of today's BBC broadcasters that emerge from the loudspeaker, not men in dinner jackets reading the news in received pronunciation English.

Radio design depended on countless variations of a basic theme centred on the tuning process, the off switch and the loudspeaker. The earliest radio I have is made by Brionvega, designed by Marco Zanuso and Richard Sapper in the early 1960s, and is based around a hinge. The loudspeaker is in one half, the tuner in the other. The two halves can fold shut, to be carried, or open up when in use. The controls move up and down, to reveal a flash of colour. For me it is the summation of a particular moment in Italian design, and an insight into the minds of two of its most gifted designers. They had transformed what had become a familiar, everyday device, and given it the promise, if not the substance, of a far more capable piece of technology. I have a Bang & Olufsen Beolit 707, designed with the austerity of a Danish town hall from the 1950s, and a Braun clock radio: a curious twin-eyed box from which the clear Perspex grille has come detached, revealing the cardboard loudspeaker drum that it once concealed.

And then there are the banknotes. I have a ten-year-old Turkish 100,000-lira note that is a lesson in national iconography and economics. Kemal Atatürk, the founder of modern Turkey, is represented on one side in his double-breasted suit, handkerchief in his top pocket, receiving a bouquet of flowers from a cluster of children in the manner of dictators everywhere. On the other side, less conventionally, he appears twice. In one cameo he is portrayed in his uniform as an equestrian statue, drawing his sword. The other, larger image shows him in wing collar and striped tie, smiling through a lock of hair flopping forward. Since this note was issued, Turkey has decided to re-denominate its currency, knocking a whole line of noughts off the banknote, but retaining Atatürk and his dress shirt. It sits in a drawer in my study, along with a Bank of China foreign-exchange certificate that looks like a cigarette coupon, a Singapore dollar with a junk on one side and the Sentosa Satellite Earth Station on the other, and a Reserve Bank of India note. The Indian note is guaranteed by the central government and shows the marks of a dozen pins that have been used by previous owners to keep it safe. I have several notes with images of architects on them. The £20 Clydesdale note with Glasgow's second-most famous architect, Alexander Greek Thomson, issued in 1999, is framed on the wall of my study. It was designed to mark Glasgow's City of Architecture and Design year. Fred Goodwin signed it personally before he left the Clydesdale to run the Royal Bank of Scotland into the ground.

The current Swiss ten-franc note with Le Corbusier on it is in an envelope, alongside a defunct Finnish fifty-markka note featuring Alvar Aalto, and the Slovenian 500-toller bill with Jože Plečnik, architect of Ljubljana's university library, portrayed in bow tie, broad-brimmed hat and beard, and an ancient 1,000-crown Austro-Hungarian banknote that my grandmother folded away for a rainy day.

I have the ten-guilder Dutch note that came as close as banknotes ever have to complete abstraction, and the Hong Kong ten-dollar note that looks remarkably like it. This is not what a collector would call a collection at all. But I am interested in what this apparently random accumulation of banknotes has to say about how nations choose to portray themselves, and what that reveals about them.

I lack the discipline to be a collector's collector. I have no desire to gather together an example of every Braun radio ever made, just as I was never very organized about stamps, never quite working out if I was after complete definitive sets or chronological completeness.

I find it impossible to fill a notebook from start to finish, but dart about from back to front, using up three pages here, half a page there, sometimes one way up, sometimes another. I am content to have a sequence of radios on my desk, one shelf away from the row of miniature modern classic chairs. These, of course, are shameless about having no purpose other than to be collected and sit on a shelf, like a line of Eiffel-Tower-in-a-snowstorm paperweights. The private urge to collect reflects a compulsion to acquire, label, place and fix, and so to instigate order.

Public museum collections have another purpose; they are used to convey messages about how countries, or leaders, see themselves, from Napoleon's triumphalist looting of Italy to fill the Louvre to the idea of shoring up a sense of national identity that underpins the modern Greek interest in the Parthenon marbles. Or in the way that the Tate in London took the decision to divide itself into Tate Britain and Tate Modern, to convey a more complex sensibility about Britain's evolving sense of itself. Public and private collections have a way of merging into each other. Some collectors are driven by a private hunger; there are others consumed by a need for public recognition, something that goes beyond personal hinterland and tips into vanity. Armand Hammer, for one, had sufficient self-belief to presume to name a folio of Leonardo da Vinci drawings the Codex Hammer, simply because he happened to have owned them for fourteen years. It's not the designation that the current owner, Bill Gates, has adopted.

One way to understand collecting is to view it as involving the accumulation of appropriate relics with which to fill the shrine that will make the founder's name immortal, a modern version of Chinese paper grave goods, or the equipment entombed with the pharaohs to furnish their needs in the afterlife. That is definitely the message you get at the Metropolitan Museum in New York, where some bequests were made on the condition that collections would be shown exactly as they were once displayed in the home of the donor, with rooms recreated in minute detail.

A more nuanced understanding of collecting looks beyond status, death and profit, and explores a collection as a chance to impose control and order on that tiny part of the disorderly universe which is within the reach of an individual. Even the most celebrated collectors may appear to have no coherent view about why they do it, but their lives offer some clues. When Jean Paul Getty was America's richest man, he kept a stream of fine-art shippers constantly on the move. Month after month through the 1960s and early 1970s, a seemingly endless supply of carefully packed crates, to be opened only in climate-controlled conditions, travelled back and forth across the world accompanied by couriers wearing white cotton gloves. Inside these beautifully made cases, each stencilled with his name, were French tapestries, rococo furniture, rare books, paintings, sculptures and silverware that Getty himself sometimes never even saw. He kept telling himself, and the world, that his collecting days were over, that he had stopped in 1964, but there was always another Rubens to buy, another vase or another Seurat.

His agents bought them in the world's auction rooms and from favoured dealers. Some were shipped directly to Malibu, to the museum that bore his name, which he paid to build, and for which he met all the running costs, but which he never visited. Some were donated to other museums. A few ended up at his house in England.

It hadn't always been that way. The twenty-five-foot long Ardabil carpet, woven in the sixteenth century, that he bought in 1931 for $70,000 and called 'the finest Persian carpet in the world' spent some time on the floor of his apartment in New York. What he did not say is that it was one of a pair acquired in 1870 by a British dealer, and that his carpet had been partially sacrificed to restore the larger version that is still in the collection of the Victoria and Albert Museum in London. Getty said that he turned down an offer of $250,000 from King Farouk of Egypt, who wanted it as a wedding gift for the Shah of Iran. Not long after acquiring it, Getty gave it to the Los Angeles County Museum of Art. 'It has been said that the carpet is too good to be seen by Christian eyes, but for me it was just too good to be seen by just a few people, and so I donated it to the museum,' Getty wrote in his memoirs.

Collecting for Getty had begun as a personal obsession with Roman and Greek relics, French furniture and European painting. Then his idiosyncratic collection began to be seen by a handful of visitors on the limited number of days that his weekend house in Malibu opened to the public. When Getty moved to Europe, he left behind a purpose-built private museum housed in an archaeologically precise recreation of a Pompeian villa. After Getty's death, his trustees poured his money into a series of new buildings for the sprawling Getty Center with its archives, study centres and its museum. The architecture, by Richard Meier, would be unlikely to have appealed to its benefactor, given his reluctance to acquire anything later than the Impressionists, and judging from his remark in 1970 that 'I refuse to pay for one of those concrete-bunker-type structures that are the fad among museum architects nor for some stainless steel and tinted glass monstrosity.'

What drove Getty to collect so compulsively when he was so financially cautious that he had a payphone installed in Sutton Place, his Tudor home in Surrey? Getty was self-confident enough to have constructed a version of the story that presented his collection as both a personal pleasure and a civic duty. In 1965, Getty published *The Joys of Collecting*, more of a pamphlet than a book, in which he said that he hoped his 'modest and unpretentious' museum would 'provide pleasure to the people from the Los Angeles region who were interested in my collection'. More revealingly, he described collecting as 'one of the most exhilarating and satisfying of all human endeavours'. Getty talks of 'the pleasure that comes from getting what you want'. The pleasure Getty took from his collection seems to have come from asserting his view of the world against that of the common herd, to demonstrate that he did things his own way. 'Following the crowd offers no real satisfaction,' Getty said. But he was not oblivious to what others said and thought of him. He was sensitive enough never to forget a sleight, and combative enough always to try to have the last word. He quoted one critic who accused him of dilettantism: 'Paul Getty buys only what he likes and lacks the singleness of purpose and the concentration that ... should characterize a collection.' He then cites in self-justification the words of Sir Alec Martin, chairman of Christie's auction house, an institution of which Getty was an important customer. Martin declared, 'I am rather fed up with these impersonal complete collections which are chosen by someone for somebody else,' and went on to praise the enormous public service that Getty's collection represented.

In his combative and garrulous autobiography, *As I See It*, Getty repeats every newspaper story about him, from non-existent assignations in the bar at the Hotel Pierre to the reception his collection and his museum got from the critics, only to swat them away. 'Reconstructing the Villa dei Papyri was seen as unconventional, and un-museum-like, by which I suppose they mean it did not look like penitentiary modern like so many museums,' he wrote. But all the un-ruffled Getty, as he describes himself, has to do is wait long enough, and pretty soon he can quote the *LA Times*'s critic claiming that there is no better museum in the USA.

Getty goes on to explain that having donated the collection, paid for the cost of building the museum, as well as the salaries and the running costs, expenditure that he itemized down to the last cent, each of the 300,000 visitors a year was costing him ten dollars or, after allowing for tax relief, three dollars.

The Joys of Collecting talks about the way that judicious contrasts between paintings from different periods can be made by relying on the enlightened eye of the collector.

'Raphael and Renoir can comfortably sit in the same room.' But to squeeze in Op Art would have been going too far for Getty.

The diaries Getty kept from 1938 to 1976, in uniform ring-binder notebooks, offer some better clues as to what it was that drove him. They have all been digitized now and, with the exception of the politically sensitive material on his dealings with the Saudi and Iranian royal families, they can be read online. In handwriting that lurches back and forth over the years from the chaotically illegible to the laboriously childish, he records visiting half-empty museums. He noted a nineteenth-century mansion that impressed him and which he thought 'must have cost $2 million complete with furnishings and works of art'. In this same laundry-list tone, he records his blood pressure, the state of his stools, the time of the train he took to Dover, and the price he paid for some oil shares. He records his first meeting with Lord Duveen, precursor of every contemporary art dealer, who, with the convenient attributions furnished him by Bernard Berenson, equipped America's robber barons with all that they desired in the way of culture.

Duveen was the Gagosian and the Jopling of his day, mixing with East Coast American new money and dealing in old masters rather than Ukrainian oligarchs and Damien Hirst, but offering them much the same range of services. Duveen, Getty said, looked '55 but was aged 69'. Getty noted that in one year Henry Frick had spent $7 million with Duveen, including the purchase of the 'Fragonard room to Frick for $1.25m having bought it from

Morgan'. Of his own first purchase from Duveen, Getty notes: 'Bought a carpet that had belonged to the Sultan of Turkey, taken in spoil in Vienna in 1689.' He then records its size, its previous owners, and what he had paid for it. Clearly questionable provenance was not something that Getty was squeamish about. As he acknowledged, the Ardabil carpet might well have been looted too. He recounts the suggestion that Russian troops took it from the shrine for which it was originally woven.

To judge by Getty's case, there is a connection of some kind between the collecting impulse and a passionate commitment to diary-keeping. It is more than wordplay to suggest that a diary is about recollection. It is certainly true that diaries are about establishing a sense of order in the confusion of the world, and perhaps to provide a similar kind of record that provenance offers a work of art. Nobody would read Getty's diaries for their literary quality. Henry James and Walter Benjamin offer rather more elegance. Getty's diaries remind us of the challenge that faces researchers when so much source material is instantly accessible. It's not enough for the academic to triumphantly gain access to an archive. They need to make something of the material.

James and Benjamin were both fascinated by the idea of collecting, and they also spent their lives collecting impressions for their diaries, listing and archiving them. They reflected on the meaning of collections and museums. In his novel *The Spoils of Poynton*, James wrote: '"Things" were of course the sum of the world; only, for Mrs Gereth, the sum of the world was rare French furniture and oriental china. She could at a stretch imagine people's not having, but she couldn't imagine their not wanting and not missing.'

Walter Benjamin famously examined the impulse behind collecting in *The Arcades Project*. He wrote that:

> For the collector, the world is present, indeed ordered, in each of his objects. We need only recall what importance a particular collector attaches not only to his object, but also to its entire past, whether this concerns the origin and objective characteristics of the thing. Or the details of its external history, previous owners, price of purchase current value and so on. All of these 'objective' data come together for the true collector, in every single one of his possessions, to form a whole magical encyclopaedia, a world ordered, whose centre is in the fate of objects. It suffices to observe just one collector, as he handles the items in his showcase. No sooner does he hold them in his hand than he appears inspired by them, and seems to look through them into the distance, like a portent of the future.

Benjamin, who was very particular about his own note-books, never saw Getty's diaries, but he could have been describing them.

Despite his huge financial success, and the breezy self-confidence of his memoirs, aspects of Getty's personal history suggest a man driven by compulsions and anxieties.

As he grew older, he experienced an increasing fear of flying. Collecting offered solace. Life has no pattern, but a collection, even one that he did not see much of but simply ordered into existence, could create at least the sense of internal consistency that offers purpose, structure, meaning and, most of all, control.

Sigmund Freud devoted considerable attention to the psychopathology of gambling, an addiction which he did not have, and to smoking, an addiction which he did. But he said less about collecting, which was a compulsion for him. In 1938, just before Freud was forced to leave Nazi-controlled Vienna for exile in London, Edmund Engleman photographed the 2,000 or so objects Freud had acquired over the previous forty years since his father had died. On his desk he had a representation of Isis suckling the infant Horus, made before 664 BC. He bought pieces of Greek and Roman statuary and ancient Chinese ceramics. Engleman's photographs provided a record that allowed his loyal assistant to replicate the desk cluttered with specimens that had always dominated Freud's consulting rooms when he got to England.

In 1899, while working on *The Interpretation of Dreams*, Freud took a fragment of his collection with him to his retreat in the mountains. 'My old grubby gods who take part in the works as paperweights for the manuscripts,' as he described them. He once told Jung: 'I must always have an object to love.'

Interestingly, when he was nearing the end of his life, Freud wrote that 'a collection to which there are no new additions is really dead'. From time to time, Freud offered more or less pragmatic accounts of his passion for objects. 'The psychoanalyst, like the archaeologist, must uncover layer after layer of the patient's psyche, before coming to the deepest most valuable treasures.' But the occasional hints that he let drop were rather more revealing of the nature of his passion for collecting. Every time that he bought a new piece, it was placed on the dinner table, 'in front of him, as a companion, during the meal', he told his biographer Ernest Jones.

There is a hierarchy among collectors and collections, and it is not one that is necessarily based on the price that objects can command. To collect art is to place yourself at the top of the hierarchy. Even if some stamps can command prices that make them more valuable than many works of art, most stamp collectors would hesitate to suggest that the objects of their desire have more cultural significance than art. But stamp collecting is probably ahead of collecting cheese labels, biscuit tins or postcards. Or at least it was. Andy Warhol spent seventeen years of his life filling innumerable cardboard boxes in his New York town house with the detritus of everyday life. Every time he filled one, it was sealed, numbered, dated and shipped off to a store in New Jersey. At the time of his death, he had completed 610 boxes. They now sit in the Andy Warhol Museum in Pittsburgh. A team of archivists spent six years examining their contents and entering the results of their work into the museum's database. A typical Warhol box has 400 objects in it, but some have as many as 1,200. Their contents range from a mouldering piece of Caroline Kennedy's wedding cake to a mummified human foot belonging to an ancient Egyptian. There is a Ramones single signed by Joey Ramone. There are newspaper cuttings, letters from the famous (the poet Allen Ginsberg) and the obscure (the Warhol cousins). And there is much, much more than even the chaos of the boxes. Warhol left behind a town house crammed with his possessions. There were bags filled with antiques, clothes and books, the product of his daily shopping expeditions. One drawer held a collection of jewellery and another was stuffed full of banknotes. There were piles of furniture, fan mail, old soup tins, and his collection of thirty-seven silver wigs that he was in the habit of wearing two at a time. It is the kind of random accumulation that sanitation departments are sometimes called on to fumigate, in houses in which an agoraphobic recluse has died alone.

The power of Warhol's name, and the resources of the Warhol Foundation – which spent $600,000 cataloguing and organizing the chaotic material from the boxes – has transformed a pile of junk into, whatever Warhol's intentions were, what might either be a collection or a kind of artwork in its own right.

It is one example of many that could be seen as having toppled or inverted the collecting hierarchy. Art is at the top of the pyramid, and design, or decorative art as it was once called, is way down. If Warhol's junk has intrinsic meaning, then why not the obsessions of outsider artists, or of Robert Opie, whose extensive packaging collection began with a discarded chocolate-bar wrapper picked up from the pavement, and which now fills an entire museum of brands in west London.

Art values, or, perhaps more accurately, art prices, are subject to a form of market-making that is shaped in much the same way that financial analysts rate corporate stock. The buyers mostly rely on the expert opinion of advisers who are not themselves purchasers. Neither financial analysts nor dealers are immune to fashion but the rhetoric is always of aesthetic achievement or fundamental financial indicators. In stamp collecting, it is rarity alone rather than beauty or technical prowess that attracts the premium. Of course rarity is an issue in art. Vermeer may or may not be an artist superior to Rembrandt, but there is much less of his work to go around and, as a result, he costs more.

Collecting is in one sense about remembering, but the digital world never lets us forget anything. Paradoxically, it has also undermined our ability to remember. Our employment prospects are haunted by our Facebook pages. Our email and text trails will last as long as the server farms that have already conferred a kind of immortality on anybody with a Twitter account,

But Google is costing us the use of our memory muscles, and, worse, we are losing the comfort that every previous generation has been able to take in its possessions. We are a society that owns more things than any other in history, but never have they been discarded so quickly. We are a species that is used to measuring out the passing of our lives through the marks and scratches, the dents and wear and tear on metal and wood, stone and leather. Dramatic or banal, they tell us about who we once were. We have an emotional need to pass things on. We remember our grandparents, and parents, through the things that they leave us. And we want to do the same with what we bequeath to our children. And yet the range of objects left to pass on is dwindling as digitalization takes over. There is an insidious and effective advertising campaign for a Swiss watch that shows a groomed and greying but still slender master of the universe with his adolescent, yet equally elegant, son. You never actually own one of these, you just look after it for the next generation, runs the strapline. This is, of course, an invitation to spend the price of a small car as a means of telling the time that is no more accurate or convenient than the average mobile phone But it is also a sharp reminder of what objects once meant and what we forlornly hope that they still might be. It's not just the precious things that are the material means of carrying a memory. It used to be the anonymous things that we used every day.

The mobile phone is not just a watch substitute, it has abolished a whole lot of other objects. And very often it goes to landfill no more than nine months after it comes out of its glossy box, to make way for the next generation, which, as Morris's law so accurately predicted, will be twice as powerful for half the price.

We are seeing technological change at unprecedented speed transforming the rituals of everyday life. There is no going back, the wristwatch hangs on a little desperately thanks only to the massive investment of the watch industry in advertising and marketing. But other objects that are usually seen as gifts to mark special events, such as the fountain pen or the clock, are on the verge of extinction. And a USB stick is not going to have the same resonance.

To judge by the number of collectors who transfer their energies apparently at random from contemporary furniture to Disney memorablia, from Wiener Werkstätte silver to suits of armour, it is not necessarily the object itself that is the primary attraction for them. Value can also serve to reflect the egotism of competition. When Yves Saint Laurent's collection was auctioned in 2009, $19.4 million of the total $28 million paid was for an Eileen Gray armchair (the highest price paid for a work of twentieth-century design at auction). This can partly be explained by the rivalry between the two collectors bidding for it. Set against the cost of acquiring a complete Gray villa, it's a price that makes no sense. But it is a reflection of another essential aspect of the collecting instinct, that relentless desire to possess an object and at the same time to deny possession of it to others. After accumulating wealth, affluence is no longer enough. To differentiate themselves one from another, the wealthy try to define themselves by the scale and quality of their collections.

Price is also a reflection of the patina of the individual history of an object. That it had once belonged to Saint Laurent could be seen to have an impact on the price, in a way in which Armand Hammer's brief ownership of Leonardo's papers does not. What price does not always do is reflect the inherent quality or interest of an object. With its ram's horn arms, the most expensive piece of twentieth-century

furniture ever made is certainly neither the most characteristic nor the most impressive of Gray's designs, but for the
pathological collector that is not always the point.

Orhan Pamuk's remarkable novel *The Museum of
Innocence* provides a more engaging insight into the psychology of collecting than a saleroom catalogue. At first
reading, it appears to be the story of a doomed love affair
between Kemal, the narrator, and Füsun, a young woman
who, though she is his distant cousin, is represented as his
social inferior. Pamuk uses their relationship as the underpinning for a miniaturist portrait of the society in which it took
place: the Turkey of the 1970s. It's a world of chauffeur-driven,
vintage American cars kept running in the absence of more
up-to-date replacements deterred by tariff walls. There are
advertising hoardings adorned by imported blonde German
models, a far-from-subtle cinema industry and venal gossip
columnists. But it was also an Istanbul, as Pamuk describes it, that had mass-circumcision ceremonies arranged
in poorer neighbourhoods for boys whose families could
not afford them. It had dance halls and belly dancers, and
certain streets ran with the blood of sheep sacrificed in huge
numbers on holy days.

Pamuk studied architecture as a young man, and
is still fascinated by the complex layers of urbanism in
Istanbul. He brings both these elements to the book, alongside his exploration of collecting: a combination that I find
particularly compelling.

Turkey had not yet fully come to terms with rapid
modernization, a word which had particular resonance in

the republic that Atatürk had built on militant secularism. Istanbul had its SOM-designed Hilton Hotel – in which a key scene in the novel is set. Perched on a hilltop, it was an architectural symbol of modernity, visible from across the city. Yet, it served as much to draw attention to Turkish ambivalence about modernity. Pamuk suggests it was one of the few places in Turkey that couples could register without producing a marriage certificate. This is all described in the novel in exquisite and affecting detail, while in the background the regular military coups, and the bombings of the period, are glimpsed from a distance, barely acknowledged by the characters who furnish the foreground.

Gradually, it emerges that the novel is not what it appears on the surface. From the opening of the book, Pamuk's protagonist starts to measure out the course of his relationship in objects: the earring that Füsun loses when they are making love; the handbag that he buys for his fiancée, Sibel, from the shop in which Füsun works, and which he is embarrassed to discover may be a locally made copy of a French original. Pretty soon he is surreptitiously pocketing Füsun's discarded cigarettes. Then, he starts to steal things from her parents' home.

But Pamuk didn't just explore the meaning of collecting in fictional terms in his novel, he built an actual collection, and a museum to accommodate it, in Beyoğlu, the area of Istanbul in which its Jewish, Greek and Armenian citizens lived until the collapse of the Ottoman empire. It was where the Sultan installed the trams, electric street lights and department stores that coexisted with an atrophied government system in the last years of the nineteenth century.

Pamuk's book is in part a reflection on the nature of the museum as physical experience. It is also an account of what it means to collect. Pamuk identifies himself with his protagonist, and the solace that he finds in collecting. 'I think that getting attached to objects happens in traumatic times, and love is a trauma. Perhaps when they are in trouble, people hoard things. People get attracted to objects. Hoarding reaches the level of collecting when there is a story that unites them.'

The novel reflects a collection that was built up over many years, both before and after Pamuk began writing it. Since his days in the flea markets and shops piled high with salvaged fragments of past lives, guarded by unshaven men, the digital world has transformed the way people collect. 'Once you did it on foot, you had to walk. With the internet, you collect by finger, click, click, click,' says Pamuk, leaping up and setting off on another of his brief tours of his entrance hall. 'We may ridicule that, but the effect was that prices went up. People never collected used toothbrushes, people did not collect liquor bottles, but they did collect small miniature bottles. Key holders used to be collectibles, suddenly, they disappeared.'

Pamuk's museum is not simply a literary device, nor is it only a species of art installation, though it could be seen as one. Installations do not, however, for the most part, come equipped with an operational fire exit. There is a director; there is a bookshop selling postcards and a

range of art books; there is a ticket office; and there are security guards. A steady stream of visitors is prepared to pay
the modest price of admission; free if you have purchased the
book. Tickets are sold from a window that looks out on to
the street: the door opens and visitors find themselves in the
midst of a hollowed-out space that Pamuk compares to the
Guggenheim spiral. Like the book, which appears to be a
love story but is something else, so the museum only appears
to be a museum of social and urban history.

Though both novel and installation give a remarkably resonant portrait of a complex city at a very particular
moment in its long history, they are in fact an exploration of
the nature of collecting and its obsessive character. And that
is what sets the museum apart from any museum of civic life
that it may superficially resemble. One entire wall of its entrance hall displays the 4,213 cigarettes that Füsun smoked
from the day she first met Kemal until the termination of
their relationship. Each cigarette is annotated in Pamuk's
handwriting, whose angular compression reveals his years
as an architecture student. The cigarettes, of course, are
elaborate fictions, or can perhaps be described as fakes.
Even if there had been a real Füsun, she certainly did not
smoke these particular cigarettes. But the handwriting is
real enough.

Pamuk has made a museum that is far from innocent. He has worked with a skilful graphic design team to
fabricate many items such as the label of the Turkish-made
fizzy drink that features prominently in the novel, as well
as the advertising featuring the glamorous German model.

It looks utterly authentic, a loving evocation of a moment when sideburns had first sprouted in modern Turkey, but is as fictitious as the wall of cigarettes. The brand never existed. The book is no more innocent: Pamuk's protagonist, Kemal, shares many of Pamuk's own biographical details, but there is also a character named Orhan Pamuk, who takes on the narrative at the close of the book. Pamuk's lovingly created mementos sit alongside artefacts which actually are old: wireless sets, bird cages, crockery, cutlery and matchbooks.

Pamuk tells me that he met the man who catalogued the Warhol boxes. But he is not convinced by them: 'Warhol was so smart about organizing his own fame. I don't see what he did as art. There is a difference between Warhol's randomly collected objects, and the contents of the Museum of Innocence, they are not random,' he says of his museum.

C is for
Critical
Design

To the touch, Tony Dunne and Fiona Raby's snow-white mohair-wool cushion has the innocence of a soft toy soothing an anxious child back to sleep from a waking nightmare. At first glance, it seems to come as close as designers can ever get to giving an object the more appealing characteristics of a domestic pet. But look at its shape, and another, far from innocent aspect becomes apparent.

The cushion's silhouette has the unmistakable form of a mushroom cloud, taken from that troubling series of photographic images of atomic tests carried out in the atmosphere in the 1950s that summed up a particular moment in history. In the increasingly desperate climate of the Cold War years, nuclear armageddon looked imminent, overshadowing every journey to school or the supermarket with a sense of unfocused but profound dread. Was this going to be the night that the horizon, lit by yellow sodium street lights, boiled with hot clouds of radioactive vapour and dust? The question was continually, distractingly, on the edge of conscious thought.

Dunne and Raby made their reputation teaching design at the Royal College of Art in London. Huggable Atomic Mushroom, as it is titled, has a hemispherical domed seat, and beneath it, impaled on a slender stalk, is a second corona-like disc forming a kind of skirt. Experts describe this as a condensation ring. William Butler Yeats, who used the words 'a terrible beauty is born' in his commemoration of Dublin's Easter Rising in 1916 , might have put it better. There were other versions in different fabrics, colours and sizes.

There are several possible ways to understand this

object. Despite its title, it might be considered as just another piece of mute furniture, an ottoman stool to be compared with all the other stools in the same category, on the basis of comfort, looks and price. It might be regarded as a piece of extraordinarily offensive kitsch, like one of those inflatable representations of Munch's screaming figure that seeks to make a novelty from the unspeakably tragic.

Is it an example of the current wave of objects that take the form of design but ask to be treated as art? Or do you take Dunne and Raby at their word when they suggest that 'Huggable Atomic Mushrooms are for people afraid of nuclear annihilation.' They claim that the basis for the stool is in the clinical treatments devised to treat various kinds of phobias, inoculating sufferers against their fears by subjecting them bit by bit to limited exposure to unthreatening doses of snakes, spiders or air travel.

Their cushions come in a range of sizes. 'Which Huggable Mushroom you might need to buy depends on the size of your fear.' The cushion emerged as one of a number of objects that were produced for a project conceived as 'designs for fragile personalities in anxious times'. As they put it, the project 'focused on irrational but real anxieties such as the fear of alien abduction or nuclear annihilation. Rather than ignoring them, as most design does, or amplifying them to create paranoia, we treated their phobias as though they were perfectly reasonable and designed objects to humour their owners.'

But that is not really what the cushion is about either, any more than, when Dunne and Raby's students at the Royal College of Art proposed breeding pigs to grow heart valves genetically compatible with individual human-transplant recipients, they were actually planning to carry out a medical procedure or to get involved with animal husbandry. What they were doing was trying to make a polemical point. Despite the deadpan tone, Dunne and Raby are not really expecting that they will actually be soothing the genuinely troubled with their atomic cushion. I am not sure that they would want to, even if they could. Atomic annihilation, along with a lot of other things from climate change to the destructive potential of overpopulation, really is something to worry about. Anxiety is an entirely rational reaction to all these manifestations of the multiple threats we face.

Dunne and Raby have a rather narrower objective in mind. What they hope their work will do is persuade us to consider design in a different way. They want us to understand that design goes beyond the superficial optimism of engineering consumer desire. The pig-transplant project looked at what is at stake when a living creature is bred to share some of our genes and is then sacrificed to ensure our own survival. If the human recipient is to survive by the harvesting of the valve, it can only be at the expense of the pig, a fraction of whose tissue will live on in its by then slightly piggy host. Dunne and Raby's students contrived an object, trough at one end, dining table at the other, that human and animal could share, signalling their intimate connection, making explicit the relationship between them and inviting the recipient to reflect on the essential nature of the transaction. It makes a more convincing case than the mushroom-cloud stool.

Dunne and Raby's works are not meant to be understood as pieces of design in the way that design is conventionally represented. They are not intended as achievable propositions or blueprints for actual products. They belong instead to the rather more nuanced category of design that wants to ask questions about the purpose of design. Design as it is traditionally defined is affirmative. Dunne and Raby see their version of it as critical. Mainstream design is problem-solving, while critical design looks to identify problems. Design that attempts to serve the market tries to provide answers, while Dunne and Raby use design as a method to ask questions.

Precisely what are the questions posed by the mushroom-cloud cushion? The most persuasive is that it asks us to interrogate the way in which design manipulates our emotional responses. 'Conventionally, design is used to create objects that make us feel better about ourselves, to suggest that we are cleverer, or richer, or more important, or younger than we actually are,' say Dunne and Raby. The mushroom-cloud cushion is a mildly sinister demonstration of the essentially ridiculous nature of this process. Our fear of the prospect of nuclear annihilation will no more be resolved by a cushion than a new kitchen will rescue a failing marriage.

For the market, design is about production, it is not about debate. Mainstream design looks for ways to be innovative; Dunne and Raby want to be provocative. As they put it, rather than looking for concept design, they offer conceptual design. Rather than treating design as science fiction they say they are interested in social fiction. They don't want design to make us buy things, instead they want to use design make us think; they are less interested in the process of design than in the idea of authorship. They see their work as critical design.

On one level the idea that design can be a critical activity, used to question the industrial system that brought it into being in the first place, is perverse. It is as unlikely a concept as critical civil engineering or critical dentistry. But critical design has a history almost as long as industrial design itself, certainly going back as far as William Morris.

Design is not entirely synonymous with industrialization. There were forms of mass production that had demanded the use of design before the Industrial Revolution: coins and amphorae, for example, which date back thousands of years. But it was nineteenth-century factories, which depended on design in the modern sense, that eventually created a new social class, the industrial proletariat, uprooted from their traditional rural communities and herded into urban slums. Social critics were horrified by what they saw as the degradation of work in the factories and by the squalor of life in the industrial cities. Cultural critics deplored what they saw as the banal and shoddy ugliness of what the machines produced as they destroyed the skills of craftsmen. William Morris deplored everything. He wanted revolutionary change, and he wanted to design beautiful wallpaper.

Morris was one of the most unforgiving and eloquent of the many critics of the industrial system. He was against mass production and the moral void that he believed it represented. But paradoxically he has also been characterized as one of the founders of the modern movement. Nikolaus Pevsner's book *Pioneers of Modern Design: From William Morris to Walter Gropius* portrayed Morris as a key figure in the evolution of contemporary design, partly, at least, in an attempt to make modernism palatable to his British audience by giving it a home-grown pedigree rather than characterize it with a litany of German and Dutch names.

And it is perhaps because of this that Morris's work has been misunderstood. It has been taken as a series of practical propositions in the classic modernist sense, and judged on that basis it was a protracted failure. He wanted to make design that offered the masses dignified objects of a certain quality. But by rejecting industrialization he made it impossible to make them at a price that they could afford. Unless one regards his work as essentially critical, as asking a question rather than offering a solution, it is hard to see Morris as a forward-looking designer. But if his furniture is understood as critical design, in the sense that Dunne and Raby mean it, as asking questions about the place of design in society, about the relationship between maker and user, then it is anything but a failure.

Morris looked back to a pre-industrial vernacular, while others were ready to embrace the contemporary world with results that made his contempt for machinery seem irrelevant. He wanted to create the sort of objects that depended on skills that the industrial world was making obsolete. He wanted craftsmen to have the chance to take pleasure in their work, because he believed in the dignity of labour for its own sake, and because he saw it as the route to achieving the highest aesthetic qualities. And he wanted ordinary people to be able to furnish their homes with worthwhile possessions.

It was, of course, a violently contradictory position. Craft-made objects were too expensive for the working class to afford them. Morris's clients necessarily had to be wealthy, and the mismatch between his ambition and the reality proved intolerable for him.

While Morris was working on the interior of a house for Sir Lowthian Bell, his client heard him 'talking and walking about in an excited way'. When Bell went over to enquire if anything was wrong, 'he turned on me like a wild animal and replied, "It is only that I spend my life ministering to the swinish luxury of the rich."' And yet Morris was prepared to employ children in his weaving workshops; their fingers could do finer work. The contradiction here is almost as glaring as the one that saw Morris struggling with the knowledge that his own freedom of action was dependent on the income he inherited from his father's investments in mining shares.

The Industrial Revolution was the cause, as Morris saw it, of the impoverishment and alienation of the daily lives of the vast majority of people. Morris's socialist impulses went hand in hand with a distaste for what he saw as the inferior products of machinery and the wage slavery that came with it for the worker. Through his company, Morris & Co., he aimed to create robust and well-made products for an enlightened proletariat, and to offer an alternative to the corrupting influences of ornamentalism run riot from the newly established factories. 'Our furniture,' he wrote, 'should be good citizen's furniture, solid and well made in workmanship and in design, and should have nothing about it that is not easily defensible, not monstrous or extravagant, not even beauty, lest we tire of it.'

Industrial methods produced affordable objects that craft techniques could not. Morris & Co. opened for business some four years after Morris's polar opposite, Michael Thonet, built the first of his furniture factories, at Koritschen, on the edge of the Austro-Hungarian empire, conveniently placed for its supply of timber and unskilled but cheap labour. By the start of 1914, Thonet had made seven million examples of its Number 14 design, the armless bentwood and cane-seat café chair. Morris & Co. made its products in batches seldom more than a few dozen at a time and barely outlived its founder.

Thonet depended on deskilling the making process, and reducing craftsmen to the role of machine minders on a production line assembling components. Its chairs were beautiful, elegant and affordable; and how they were made was not the issue in their appeal. Morris's workshops produced small numbers of objects which were never affordable and were not always beautiful.

Perhaps the biggest and most hostile postbag I had as a journalist was when I reviewed Fiona McCarthy's impressive biography of Morris. I found myself tentatively pointing out the curious echoes of Morris's loathing for cities, machines and all their works, expressed in his vision of an anarchic and bucolic utopia in his prophetic novel *News from Nowhere*, and the forced depopulation of Phnom Penh by Pol Pot. Morris enthusiastically described an abandoned London. Parliament Square had been turned into a dung heap, with worthless banknotes fluttering across it in the breeze. I wasn't suggesting, of course, that Morris was a mass murderer, but that there is something of the Khmer Rouge's loathing for urban elites in Morris's distaste for the modern city. As I have got older, I find myself becoming less impatient with Morris. Walking through the bleak pebble-dashed streets of Bexleyheath to find the Red House, the home he built for himself when he was first married, it's impossible not to be moved by what Morris had achieved. There would have been orchards here once, stretching all the way towards the Kentish hills. Now there is nothing but the joyless detritus of a brutal economic system based on expediency and mean-spiritedness, dreary terraced houses and joyless shopping streets. There is nothing spirit-lifting anywhere in the town until you find the now mellowed sheltering red-brick wall that curves around what had once been Morris's home. And it is then that you understand that you are being offered a vision of life as it should be rather than as it is. You see a remarkable experiment by a remarkable man, who was ready to invest time and money to show what a house could be. It's a house endearingly full of mistakes. Philip Webb, who designed the Red House for his friend, wrote much later that no architect should be allowed to design a house until they are past forty. He built the Red House for Morris when he was twenty-eight, and he conceded that it was facing the wrong way to get the best of the sun. But it was a manifesto that was to prove enormously influential. And here the house still sits, a mute reproach to all that surrounds it, a reminder that architecture at heart has to be about optimism.

Morris's furniture was political, but at the time few understood the political point that he was trying to make with it. And in the end, how political can any object be, when set against making a manifesto, or a speech, or a street protest, or starting a political party? It is not surprising that Morris ended up doing all of those things, and doing rather less as a designer and an entrepreneur.

The idea that it is possible, even an obligation, for design to criticize itself is a continuing one. Victor Papanek, the Austrian-born critic, began his book *Design for the Real World* with the ringing declaration 'there are professions more harmful than industrial design, but only a few of them', and then suggested that 'by creating whole species of permanent garbage to clutter up the landscape, and by choosing materials and processes that pollute the air we breath, designers have become a dangerous breed'.

Papanek's view was that the job of the designer is to work on socially useful projects, not to help their clients to sell overpriced consumer goods to people that neither need nor can afford them. He was a forerunner of the environmental movement with his interest in designing radios for communities without access to mains electricity, recycling and wind power.

Papanek described his position as being anti-design, which though it might sound close to the kind of critical design now practised by Dunne and Raby, actually has a rather different character. Papanek took the overheated view not just that any kind of formal design language was essentially manipulative and dishonest, but that almost any relationship between design and commerce was unacceptable. Given the roots of design in the Industrial Revolution it was an ultimately self-defeating position. His books are consciously artless; the projects he set his students, the consultancy work he did for Third World governments, all were inevitably low technology, utilitarian, unambiguous, entirely without guile and mostly futile. Dunne and Raby are critical too, but they are also interested in understanding and working with the formal language of design, and in using it against itself. This is an approach that emerged in the Italy of the late 1960s and 1970s, a troubled and narcissistic society in which the idea that the children of the rich could kill policemen, in the name of the revolution, or that millionaire yacht-owning publishers might attempt to dynamite electricity pylons to undermine capitalism did not seem far-fetched. In a climate such as this, design could become pure research, freed of the demands of production, price or brand. Designers could stop listening to anything as tiresome as a brief, or a budget, or a marketing strategy, and get on with the altogether more congenial task of speculation and criticism instead.

Not every design culture approaches this division between production and dissent in the same way. Some take a more ideological view than others. Italy gave designers the chance to work on industrial projects, within the system, but at the same time to try to explore the idea of what was sometimes called anti-design, or radical design, and which is now more commonly described as critical design. At the same time as they were designing the sofas or cutlery that furnished bourgeois Italian living rooms, Alessandro Mendini and Andrea Branzi were also working on objects that subverted and mocked bourgeois taste. Italian mainstream manufacturers were ready to commission designs that they had no chance of making in industrial quantities to demonstrate how culturally sensitive they were, and to attract media coverage.

Berlin in the 1990s took a more militantly anti-consumerist viewpoint than Italy. The Netherlands developed its own aesthetic, mostly by a process of deconstructing the language of contemporary design. Britain, or perhaps more accurately London, had a complex enough local ecology to allow multiple approaches to design to coexist.

Bit by bit, critical design managed to carve out an independent territory for itself. There were enough faculty positions in design schools, commissions for installations at the Milan furniture fair, galleries selling limited editions to collectors, and to museums, to make critical design a feasible career proposition.

Critical design has seemingly had more appeal to those museums that have taken on the role of shaping our understanding of design than the mainstream represented by technical and formal innovation. Of the eighty-four acquisitions made by the Museum of Modern Art in New York between 1995 and 2008 that could in even the most tangential way be described as British design, only a handful are industrial design in the conventional sense. The charismatic E-Type Jaguar roadster or the Vincent Black Shadow, the motorcycle manufactured from 1949, the Moulton bicycle, and a collection of work from the Cupertino studio of Jonathan Ive – culminating in an iPod, which, of course, natural British modesty prevents anybody from claiming as being an example of British design. And there are one or two pieces of design history. Gerald Summers's remarkable armchair made from a single sheet of bent, moulded and cut plywood is the highlight of these, but by far the larger proportion are the product of the critical thinking of Dunne and Raby, and their students, or those of Ron Arad, whose work is less obviously polemical but no more ready to be complicit in conventional readings of design.

These are all objects that are produced as limited editions and which present themselves as challenging the status quo. The question that arises is whether this is a redefinition of design, and the introduction of a new discipline of critical, or conceptual design. Or is it an abdication of design's responsibility to engage with the world? From this perspective, design has moved away from centre stage, as an economic and social force, and retreated into the museum and the auction house.

Dunne and Raby's strategy has been to use design as

a provocation, as a means of inoculating their students against the market, to encourage them to ask 'what if?', to invite designers to confront the uncomfortable and the disturbing, not just to unquestioningly provide a shape for an object.

> We need to move beyond designing for the way things are now and begin to design for how things could be, imagining alternative possibilities and different ways of being and giving tangible form to new values and priorities. In the field of design, users and consumers are usually characterized in narrow and stereotypical ways, resulting in a world of manufactured objects that reflects an impoverished view of what it means to be human. This project set out to develop a design approach that would lead to products that embodied an understanding of the consumer user as a complex existential being.

The issue, though, is how many times the same questions about design can be asked until the answer becomes predictable even before it is posed.

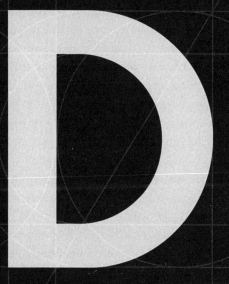

is for Design

I went to a school that was both theatrical and sporty. Lacking proficiency in either field, I took to spending my free periods in the library as a self-defence strategy. It was there, through the writings of Reyner Banham in the long-defunct weekly magazine *New Society*, that I discovered design for the first time. I was meant to be reading the key text for my A level in art history, Nikolaus Pevsner's *Pioneers of Modern Design*. It struck me as slightly musty. By comparison, Banham, once a student of Pevsner, seemed like an electrifying literary stylist. He had a way of putting half-formed thoughts that had already occurred to me into words with a sharpness and wit that made an indelible impression. I remember that he once described the clipboard as the 'power plank'. He was pointing out that the meanings of an object sometimes go beyond what its designer intended. He seemed to be offering a new way of looking at things: a modern way of understanding the modern world.

Banham could claim as his greatest achievement his transformation of the conventional Anglo-Saxon view of the modern movement. He demonstrated the significance of figures as far apart as the Russian Constructivists and the Italian Rationalists, who had previously been excluded from the usual narrative of mainstream twentieth-century architecture. In so doing, of course, he made room for himself as a new critical voice to supplant his predecessors.

In the 1950s he was one of the first to discover the work of Peter and Alison Smithson, the so-called Brutalists responsible for two of Britain's most internationally celebrated buildings of the time: a school in Hunstanton, a steel-and-glass evocation of Mies van der Rohe's Chicago, mysteriously transplanted to Norfolk; and the Economist tower, a travertine slab just off St James's in London. Banham championed Cedric Price, architect of the aviary at London Zoo, for his pragmatism. For Price, every building was out of date by the time it was finished. Banham was attracted by what he saw as the Smithsons' sceptical view of monumentality. Later on, he was clearly disappointed by the reluctance of his protégés to conform to his idea of what made architecture culturally relevant. He turned his attention to the young Norman Foster, who was capable, in those days, of telling potential clients that the answer to their needs might not be to build anything at all. Most unsettlingly of all for those who took a conventional view of architectural aesthetics, Foster spoke of his admiration for the maverick visionary Buckminster Fuller and his geodesic domes.

As time has passed, design history has emerged as an academic subject, somewhere between cultural studies and social anthropology, a shift that I don't find particularly appealing. But design keeps changing shape, which is why it matters. The clearest, but still not entirely satisfactory, way to define design is through its relationship with mass production. Some objects were mass-produced far earlier than the late eighteenth century, when the Industrial Revolution is conventionally understood to have started – coins, amphorae, Venetian galleys, bullets and arrows, for example – suggesting that design has a longer history than is sometimes claimed. But these exceptions apart, before the coming of the factory system, there was an intimate connection between the maker of an object and its user. Industrialization broke that link, and created the role of the designer in its modern sense. Now that the kind of factory where rolls of sheet steel go in at one end and completed cars come out at the other has gone, design has not disappeared, but it is being redefined once again.

Before the Industrial Revolution, a skilful craftsman could create a piece of furniture shaped to accommodate the individual needs of a specific user. He could craft a weapon for a left-handed swordsman, or make a piece of farm equipment tailored to the particular landscape in which it would be used. Objects made in this way existed in the mind of the maker before they took on physical shape. They were based on inherited forms and skills. A craftsman could make a chair working from a combination of memory and intuition. Just as a skilled cook does not need to follow a pre-planned recipe, or a musician can play an instrument without being able to read music, the craftsman does not need a drawing or a prototype to test his intentions. Such a process arguably does not involve anything that can be called design, or if it does, it is the synthesis of designing and making into one single seamless process that is closer to craft than to design. For more elaborate projects – a suit of ceremonial armour with an inlaid, elaborately figured breastplate, never intended to be used in battle, commissioned for the start of a new campaign, perhaps; a set of silver candlesticks to make a wedding dowry; or the baptistry doors for Florence's cathedral – it was different. In such circumstances the commission might involve an artist as well as a craftsman.

The artist's role was to provide the creative direction through drawings, or 'designs', that could be used to guide a network of makers who would physically carry out work to create pieces with a cultural ambition that less elaborate vernacular objects lacked. Such 'designers' were often engaged in a range of creative activities from art to architecture, by way of sculpture. They were commissioned to transform functional objects, to embellish them, and so to give them symbolic significance. Such objects could be used in a ceremonial or ritual sense, to mark a marriage, a diplomatic alliance, as a memorial, or simply as a display of wealth and status.

From the perspective of the decorative arts the relationship between maker, user and artist continues to define the essential nature of design. It is the spark that brings skill to life. But although Lorenzo Ghiberti, the goldsmith, sculptor and architect, and rediscoverer of the lost-wax casting process that was used to make the baptistry doors, can also be called a designer, looking at his working methods and ideas does not offer much help in understanding the rather different version of design now practised by Jonathan Ive at Apple, say.

When mass production severed the connection between maker and user, design started to take on meanings other than those given it by the decorative arts. Design became an assertion of modernity.

It was mass production that demanded the emergence of a new role for an individual who came to be called the designer, an individual who was not the physical maker of an object, any more than a contemporary architect is a stonemason or a carpenter or a mixer of concrete, even if their profession has its roots in these craft skills. Art too has moved in this direction, as so many artists sever any connection between art as a conceptual idea and art as the physical realization of that conception.

The factory system required the marshalling of sufficient information from the designer to define a design in enough detail for the object to be made efficiently. That is to say, it needed the drawings, or designs, that represent an object before it exists. The system also requires an understanding of how an object will be manufactured. This understanding may come from the production engineer, or it may come from a challenge by a designer who has an instinctive predisposition to ask why something cannot be done rather than to accept the limitations of a method. In either case, a prototype will be made before a production version.

The designer was needed to give a definitive form to the new categories of object that industry was inventing, and to give them a character that would persuade consumers to buy them. It became the role of the designer to create the signs that could make an object look and feel valuable enough to justify its price, and to give those objects a sense of gender when considered appropriate. A hairdryer or a razor aimed at male users, for example, could be made to look different from similar devices aimed at women. The stereotypes are insultingly obvious: soft and rounded forms are supposedly feminine. Objects aimed at men are given aggressive forms, and hard materials. The designer was also required to make an object intelligible, to equip it with the signals that communicated its purpose to a user, and the way in which to put it to use.

Vestiges of an older relationship between maker and user still linger, in the shape of a tailor-made suit for which tape measure, chalk and thread chart out the pattern for a set of clothes that will shape the perception of an individual. A similar connection is to be found in the work of those jewellers who make to individual order. It is much the same in the furnishings of a house for a wealthy patron, or in the continuing appeal of the limited edition. Such work is based on skill and expertise. In the past, this was built up often over several generations, passing from one to the next through the process of an apprenticeship, or of folk memories. The pace of change is much quicker now and the range of materials and techniques available to makers has expanded enormously.

Craft, presented rightly or wrongly as the outcome of a constant process of modest refinement, of one generation building on the precedents defined by their predecessors, was effectively contrasted by John Ruskin and William Morris – who inspired the Arts and Crafts movement – with the shallow industrial pursuit of lifeless novelty made possible by machinery.

In fact craft has its egotistical aspects too. To call yourself a craftsman or a maker is not to amputate the ego. Dale Chihuly's ubiquitous and unnecessarily energetic art glass, or John Makepeace's furniture, is as signature driven as

Philippe Starck's designs, and is neither modest nor anonymous. And that is true of every generation. It seems unlikely that, let's say, a virtuoso goldsmith such as Jacques Bilivert from sixteenth-century Delft, known for his work with Bernardo Buontalenti on a lapis lazuli vase, or Roger Fry and the amateurs of the Omega Workshops, or an eighteenth-century English cabinetmaker such as Thomas Malton were any more reticent about their accomplishments, no matter how much William Morris might have wished the contrary.

The emergence of industrial design in the modern sense has done a lot to weaken the practice of craft. When craft skills lose their practical underpinnings and become the preserve of the self-conscious craftsman, or maker as they now call themselves, rather than the traditional artisan, the urge for self-expression pushes once functional objects into baroque excess. Potters now make vases that can no longer hold flowers; bookbinders bind books that cannot be read. Look at the glasswork of a Chihuly, and you may see skill, but very little in the way of taste. Such objects bring home the sense that without the intelligence of design to provide a template for an object, skill by itself is not sufficient to produce a convincing object. Without the intelligence of design, craft has become a cultural backwater. Skills have migrated to different areas: the fibreglass pattern cutters at the McLaren car-building plant, the blades of a turbofan jet engine, the toolmakers for the presses that mass produce castings.

Skill is an accomplishment that enjoys an uncertain status. The fact that something can be done at all may be impressive, but it is the use to which a skill is put that really counts. And it is this distinction that accounts for the continuing insecurity of craft's position. There were two currents to the twentieth-century's rediscovery of its craft traditions. One, which paralleled the folk-music revival, was about the preservation of threatened traditions. The other was the sense that for craft to remain vital it had to reinvent itself, to innovate in form and materials. The former was the less problematic approach. It depended on the acquisition of the requisite skills, and could then rely on the formal archetypes developed by tradition. Innovation was more troublesome. It required more than the skills to turn wood, weave baskets, shape porcelain or chase metal; it also needed the conceptual intelligence and the formal perceptions to be able to put the skill to work in an appropriate or creative way.

The most pressing issue for the contemporary crafts is the way in which visual imaginations have been shaped by the industrial world. When we are accustomed to the forms that injection-moulded plastic or pressure casting make possible, there is a sense in which they have shaped our visual imagination, and it is hard not to see handwork through the same filter. These precedents provide a repertory of forms and materials that easily come to overshadow the possibilities of a craft maker, even if the materials and the tools he has to work with are unsuited to them. In the 1970s, the tensions between design and craft became more complex. When art schools started to produce more industrial designers than Britain's shrinking industrial base could possibly support, some of those graduates put their skills to work to produce objects in small numbers or batches in their own workshops, as a survival strategy. They were careful to emphasize that what they were doing could not be described as craft. They had been trained to do something else, and to understand that there were negative connotations to the word 'craft'. This was noticeable in how they looked to find ways to achieve the physical quality of machine-made production given that they had no means of investing in the costly tools on which true mass production depends.

It was what Jasper Morrison began to do as a student, when he put together a pair of salvaged bicycle handlebars, a piece of wood and a glass disc to create a table. And at the Royal College of Art, he made a series of wing-nut chairs and tables using the techniques and materials used for manufacturing laundry baskets. It was a strategy caught in the cracks between art and design and craft. For some it became an end in itself, for others it was a stepping stone.

David Redhead's exhibition in 2001 at the Crafts Council had the succinct and suggestive title 'Industry of One'. It perfectly captured the curious history of the relationship between 'making' and 'designing'. Making is intimately connected with skill, but design is, or ought to be, about ideas. There is in the word 'craft' a sense of defending traditions threatened by industrialization, yet also of connoisseurship. Craft continually oscillates between the impulse to reinvent, to innovate and to safeguard; while design has been seen as both a threat and an opportunity.

Few designers have had a closer acquaintance with this dichotomy than Konstantin Grcic. He began by studying at the John Makepeace School for Craftsmanship in Wood at Parnham in Dorset. Grcic remembers the gradual transition from seeing the world from the perspective of a workshop to that of a studio. To be a maker, to use the word 'craft', is in some senses to take an oppositional stance to the world around you. It is to question the values of mass production, and your place in the world that it brought into being. When Grcic arrived at Parnham, a school that could be understood as the last gasp of an arts and crafts tradition that had seen semi-utopian communities taking to the Cotswolds and the backwoods for the better part of a century, Grcic had that view, and then lost it. As he puts it, after a while at Parnham,

'even the word "making" turned into design. It includes the question of what you make, how you make it and who you make it for. It was a process. At the same time, I discovered the history of design and the work of certain designers and began to understand the larger picture. Design evolved from manufacturing, from craft and small industry. It could not be a local craftsman who drew the chair he would build. It became more complex and specialized, whether it is furniture or the more sophisticated varieties of industrial design or services. But in the end the idea of design always comes from the reality of making, it's not just a theory.

'Design can be a form of creative self-expression.

That's the way I work, it is what distinguishes design offices like mine from the ones that have a more pragmatic approach. We don't just offer a service to somebody who needs a product. We can add something extra. Authorship is part of good design, it's something that we appreciate. It's what we want in a product. A design may be good in how it functions, but it isn't interesting unless it has something that makes it appealing. Only the design can give that quality, whether or not you know the name of the person who did it.

'Design is an added value. Maybe that means the price is higher. It certainly is sometimes used in a cynical way, and people do sometimes mistrust it. A "designer" something does not stand for more quality, it is perceived as a marketing trick or as fooling us. I am not sure what the way out of this problem is. Design should still be a signature, but one that represents quality.

'There are no "non" designed products. But look at the ones where you can see that someone has sat down and tried to be original. At their best, they are reassessing, refining and rethinking – taking an object on to another level. Design can be anonymous but still represent real development. Designed products are the best ones. It's interesting how "design" has lost credibility in the product design sector, but in services we use technology design to create credibility. You design a timetable to be more reliable. In this context, design still means something. It stands for all the virtues, somebody is trying to improve things, to make them more efficient, that is how I see design.'

Design is not sculpture, although it does have a formal aspect. It is a discipline that has had much of its ideology shaped by architects, which is curious because the essence of architecture must be an interest in space. Designers have different concerns. But the two do have important things in common, which are used for similar ends, to create a sense of identity, to convey a message. This can be, at its most blatant, to give objects sales appeal, to make them appear novel and desirable.

But design is now increasingly about the need to create an experience. The sequence of questions that you are asked in order to identify yourself when calling a credit-card company. The means by which you cast your vote. The way in which you check into a hotel. The way that you pay for a mobile phone, the deliberate obscurity of the tariffs you are offered, these are all examples of experience design.

And while design has been defined by mass production, the way in which the world is making things is also in rapid transition. The system of factories, the role of the designer and the technology of tooling, they are all vanishing. The impact of digital fabrication and the process commonly described as printing will radically change the way in which things are designed and made. Sooner or later, a small box in the living room, or the shed, will have the power to allow an owner to select a design for almost anything and produce it for themselves. It's hard to imagine this as a way to produce a chair or a laptop, but it is already the way in which America's aircraft carriers replace spare parts while at sea. Elon Musk, the entrepreneur behind the Tesla electric sports car, is determined to manufacture cars in this way.

When this does become the norm, design will undergo another change of direction, one that will have consequences even more far-reaching in their impact than the coming of the factories.

IS FOR

DESIGN ART

Design has more often been defined by what it is not than by what it is. More than anything else, what design is not is art. It has at various times been referred to as commercial art, or decorative art. Deep down, design is understood as being useful, and therefore to be taken as having lesser significance than a work of art, which is unburdened by utility.

It's a tension that has left artists largely unmoved, but designers, and those fascinated by design, continually try to explore the scar tissue that divides them from art. While there is no shortage of designers who wouldn't mind presenting their work as if it were art, very few artists would have it the other way round. That does not mean that art fails to explore design as a source of subject matter. Nor that art and design lack shared interests and territory. Duchamp was intrigued by the ready-made; Richard Hamilton explored the sheen of industrial design; Damien Hirst's work is on one level about the alchemy or snake-oil salesmanship of branding.

Like two magnetized needles impaled on pivots, simultaneously poised between attraction and repulsion, artists and architects warily circle each other. They are intrigued and suspicious, jealous and dismissive of each other. It's a phenomenon reflected in the confrontation between the artist Robert Irwin and the architect Richard Meier over the Getty Museum's garden, about which one of their mutually exclusive conceptions would predominate. The well-documented tension between Frank Gehry and Richard Serra reflected a similar lack of a shared view. They were once close friends, then Serra started to complain about Gehry, who, as Serra saw it, was invading his turf to posture as an artist.

The relationship between art and design can be equally tense. The continuing doubts in the art world about Isamu Noguchi can be traced to questions about his success as a designer of paper lampshades, coffee tables and even a mass-produced Bakelite case for the Radio Nurse baby alarm. These were not the kind of things that an artist could take on before the age of irony and still retain his or her credibility. But when Pharmacy, the restaurant designed by Damien Hirst, closed, the furniture, fittings and tableware – suitably augmented by replicas – were auctioned off as if they were artworks, even though they were mostly the work of Jasper Morrison.

The conflict between art and design is, at least in part, about control. When Matisse accepted a commission to take on the art, the stained-glass windows and the vestments for a new chapel in Saint Paul de Vence, he was offered the chance to work with Le Corbusier to design a building that would be an appropriate setting for his work. According to Hilary Spurling's biography of Matisse, the offer from Père Marie-Alain Couturier, the Dominican intellectual who was trying to reinvigorate the cultural life of the Church, was rejected. Instead, Matisse chose to work with the elderly Auguste Perret, 'because he will do what I say'. The result is great art, in a bland building. To suggest that great art inside a great piece of architecture would be a better combination is to beg a lot of questions.

Unlike art, design has its roots in usefulness. The questions about what art is, and what looks closely related to it but may or may not be art, continue to trouble us. We persist in treating art as some special hybrid of magic and religion, even while we are fascinated by its place in the market. This collision between money and the supernatural makes any discussion of significance difficult. Like popes, artists need to present an air of infallibility. Once a new art-world religion has been established, every further revelation of the faith needs only to show itself as belonging to the appropriate congregation to prove that it is among the elect. If art is a belief system, then each work, no matter by how minor an artist, is part of the same divine revelation. To question its value is to doubt the faith that underpins it. And, in the process, art and branding have converged. Julian Schnabel used to do a lot of canvasses that involved smashed plates. When he stopped making them, how could anybody know they had an authentic Schnabel? Damien Hirst was so convinced that he owned the exclusive rights to the artistic deployment of dots that he tried to sue a British airline when it painted the hulls of its Boeings with dots. Lucio Fontana found his work traduced by an advertising campaign for a cigarette brand called Silk Cut.

One theory to account for the regard in which art is held is that it does not compromise. Yet Rembrandt was ready to paint to order – his fee shared among all eighteen members of *The Shooting Company of Frans Banning Cocq*, otherwise known as *The Night Watch* – to a given size, and with specialist help from his studio assistants.

Another version of the meaning of art is that it has a relationship with time that is different from the transience of design. A washing machine or a typewriter, or even, to an extent, a chair, is the response to issues that emerge from precise moments in time, the outcome of particular technologies, social practices and methods of distribution. When those technologies and customs are no longer current, the objects that embody them lose much of their significance. Out of time, they are left naked and vulnerable, if not actually irrelevant. The same, or so we comfort ourselves by believing, is not true of art, which is portrayed as if it were capable of relevance in any context. If we did not believe this, we would lose the comfort that art offers, the sense that there is something of spiritual value in the midst of our compromised world. Let's call that quality, just for a moment, beauty. It's the kind of beauty that does more than seduce, but which seems to offer some kind of truth, some kind of lasting value or quality. Yet art is also mediated by fashion and the market, as the rise, fall and resurrection of the prices commanded by the Pre-Raphaelites demonstrates.

Paradoxically, there are times when becoming technologically redundant has the effect of turning design into something that starts to take on the aura of art. When Jean Prouvé was alive, he had a special place in the minds of a generation of British architects. His pragmatic approach to manufacturing and prefabricating buildings made him crucial to the development of high-tech architecture, which celebrated the aesthetics of engineering. But his designs never had the same reach as those of Charles Eames. Prouvé seemed to belong more to the 1930s than to the 1960s, and to be involved with a dustier version of modernity. But after his death, just as his production methods were beginning to look frankly outdated, something entirely unpredictable happened. Thanks to the diligent efforts of one or two Parisian dealers, his furniture, and even his architectural relics, turned into something else. They became collector's pieces. Prouvé, a devout socialist, had designed robust, low-cost fixtures for schoolrooms and hostels as a thrifty way to civilize the public realm. Others may have given these objects a new meaning, but Prouvé never designed anything that was self-conscious, or intended to be understood as anything but utilitarian. With unbearable pathos, as they grew in value, the remaining Prouvé interiors were treated as pitilessly as an elephant reserve by an ivory poacher.

Carlo Mollino was primarily an architect, but one who was also responsible for some remarkable furniture that is much rarer than Prouvé's and so even more valuable. In addition, he produced a racing car, and a rich stream of erotically charged photography, a combination that has given him an audience that is more rooted in the art world than that of design.

Most artists in Britain in the 1960s survived by teaching rather than by selling their work. To be a designer or an architect looked like a more secure career option. Art can seem a better bet now, when a significant number of artists make the kind of money that allowed the nineteenth-century academicians to build themselves prodigious studios in Kensington or Chelsea. Another generation of prodigious studio houses is rising in Hoxton and Shoreditch, with David Adjaye providing the architecture rather than George Aitchison in Holland Park.

Design, on the other hand, can support fewer individual successes. For most designers, their work is either a salaried job or a precarious hand-to-mouth question of survival. At the beginning of the 1980s, what are now called limited-edition designs, or even design art, were part of that survival strategy for designers. When there was no demand from manufacturers for designers to work on industrially produced objects, the only strategy that they had left was to make things themselves. A chair created in this way can be understood less as a chair than as a sculptural representation of a chair. When these pieces first appeared they were on the periphery of the design world. As the auction houses and the galleries have shown an increasing interest, they have commanded higher and higher prices and, for some, have moved from the edges to occupy the centre ground.

If there is one man who has danced on this fault line between the two mutually suspicious worlds of art and design, it is Ron Arad.

He got his first major show in 1987 in Paris at the Pompidou Centre, an institution which itself was originally conceived as attempting to abolish class distinctions in visual culture. The museum celebrated its tenth anniversary with 'Nouvelle Tendences', an exhibition supposedly based on a new generation of designers. Arad was allotted 300 square feet alongside Philippe Starck, Hans Hollein and Alessandro Mendini. At thirty-six, Arad was the youngest of the group, though in sharing the stage with Starck he wasn't the only *enfant terrible*. Starck came up with a variation on the Smiley face, and used it to create a set of branded products. Arad chose to show an electric-powered metal compactor, made by a firm he had found in the telephone book, specializing in the needs of the waste-disposal community. When switched on, it made a fearsome noise. Hardly camouflaged by the message 'Sticks and stones may break my bones', rendered in hand-cut foot-high metal letters tacked on to its extremities, the machine could not fail to make its presence felt. With its mechanical jaws equipped with crocodile teeth, it was capable of reducing mountains of junk into neat cubes of mesh-bound crushed metal within moments. Design, in the sense that it would once have been understood, it certainly wasn't. Nor did the beast have much to do with craft, or decorative art.

Arad invited visitors to donate unwanted chairs to the museum. In exchange for a lender's certificate, their contributions would be fed through *Sticks and Stones*, and the results used as building blocks to gradually create a wall stretching across the gallery. Part César Baldaccini, or John Chamberlain, who did something similar with squashed cars, part shameless provocation, it was also a sly suggestion that there were too many chairs in the world already.

Sticks and Stones was an early demonstration of Arad's weakness for puns. He was already playing design by the rules of the art game, with some sophistication. So much so that there were some in the design world who didn't get the point of what he was doing. His work in those early days was raw, and he took a stance that could only be called blunt. At times, he came across as a kind of punk. Arad inspired a TV commercial for designer beer in the 1980s that involved a stubbly chinned creative type moodily tossing postmodern chairs out of the window of his Wapping loft to make room for the product of his welding lance.

There were rumours at the Pompidou of the

unauthorized feeding of chairs from the museum's offices into the machine, and a row about the attempts of the exhibition sponsor, Louis Vuitton, to use the machine in a public destruction of a mountain of counterfeit bags.

Arad was back at the temporary gallery on the ground floor of the Pompidou two decades later with a no-less combative solo exhibition. It subsequently moved from Paris to the Museum of Modern Art in New York, and was scheduled to end up at the Stedelijk in Amsterdam. This time there was a back catalogue to deal with, as well as new work. There was plenty of noise and spectacle. A huge hydraulic ramp sent a steel disc spinning from one end of the gallery to the other, while a massive model of a slice through one of his architectural projects had been executed at close to full size.

Since that first show in Paris, Arad has oscillated between art, architecture and design. He is represented now by a mainstream art dealer. He has shown at the London art fair Frieze. And he is one of the very few designers whose work has managed to command six-figure prices at auction. But he also works with Alessi and Kartell, Moroso, Vitra and other manufacturers to create mass-produced objects that demonstrate all the qualities of successful industrial design. A designer working in this way has to think about how something will be made in an economical way, as well as how it will be packaged, and sold. These are not issues that sit comfortably for those designers who attempt to present themselves as essentially concerned with creative self-expression. But over the years, Arad has been able to address both aspects of design: the emotional and intuitive, as well as the technical and the commercial.

With the opening of the new design museum at Holon in Israel in 2010, his most significant piece of architecture to date, he was also able to prove himself capable of successfully making the scale shift from object to building that has eluded so many designers.

Arad has had no shortage of turning points in his career. For one, there was the moment that he decided to come to London after leaving the Bezalel Academy of Arts in Jerusalem without a diploma. Then there was the day that he decided not to return after lunch to his drawing board at the small practice in Hampstead where he got a job after graduating from the Architectural Association. The routine of preparing door schedules was not what he had come to London to be part of. Peter Cook, his tutor at the AA, had no interest in preparing him for that aspect of architectural practice.

As Arad tells the story, it was on the way home from the office that day that the idea of making a chair first came into his mind. Walking by a scrap yard, he saw the remains of a very solid, very reliable British car from the 1960s, the Rover 2000. He picked up a couple of leather seats from the rusting hulk of the car, which were to become the first Rover chair. They were red, which as he later discovered were remarkably rare. With the aid of some bent scaffolding, and a few Kee Klamp joints, originally intended for use on construction sites, he converted the seats into a plausible sofa.

Arad had already used Kee Klamp components, to form tables, beds and mezzanine platforms from scaffolding, but they were more like architectural installations than furniture. The Rover chair was an object in its own right – with a certain coincidental resemblance to an adjustable armchair that Jean Prouvé had produced decades earlier – rather than a fragment of a car.

Another turning point came one day in 1987 in Kassel, the small aristocratic town in what was still West Germany. As an experiment, the organizers of Documenta 8, the sprawling quinquennial art show, had asked the curator, Michael Erlhoff, to pick a range of designers to show their work alongside that of the artists. Arad was one of them. Alessandro Mendini and Andrea Branzi represented an older generation. And a range of the Berlin-based Germans provided an anxiously neurotic alternative to the more flamboyant work coming from Milan at the time. Predictably, there was trouble from some artists uncomfortable about the conjunction of design with their work. Ange Leccia's installation took the form of buying a shiny new Mercedes Benz and mounting it on a plinth that rotated very slowly, in the name of art. He was unimpressed to have, as he saw it, his work diminished by the association with a car treated as a piece of design, tainted by a lingering hint of commercial utility, just across the corridor.

It was a confrontation that prefigured Arad's later experiences at Frieze. Ernest Mourmans, the gallerist on whom he has often relied for support, was denied a space by the organizers. Instead Arad showed his work on the Jablonka booth, a name with enough art-world clout to overcome any questions about who qualifies as an artist in Frieze's eyes and who does not.

In retrospect, perhaps Documenta was the point in Arad's life at which he was confronted with the sharpest of all the choices that he has had to face over the years, even if he wasn't necessarily aware of what was at stake at the time. It was a decision that eventually led him into industrial mass production, working with furniture makers such as Kartell, who extrude plastic by the kilometre to make Arad's technically ingenious and functional shelving, with Magis to make rotationally moulded plastic armchairs, with Moroso, and with Vitra for café chairs. These projects were followed by an assortment of watches, wine racks and wine coolers, cutlery and spectacles. This was the kind of work that reflected the traditional role of the designer. It follows a path that originates in the middle of the eighteenth century, when mass production overtook the decorative arts, and industrial design filled the gap left by the demise of the craftsman. The designer was being asked to provide a service, to keep a factory busy, to build a brand and a range.

It was a trajectory that reflected only a part of Arad's interests. His real motivation is the pursuit of a much more free-floating, uncategorizable form of creativity, one that was clearly signalled by the nature of the work that he showed in Kassel that year. He called it *Full House*. It was made from a thick slab of aluminium. It was raw to the point of brutality. He scored the metal with jagged cuts, gouged and wired it up with an array of cables, makeshift hinges and winches that could be pulled tight to convert a flat carpet into the semblance of a three-dimensional sofa. You could, just about, sit on it, and then when you had finished with it, you could make it disappear by winching it back down to floor level, completing the performance by folding back the winch handle into a position flush with the metal sheet. It had the same relationship to the conventional idea of what constituted design as Sid Vicious's rendering of 'My Way' had to Frank Sinatra. And it was just as attention-grabbing, in that it suggested a new option for design at a moment when it seemed that design had run out of ideas.

On the day of the Documenta opening, Rolf Fehlbaum, Chairman of Vitra, had come to see Arad, and asked him the price of the piece. Fehlbaum was fascinated by the new directions that design was taking. He saw Arad as offering a kind of research lab for the mainstream projects that would shape the future of his business.

He wanted to buy Arad's slab for his own collection, and to talk about designing something for his factory. He left with a handshake, but without confirming a sale. Later that same day, the Swiss art dealer and gallerist Bruno Bischofberger also stopped at Arad's exhibit. Was the piece for sale? Arad hesitated. 'I told him that I had already had some interest in it.' Bischofberger told him that he would pay the price that Arad was asking. Arad asked for time to call Fehlbaum to check that he was serious. Bischofberger told him it was a take-it-or-leave-it offer, and Arad said no sale.

It was a career-defining move. If he had sold to Bischofberger, he would have opted for the art world. To sell to Vitra was to definitively place himself in the design camp, although Arad being Arad, he always did things on his own terms.

When Fehlbaum asked him to work with Vitra, Arad ducked the chance of using industrial methods to make a piece that could be produced in tens of thousands. Instead he designed the *Well Tempered Chair*, a piece that might just as well have been made in his workshop in London as in Fehlbaum's factory. It depended on cutting tempered steel sheet and bolting it together with wing nuts, not the most sophisticated production methods, although daring enough in the way that it attempted to stabilize highly unstable, flexible sheet metal.

In one sense, Arad has spent much of his career since then attempting to reverse what had happened that day. If he had gone with Bischofberger, it's possible that he would never have been involved in design on an industrial scale – which would certainly have been a real loss to the history of contemporary design.

Arad has the agile and restless mind of a chess player, with a passion for material and the inventiveness that has given his mass-produced objects their distinctive character. But it is clear that they do not fully satisfy him. A different level of cultural ambition moves him.

And yet his design work has served Arad's career well. He could be described as an artist whose subject matter happens to be design. It is a working definition for a man who is also a gifted architect – though perhaps still not entirely satisfactory, especially for someone who has Arad's fascination for the workings of the art world, and a fencer's skill in parrying any attempt to categorize him.

As with other artists, you can see a body of work emerging from his studio in which certain themes recur. It's not that Arad is designing the same chair again and again. He uses certain formal archetypes in different ways, and different materials, and for different purposes.

Arad has kept coming back to the *Big Easy*, a form that he first made in the early 1980s, when he was still welding and cutting metal himself. It has subsequently been produced in a variety of materials and finishes, from mass-produced, blow-moulded plastic to carbon-fibre editions, some polished, some painted, and in a variety of scales. The first *Big Easy* and a late one are essentially the same form, but one is about rawness, and everything but finesse. The early versions are 'badly' welded and bent, and that was their charm. The later ones are much more polished in their execution.

The latest in the *Big Easy* series is a pair of chairs, in positive and negative versions. One is intricately cut full of holes like a lace tracery, the other a matching version, with spheres that precisely match the voids in the other chair, which is a kind of negative twin. The whole has the shimmering immaterial quality of a digital image, or a soap bubble about to vanish in a burst of air.

In the run-up to his second Pompidou show, Arad was working on a new shape. It's a figure that he calls the Gomli, after the British artist Antony Gormley. It was a new addition to his repertoire, a figure to be used in a range of ways. And it can also be seen as a response to his own reactions to a career in which he has worked on so many chairs. The point is not the shape of the chair, but the form of its occupant. 'As a designer you are always working on doing a container for someone you don't know. It could be Pavarotti, or it could be Twiggy, but it's the same chair. You spend your life doing this for the invisible sitter. So you start to think, what does he look like, this invisible sitter? We made a figure designed not for beauty but for the imprint of the backside. It's called the Gomli. I showed him the figure, and we discussed the project.'

This is not the first figurative piece that Arad has done. In the 1980s, there was a project that he worked on based on technology developed by Eric Victor known as the Transformer. Victor created a method of supporting broken bones – so that accident victims could be moved to hospital without making their injuries worse – that involved vacuum-formed bags of foam granules. Arad used it to produce seats moulded to the form of the user's body. 'In a way, the Gomli is the opposite of the foam vacuum. That was a kind of instant customization. What I learned was that you don't really want to sit in your own body shape. It's not a comfortable feeling for furniture. That was made-to-measure; the Gomli is prêt-à-porter.'

For Arad the pursuit of the ready-made has always been a potent theme. In the early days, he was appropriating objects: the Rover chair, the Kee Klamp scaffolding system. Then there were industrial meshes used for conveyer belts, and car aerials for desk lamps. Recently he has used the idea of the ready-made as a way of concentrating on the important decisions in a work, and being prepared to accept the aesthetic consequences of trusting in the nature of materials, and the dictates of geometry and detail.

> 'I can do a complete computer rendering of an object which will show what the effect will be, but you can't predict. You make the first decision and you see what happens. You know there will be six of

the Gomli and 60,000 of a mass-produced chair. In those circumstances, success or failure is completely different. With the Gomli, I have freedom. I don't have to do any persuading. The piece just has to be liked by someone who will like it enough to buy it. Even that is not necessary all of the time. You could say art and design are completely different. It depends on what sort of discussion you want to have. You can see that an artist who champions abstraction would say, "This is not a chair, it is a sculpture." And sometimes it doesn't matter what people say. If it is furniture then the back has to have a rake. It is not doing it because it has another agenda. It's not an ideology, it's a commercial issue.'

Rehearsing the overfamiliar arguments about the division between art and design makes Arad impatient. He compares it to previous tensions between disciplines.

'There was a time when photography was not allowed into the art world. Then it was video that was not allowed. It's a self-fulfilling prophecy. Design art comes as a reaction to being refused by the other world of art. If the art world had no problem with things that may have some connection with furniture then we wouldn't need this world of design art. Perhaps we still don't need it. The market has shown that there is a different thing happening. There is a market for these objects, whatever we call them.'

For Arad the definitions are less important than the context. 'It's maybe not a question of what do we call it, but where do we show it? I feel less of a problem to show in the Downtown Gallery, with its tradition of selling Prouvé. I have an affinity with that world, though of course we don't know what Prouvé and the others would do now. For me the trouble with design is that it was kidnapped by lifestyle. I don't care about the sink, or the colour of curtains. I am not interested in taste and magazines.'

Arad has questions about art as well as design. 'All those slogans may serve some people some of the time. There is not one true way of working; there is no right and wrong. There is exciting, interesting, engaging, charming, and there is boring, and tedious.' It's a view that makes him reluctant to be drawn on the criteria that might be applied to understanding the form-making that has transformed architecture. 'What we grew up thinking is naughty has become normal. The computer-generated blobs are being done by the Game Boy/Nintendo generation, working for the old masters.'

Arad has adroitly managed to have it both ways. He is one of the handful of contemporary designers to have succeeded in creating a substantial market for his work at auction, and also in making successful mass-produced products. He plays by his own rules, and he has changed the nature of the game.

E
IS
FOR
EXPO

It would be wrong to portray the Great Exhibition as an un-nuanced celebration of modernity. But the structure built to accommodate it, the Crystal Palace, was, to a remarkable extent, exactly that, and it was perhaps the greatest of all the Great Exhibition's achievements. It was the palace, rather than its contents, that was to haunt the imagination of the nineteenth and twentieth centuries. The Crystal Palace was like nothing that had previously existed. At the start of the Gothic Revival that represented the most flamboyant peak of High Victorian architecture, which attempted to recreate the thirteenth century in the midst of railways, canals and factories, the Crystal Palace was like a time-travelling spaceship returned from the future.

Ever since ambitious cities struggling with each other to make their mark. A few have come close. The Eiffel Tower was the product of the 1889 Expo. Montreal almost bankrupted itself in 1967. In 1992, Seville persuaded the Spanish government to build a high-speed railway line, bringing visitors from Madrid to their city, and construct a new terminal for the San Pablo International Airport. But Seville's dreams of using the Expo to turn itself into a high-tech gateway between America and Europe drowned in the mud of the site.

The Crystal Palace was designed by Joseph Paxton, a polymath who had begun his career as the Duke of Devonshire's head gardener, and whose first architectural experience was the creation of a series of greenhouses for his employer. The palace was the embodiment of the new industrial system. It was built in just eight months, using an

unprecedented degree of prefabrication, a cast-iron structure and so much glass that it accounted for fully one-third
of Britain's annual production of the material. The glazing
was installed using special trolleys that allowed 108 panes
to be fixed in a single day. The palace was huge, big enough
to accommodate full-grown trees, and over 500 metres long.
Building it took 2,000 men and cost £79,800; they needed
4,500 tons of iron and 293,000 panes of glass.

The Crystal Palace was a condensation of many
different kinds of urban space – promenade, piazza and
forum – into a single gigantic object. And it represented a
new approach to injecting design into every aspect of life.
Despite the ruthless utilitarianism of Paxton's structure,
the interior encompassed a much broader range of styles.
Among the group that worked on the interior were Owen
Jones, whose book *The Grammar of Ornament* was perhaps
the first visual encyclopaedia of decorative design, and
Augustus Welby Pugin, responsible for the design of the
Medieval Court.

Henry Cole used the profit made from ticket sales
to the palace to help fund the creation of the Royal College
of Art, to train designers and also to start the construction
of what would eventually be called the Victoria and Albert
Museum, the world's first design museum. The V&A was
intended as an instructive demonstration to students and
manufacturers of what design could achieve, but it very
quickly turned away from Cole's vision and took on a much
more diffuse role as a historical collection of the decorative
arts in all forms.

If William Morris despised the Great Exhibition and refused to set foot inside the Crystal Palace, Christopher Dresser, born in 1834 (the same year as Morris), can be seen as the designer who most productively understood its significance. At seventeen years old, Dresser was already a graduate of the Government School of Design. He went inside the Crystal Palace and emerged impressed by what he had seen, at least by the inventiveness of pattern and decoration from the non-European exhibits. Morris rejected the industrial system, while Dresser was prolific in his work for it, acting as a consultant for many different companies, creating hundreds of machine-made products, from textiles to wall coverings, ceramics, glassware and metalware.

At a time when the fast-expanding middle classes were looking to furnish their homes in ways that reflected well on them, Dresser designed all the objects needed for their tables: claret jugs, tea services, serving dishes, toast racks, candlesticks and cruet sets. Dresser's designs were radical in the context of a period when many designs combined a giddy mix of cultures and periods with the highly decorative Rococo Revival style dominating silverware. His sharp, geometric forms look startlingly contemporary even now. But it is Morris's name that lives on as a pioneer of design, while Dresser's is known only to the specialists.

The Crystal Palace was dismantled and relocated to the south London suburb that still bears its name. The structure was used for a variety of events over the years, before finally being destroyed by fire in 1936.

The first *Exposition publique des produits de*

l'industrie française was held in the year VII of the revolutionary calendar of the French Republic, or 1798, on the Champs de Mars, close to where the Eiffel Tower now stands. There were just 110 exhibitors, and apart from a tethered hot-air balloon hovering overhead, the displays of cotton yarn, watches, paper and cloth were worthy if hardly spectacular evidence of the first tremors of the coming Industrial Revolution.

France had recently occupied Geneva, and tried to land troops in Ireland in an abortive attempt to support a rebellion against the British. Napoleon had yet to return from Egypt and declare himself first consul of the republic, let alone the first emperor of the French.

As developed by the French, the exhibition hall quickly became an essential part of the modern city, as a form that was put to work in a range of different contexts, from the convention centre to the department store. The expo itself evolved into a curious mixture of high-flown but empty rhetoric about international goodwill and utopian futures, with bombastic nationalism and fairground entertainment. The Paris Exposition Universelle of 1889, celebrating the centenary of the French Revolution, was an even larger and more flamboyant event than the Great Exhibition. Attracting all of twenty-eight million visitors, its swaggeringly ostentatious national pavilions set a precedent for future fairs. Alongside the engineering tour de force of Eiffel's famously controversial tower (the 'useless monstrosity' so angrily denounced by its contemporaries) and the vast, clear spans of the Halle des Machines, a crop of bizarre new structures made their startling if temporary presence felt on the Paris skyline. Ignored as kitsch by the more squeamish of architectural historians, it was the fantastical aspects of the exposition, the replicas of the pagodas of Angkor Wat, Senegalese villages and Indochinese palaces incongruously silhouetted against the dome of Les Invalides, that were to have as much of an impact as Eiffel's engineering brilliance.

Once inside the turnstiles, paying customers could wander along a replica of a twisting street in old Cairo, past a reasonably faithful reconstruction of the Bastille, stormed in re-enactment every hour, and the Faubourg Saint-Antoine, in which they could pause for refreshment at an open-air café. It was Disneyland before the animated cartoon, let alone Mickey Mouse, had been thought of.

At the Paris Exposition of 1937, the Nazi and Soviet governments attempted to outdo each other with bigger and more imposing national pavilions. Speer's obelisk was confronted by hammer-and-sickle-wielding Russian peasants. It was the same expo that saw a much more resonant political statement: the Spanish pavilion – designed by José Luis Sert – housed Picasso's *Guernica*.

Germany did not go to New York in 1939, but Stalin's architect Boris Iofan built a remarkable celebration of the Soviet Union in Queens. Robert Moses, the J Edgar Hoover of twentieth-century urbanism, who controlled New York's infrastructure for forty years with implacably fixed views, organized two expos, the first in 1939 and another in 1964. The difference between the two reflects the way in which the expo has declined into commercial banality. In 1939, Wallace Harrison's Trylon and Perisphere provided a soaring landmark, reflecting a world still lost in adolescent wonder at nylon, chrome, motorcars and air conditioning. Norman Bel Geddes designed Futurama, the enormous General Motors display, which proudly claimed to be the city of tomorrow – its 500,000 scale model buildings, its one million trees and 50,000 cars, 10,000 of which actually moved, defining the idea of the modern world in the popular imagination. The models were wonderful, but they reduced the individual to the scale of an ant, paving the way for Moses to start driving expressways through the Bronx, and demolishing swathes of Manhattan for the building of the Lincoln Center during the 1940s and 1950s.

By the time of the 1964 New York World's Fair, once more dominated by Robert Moses, by now already under attack as the dark genius of urban renewal, the very idea of the city of tomorrow had gone senile. Moses distrusted modern art even more than he distrusted modern architecture, and his one attempt at involving the younger generation of artists ended in embarrassment. Warhol painted *13 Most Wanted Men*, a mural that caused a brief scandal before being obliterated on orders from Moses.

The 1964 fair marked the convergence of the expo tradition with that of Disney. Walt Disney had set up his first theme park in California ten years earlier and, in the run-up to the Expo, he offered his services to several of the big commercial exhibitors. He designed a troupe of animated dinosaurs for the Ford pavilion, and a chorus of walking talking dolls for Pepsi, who sang the joys of cola in a dozen languages.

From the first Paris exposition to the starry-eyed futurism of New York in 1939, from the welfare state optimism of the Festival of Britain in 1951 and the tawdry corporate vision of New York in 1964, each of the fairs sloganized a particular view of urbanism. The most extreme embrace of drip-dry modernity was the Montreal Expo of 1967, with its concrete housing ziggurat designed by Moshe Safdie, its Buckminster Fuller dome for the United States pavilion, and its monorails.

The expo, despite all the dross and the expense, is still refusing to lie down and die. The Shanghai Expo of 2010 was the most well attended of all time, the product of the burgeoning mobility of the Chinese labouring class and the determination from governments around the world to make the best possible showing in front of this potentially enormous new market. But in the world of the jaded consumer in Europe and America, the idea of the expo has lost the cultural significance it once had.

London's Millennium Dome – strictly speaking the structure was neither a dome nor were the contents that of an expo – demonstrated all too clearly just how pallid the species has become. It was too polite to follow in the full-blooded vulgarity of the great expos, and its exhibits were too bland to have the redeeming architectural brilliance of the Crystal Palace. It was left to deliver morally improving but empty rhetoric about sustainability and new technology that Prince Albert might have recognized, but not much in the way of innovation.

The more superficially sophisticated that the world appears to become, the more its public rituals signal that its underlying preoccupations remain as intoxicatedly atavistic as they have ever been. Like the Olympic Games and the Grand Prix circuit, the expo movement comes wrapped in the appearance of a glossy sense of modernity. For all the alibis of urban renewal, the real significance of the expo is closer to the motivations of the Easter Island head builders, or the ritual festivals of the Mayans. They are massively profligate undertakings that involve pouring huge resources into events that in the case of the Grand Prix races last less than two hours. The calculations of everyday reality do not apply. These are events that are to be understood as reflecting national prestige, or the imposition of cohesion, or else the rampant pursuit of sheer spectacle for the sake of spectacle.

F IS
FOR
FASH
ION

The first item of clothing with any kind of fashion ambition that I can remember buying for myself was a corduroy tie, printed with a vivid turquoise paisley pattern. It was not the kind of thing that you would want to keep after its moment had passed. Nor was the four-inch-wide hipster belt with orange-and-yellow-zigzag stripes on its fabric inlay, and a big rectangular metal buckle, or the donkey jacket, or the sharkskin-print suede boots. They were the kind of thing that on a Saturday night you could add to a wardrobe based on a sensible brown tweed jacket with leather-covered buttons to make some tip of the cap towards fashion, in a way that was affordable on a teenage budget and would not lead to parental ostracism.

Fashion in the London of the late 1960s was a matter of social and sometimes even physical survival. It was the means to signal allegiance to the values of one tribe against the others, and so to claim its protection. For me it was the choice between *Sgt Pepper's Lonely Hearts Club Band* and Chelsea Football Club. It was either try to look like the Beatles, or sign up as a skinhead, with a Ben Sherman shirt, Dr Martens cherry-red boots and Sta Prests. I did, briefly, try a crop that left each hair on my scalp so short that it was standing perpendicular to my skull, but football was not for me.

Instead, I remember a particularly impressive music teacher rushing into class with the *Sgt Pepper* album on the day it went on sale. He played both sides from start to finish in an overwhelming burst of enthusiasm that left a deep impression on me. A Grenadier Guards red tunic from I was Lord Kitchener's Valet, the stall at the top of the Portobello

Road, was out of reach financially. But a Civil Defence great-coat from the Laurence Corner army surplus store behind Euston station was the next best thing, and could be presented to parents as both practical and economical.

Second-hand clothes were the staple of university life. I had a Swedish army sheepskin, which I sold when my student grant ran out, and something a far hipper student than I described as a 'canoe-club blazer'. Then came brushed denim, T-shirts with American-football-style numerals, worn with desert boots that laced up to mid-calf and beyond, but were invisible under narrow-leg pink needle-cord jeans, and finally a brown velvet suit, along with a pair of art nouveau-style cufflinks from Biba. The jacket had the exaggerated tulip-shaped lapels of the period that certainly stood out at pub-closing time in the streets of Edinburgh. The trousers flared out at the ankle to cover almost entirely the green platform-heel boots, and hovered just above the ground in the manner of the shadow-gap skirtings that were later to be such a feature of John Pawson's architecture. It was the glam-rock alternative to the dominant mode of student dress, which involved collarless shirts and a certain amount of Fair Isle knitwear. None of these once essential aspects of my identity as an adolescent survive. Nor do the shirts that I bought, then and much later. They represent a personal history of taste, one that I hesitate to call my own. It's a history that spans fabrics from Aertex to cheesecloth, from madras cotton and linen to whatever the rubbery fibres that Miuccia Prada has woven into her mad-scientist lab-technician outfits. But shirts never last.

What is left are the things that are harder to discard, the clothes that bring back particular moments that still seem too significant to consign to the thrift shop, even after thirty years. The oldest-surviving garment that I still have hanging in my wardrobe was, at the time that I bought it, punishingly expensive. It is a jacket made from corduroy so heavy-duty and so stiff that it was once fully capable of standing up on its own. It came from Margaret Howell, a kind of anti-fashion fashion designer, who based her look on those student Fair Isle knits. She made *Far from the Madding Crowd* trousers that had curious flaps at the back to hold your braces in place. I preferred her brightly coloured check wool shirts, which were less specifically period. But the jacket – I wore it with equally imposing corduroy trousers that expired long ago – had professorial leather patches already in place on the elbows, as well as leather edging to the cuffs. It had an impressive array of pockets, and was made so conspicuously well that thirty years later I can still wear it. Only now it has actually achieved the well-worn patched-and-faded look that it was aiming for when it was new, but had not yet earned.

Not long after that purchase, I bought my first – and only – dinner jacket from Crolla in Dover Street. Scott Crolla started one of the great fashion might-have-beens with Georgina Godley. In 1983 there was nothing else quite like it, a kind of grown-up baroque idea of glamour, the sort of place that you could imagine Bryan Ferry coming in to change his suit. There was a branch in Tokyo before you knew it. But Crolla signed an ill-advised contract which did not allow him to hedge against currency fluctuations.

Because not many people make more than occasional use of them, dinner jackets, once the casual alternative to evening dress, tend to outlive the style that they were born with, and so have a way of always looking outdated. People who bought one in the 1960s will have inappropriate colour schemes. Others dating back to the 1950s have the look of Demob suits and utility clothing. When I bought mine, its fashion content lay in the way it quietly hinted at the recent past, with turned-back buttoned cuffs on the jacket.

By this time I had been through a couple of suits after the brown velvet. There was the loud check pattern with enormous notched lapels from the Village Gate, worn, I am reluctant to admit, on at least one occasion with an outsize brown pre-tied bow tie with cream polka dots. It was followed by my first Paul Smith suit, acquired from a shop in Bath along with a Paul Smith tie and shirt. I knew there was something special about it. This was Smith even before he had discovered the classic with a twist idea. It was the kind of outfit that Phillip Marlowe could have worn to patrol the mean streets of LA. A double-breasted jacket with pointed lapels, a cream-coloured shirt with a very small collar, and an argyle-pattern tie. Actually it was the kind of suit that my father had worn in the 1940s, though I was only hazily aware of that when I bought it.

Paul Smith shortly afterwards opened his first shop in Covent Garden, from where the vegetable market was still in the final stages of withdrawal. It had bare concrete walls, Italian lights with outsize milky glass shades, and a window to the street that Smith filled with slide projections.

I got to know Smith when I was editing *Blueprint*. He was in the midst of expanding throughout Japan, which in the mid-1980s was still in the throes of the bubble years, when *Japan as Number One* was the title of a book written by an American sociologist, when it was possible for Japanese companies to buy anything. Life in Japan was as mysterious as life on Mars. We flew out on the weekend of the Chernobyl disaster. It was on that trip that he introduced me to Rei Kawakubo, his polar opposite in terms of her approach to fashion at Comme des Garçons.

I was fascinated by a woman who could countenance a shop so reduced to its minimum essence that there was nothing at all to see, just a counter. If you asked for anything, it would be brought out for inspection from behind a screen.

I ended up writing a monograph that involved following her through a collection from design to textile selection to Paris show. And that is how I come to have a jacket from the 1989 Homme Plus collection that she gave me. The silhouette looks exaggeratedly bulky now, with shoulders that cantilever over my arms, but at first sight there is nothing else trickily Japanese about it. And then you notice that it is actually two jackets. The inner lining is a check-patterned blouson with long sleeves and elasticated cuffs that can be buttoned into the outer jacket. It comes with a wealth of secret pockets. Flying back from Tokyo via the Polar route, I put the jacket on during the refuelling stop at

Anchorage, and spent the rest of the way home feeling smug that it would be the only one of its kind anywhere in Britain.

Almost as old, and still hanging in my wardrobe, worn rather more often than the Comme jacket – which has finally started to fray at the edges, despite the formidable Japanese craftsmanship and attention to detail that went into it – is the Paul Smith suit I bought myself after a lengthy lunch to celebrate my fortieth birthday. It's grey wool, and made in Italy. While wearing it is no embarrassment in style terms, it has gone from sharp to distinctly cosy over the years.

The shirts have all gone. I can remember the ones I liked wearing, and could never find anything to replace them once the collars started to fracture. Long ago there was a candy-striped cotton shirt with wide collars from Austin Reed. Much later there was the searingly fluorescent pink shirt from Comme des Garçons. There are a few ties, mostly with broad horizontal stripes.

At the time of purchase, these were not the kind of things that seemed as if they had anything to do with fashion. They just made you feel better. But they are fashion moments. Mostly they are focused not on shirt collars but on the fluctuating diameter of trouser legs. I can remember when the skin-tight needlecords started to sprout flares: in the most egregious examples with contrasting-fabric insets; and then I can remember the day when skinny legs suddenly looked acceptable again, closely followed by narrow ties.

Britain's default position is to look down on those who try too hard with their clothes, but to look down even harder at those who get them wrong.

I find it difficult to buy clothes, and tend to do it in short bursts, followed by years of inactivity. Armani passed me by; but I did eventually catch up with Prada, at about the same time that Miuccia Prada hired Rem Koolhaas and Jacques Herzog to design her shops, and then with Jill Sander's sternly Teutonic version of modernism. The most recent example is the raincoat that I bought in a Hong Kong discount outlet, a 28-storey concrete hulk that was once a multi-storey factory. When Shenzhen set up as a manufacturing centre, such places went out of business, and this particular example has found a new life as fashion's equivalent of limbo. Far away from the glossy stores of Hong Kong Central, with their travertine floors and their exquisite window displays, here in Aberdeen is rack upon rack of the clothes that the boutiques cannot shift before the next season's collections come in. The price tags have three dates on them, past each date there is another 20 per cent off.

I like my raincoat. It's made of the kind of rubberized black gaberdine that the police used to wear back in the 1950s. There are popper-stud fastenings backed up by a zip hidden behind the fly front. The silhouette is stylishly severe, with the pockets neatly flush with the surface. There are metal eyelets and a discreet collar. And then there is the vivid pink lining.

I like wearing it every day, but I know that I am shortening its life. So I try to extend its stay in my wardrobe by rationing its outings, to ensure that it maintains the crisp outlines its makers intended it to have. And I know that sooner or later it will be making way for something new.

Howard Roark is, up to a point, a plausible-enough name for an architect, but I am less convinced by Stourley Kracklite, the lard-tub protagonist of Peter Greenaway's *Belly of an Architect*, played by Brian Dennehy. Gary Cooper's Roark in King Vidor's schlockfest *The Fountainhead* (based on Ayn Rand's novel of the same title) is a picture of toned muscle and angst, handy with a rock drill and brutal in his wooing of the boss's daughter, Dominique Francon, when he takes a job as a day labourer in a quarry. Dennehy's Kracklite comes fully equipped with a waistline that authentically overwhelms his belt in the manner pioneered by the twenty-something-stone James Stirling. They are both films that have always fascinated me. In the case of *The Fountainhead*, it's not so much Roark, a tortured genius somewhere between Louis Sullivan and Frank Lloyd Wright, that was the special attraction, although it's hard not to warm to an architect who, rather than see his work compromised by lesser talents, breaks into the building site and lays the dynamite charges to blow it up, appalled at the decorative frills that lesser hands have tacked on to the sheer walls of his thrusting tower. Even if you might not want to actually hire him, he gets your attention. But what makes *The Fountainhead* irresistible is that its villain-in-chief is an architecture critic. The silkily evil Ellsworth Toohey is portrayed undermining his proprietor by luring away his star columnists, and inciting his readers against Roark. If only.

Kracklite, even without the same virile menace as Gary Cooper, was equally fascinating as a kind of awful warning of the worst things that can happen to a curator.

I saw the film when, much like Kracklite, I was curating an architectural exhibition in Italy. In his case, it was on the subject of Étienne-Louis Boullée in Rome. For me it was the Venice Architecture Biennale, although I managed to get through the experience without being poisoned, which was more than Kracklite did, even if the undercurrents of architectural politics at the biennale had a somewhat sinister reputation. 'Be careful of the people of the lagoon,' Renzo Piano told me. 'On the surface it's all sunshine, but below the water they bite.'

Cinema and architecture, on and off screen, have a relationship that goes back a long way, and which is both superficial and profound. Half a century before Brad Pitt started hanging around Frank Gehry's studio, and working on sustainable low-cost houses for New Orleans, Alfred Hitchcock was already fascinated by architecture. He filmed it, he designed it, he evoked it. *North by Northwest*, a film that I can watch again and again, is full of architecture, starting with Saul Bass's titles, which begin as an abstract grid that is gradually revealed as Wallace Harrison's glazed façade of the UN building in Manhattan. In the film, you see Hitchcock's version of the UN's lobby, recreated in a Hollywood studio, which through the lens looks much like the kind of buildings Zaha Hadid is designing today (she confesses a weakness for *North by Northwest*). Later in the narrative, there is the Vandamm house, allegedly in North Dakota, which looks more like Frank Lloyd Wright than Frank Lloyd Wright, but which was actually a set built by Hitchcock. Camille Paglia pointed out Hitchcock's continuing architectural obsessions years ago, even if the nearest that he came to an architectural hero was Eva Marie Saint's industrial designer. The architectural critic Steven Jacobs documents Hitchcockian architecture in minute detail. Jacobs has painstakingly examined, shot by shot, all of Hitchcock's key domestic interiors, and used his research to draw each of their floor plans. He published the results as a book entitled *The Wrong House: The Architecture of Alfred Hitchcock*. It's an exercise that shows the precise point at which physical reality overlaps with dreamlike images, and demonstrates the unpredictable interaction between the kind of spaces that can exist only in film and those that are more physical and can be realized in the architectural world.

We know what the flat in the Maida Vale crescent that is the setting for *Dial M for Murder* ought to look like on the basis of the exterior shots. Jacobs's drawings show that the simple orthogonal plan, implied by how the spaces looked through the camera lens, would actually have had to have been overlaid by wedge-shaped projections that were required to achieve the shots that Hitchcock wanted in his films. Two different forms of architectural notation create what appears to be a version of the same implied architectural experience, but which demand a different physical plan.

There are other connections between film and architecture worth pursuing. They are activities that require both introversion and extroversion of their practitioners. To design a building, just as to make a film, demands a creative impulse as well as the business acumen to assemble the necessary finance, and the personality to stand on a building site or a film set and impose their will on sceptical construction workers, actors and crew.

What is not always clear is the precise terms of the comparison. Is the architect playing the part of director, or of the star – the headline name that can get a development funded, in the same way that signing up Colin Firth or George Clooney can green-light a film? It does happen occasionally when a developer, looking for a degree of visibility or an easy planning consent, commissions Norman Foster or Frank Gehry, and the bankers come up with the mezzanine finance to build a business park or a block of flats or a skyscraper on the strength of that architect's involvement. But a more plausible analogy for the architect is with the script writer, whose work is written and rewritten until everything that made it distinctive has dissolved under layer upon layer of mush.

Simply because a film has an architectural theme does not necessarily mean that it will tell us much about architecture. Watching a life-size replica of the spiral at the heart of the Guggenheim Museum getting obliterated in a firestorm of automatic gunfire in the beyond-dire thriller *The International* is more architectural product placement than spatial insight. Michael Caine's walk-on performance as an architecture professor at the beginning of *Inception* is no more helpful as an insight into the mother of the arts than the random job description of Woody Harrelson's character as an architect in *Indecent Proposal*.

It's not simply a question of the distinction between art house and blockbuster. Both can cast light on architecture. *My Architect*, the art-house documentary, tells you a lot about the inner life of the son of an architect, and the architecture that ultimately deprived Nathaniel Kahn of his father, Louis, the revered American architect responsible for Bangladesh's Parliament building and the Yale Center for British Art, who managed to combine modernity with monumentalism. It is a sharply observed, witty film in which Nathaniel scrutinizes his father's life with a forgiving, sad, sweet eye, assessing his shortcomings and his creative achievements. It is also an emotional rollercoaster as Kahn asks his two half-sisters, his mother, his father's surviving lover, his aunts and an assortment of taxi drivers, rabbis, former employees, clients, critics, famous architects and, most of all himself, a series of searching, impossible questions.

Louis Kahn had a complex relationship with Harriet Pattison, Nathaniel's mother. He would arrive, announced only by a last-minute phone call, at her house once a week. He would play with his son on the lawn, stay for lunch and dinner, and drink a chilled martini or two. Then Harriet would drive him into town and drop him at the end of a darkened street, with Nathaniel, wrapped under a blanket, watching as his father vanished into the night, back to his wife. Kahn does not spare us his mother's humiliation at his father's hands. The door to her office at the studio would be locked when Kahn's wife visited. She had to cajole Kahn's secretary to find out where he was. She was crossed off the guest list for the opening of the Kimbell Art Museum in Fort Worth, one of the greatest triumphs of Kahn's career, where she was responsible for the landscaping.

After leaving Yale, where he studied philosophy, and finding himself continually exploring the monumental spaces of the two art galleries his father designed for the campus, Nathaniel Kahn became an actor. He recognizes his father's self-dramatizing tendencies in himself. 'He was always playing the part of an architect; his outfit was a bit of a costume,' he says of his father's trademark floppy bow tie and occasional cape. ' "You know, even when I get a haircut, I'm an architect," he would say. That says so much about my father's sense of identity. Architecture was more than a profession for him. It was, in the romantic sense, a calling. And, in a practical sense, it helped with the ladies; it's an enormously attractive profession to have.'

Nathaniel brings his mother to the edge of tears when he asks her why she never married. He sits down with his two half-sisters to talk about their father's funeral, at which they met for the first time, and from which Louis Kahn's wife tried to exclude two of his children and their mothers. 'I wonder if that really is true,' muses her daughter, hinting at years of anger and betrayal.

There are unbearable moments. Nathaniel meets the site architect of a research laboratory his father designed for Jonas Salk, the discoverer of the polio vaccine. 'Did you know my father well?' asks Kahn lightly. 'Oh yes, he used to spend Christmases at home with us, playing with my kids.' The camera stays on Kahn's face. You see him jolted, white-faced, as if reeling from a slap, but not missing a beat.

At one point, Nathaniel reads to camera what he calls the first letter that he has written to his father after all these years. 'Did you ever really mean to come up to Maine to spend the holidays with us, or was it just something that you said to get my mother off the phone? Because I have to tell you, Lou, that we waited for you.' Despite everything, *My Architect* is neither a bitter nor an angry film, and nor are the people in it. It paints a lyrical and affectionate picture of Louis Kahn, just five foot six inches tall and terribly disfigured by burn scars from his childhood in Estonia, his fingers black with charcoal from his drawings. In one memorable sequence, Nathaniel Kahn goes rollerblading in languid, effortless loops across the sublime courtyard of the Salk Institute. Kahn's architecture seems to hang over the lip of the Pacific, water trickling across its courtyard, and his son looks like a small boy showing off a new skill to his father. The film shows archive footage of Louis Kahn with his students, sitting on a table, hanging on his every word as he delivers his most famous aphorism about the need for an architect to listen to the brick and ask it what it wants to be: 'Hello, brick.' 'The brick business was embarrassing for me. The kids in my class in high school, when they really wanted to annoy me, they would go and put an ear to a wall and go, "Shhh, I'm listening to the bricks,"' says Nathaniel.

Hollywood producer Joel Silver (who collects Frank Lloyd Wright houses the way some people collect vintage cars) represents the blockbuster end of the depiction of architectural space, at the opposite end of the spectrum from Nathaniel Kahn. In the first two *Die Hard* franchises, he took his audience deep into the entrails of skyscrapers and airports, to demonstrate how buildings and complex spaces work, drawing a much less two-dimensional portrait of them than he achieved of his human character with Bruce Willis.

In the Australian thriller *Heatwave*, director Phillip Noyce provided another take on *The Fountainhead*. Richard Moir plays Steve West, an idealistic but ambitious architect with a ruthless property-developer client, on the verge of his breakthrough project, a housing complex called Eden, in a run-down part of Sydney. 'Why are you doing this?' asks the community activist, played by Judy Davis, who is trying to stop the project from demolishing her neighbourhood. 'Because if I didn't do it, somebody with half my ability would.' Later, West echoes Roark: 'It's not what I designed.' In real life perhaps, most architects would be more cautious about spelling out such unshakable self-confidence, no matter how much of it they might possess.

Some films can capture a shift in architectural mood even before architects are aware of it. *Bladerunner* really did detonate an interest in dystopia, and an exploration of the city of the future as messy and dark with machines dripping steam, and backstreet DNA analysts. It became the subject of seminars and conferences at architecture schools around the world. Others, such as Antony Minghella's *Breaking and Entering*, manage to convey something of the essential nature of city life, in the way that a city is multilayered, an environment in which very different groups of people exist side by side in the same space but hardly acknowledge each other's existence. Jude Law's landscape architect has his office in a sandblasted brick warehouse in the midst of London's King's Cross redevelopment, which by night is overtaken by Albanian drug dealers and Nigerian cleaners.

It's not the film namechecks or the plotlines that can really tell us something new about architecture any more than Frank Sinatra's portrayal of Sam Laker, furniture-designer-turned-hitman, tells us about Charles Eames – even if Laker's studio is set in what later became Jeffry Archer's apartment. Of course, there is a certain narcissistic flutter when Maria Schneider in Michaelangelo Antonioni's *The Passenger* makes her appearance as an architecture student – would anybody else be discovered lurking in quick succession both outside the brutalist raw concrete of the Brunswick Centre in London, and on the roof of Gaudí's La Pedrera in Barcelona? But there is more to it than that. The real architectural quality of the film is in the climactic, uninterrupted, seven-minute continuous take that begins inside Jack Nicholson's hotel room in southern Spain, moves round the room and through the window to make a circuit of the square outside. It's the same sort of crystallization of space that Bertolucci's cameraman Vittorio Storaro achieved in *The Conformist*, when Jean-Louis Trintignant is lost in the endless spaces of some fascist minister's office, and the screen is suddenly filled by a vast bust of Mussolini's head that is carried across from left to right. This is the kind of magic that architects always wish they could work, but their buildings are static, and they can't impose their viewpoint on the people who experience their buildings. Though it doesn't stop them from trying.

F is for
Function

Functionalism is a quite remarkably persistent idea that simply refuses to lie down and die. As a pragmatic proposition, it's unarguable that design begins with a systematic exploration of practical requirements. But functionalism is also a philosophical idea about the nature of things, one that is more complex and less useful than the old slogan 'Form follows function' would suggest.

The belief that a close enough scrutiny of the technical purposes of an object provides everything that is needed to dictate its shape had become as much an aesthetic as a practical question long before the term 'functionalism' was first coined. It is a view of the world that suggests not only the means with which to achieve efficiency, but also the conviction that perfect efficiency is the route to visual perfection. It is an echo of the teachings of Plato and his belief in ideal form. It reflects the marketing pitch of the Roman architect Vitruvius, with his guiding principles of firmness, commodity and delight. Vitruvius' ideas were delivered to the English-speaking world through a translation made by England's ambassador to Venice, Sir Henry Wotton, who was to become notorious for suggesting somewhat ambiguously that an ambassador was 'an honest man whose role was to lie abroad for the good of his country'.

Mao Tse-tung is alleged to have said something much like Vitruvius of his plans for rebuilding Beijing. 'Utility, Economy and, if possible,' as he put it, 'Beauty,' were his priorities while demolishing the city's walls and toying with the destruction of the imperial palace. And at a poetic level, the functionalist ideal recalls John Keats's lines in *Ode to a Grecian Urn* that ' "Beauty is truth, truth beauty," – that is all/Ye know on earth, and all ye need to know.' Keats's words are a reminder that the functional ideal may be more aesthetic than utilitarian.

We are accustomed to the idea that there is beauty to be found in the craftsman-made object, honed, tested and perfected over generations to produce the optimal response to a physical and material demand: the Norwegian wooden ski, the steel blade from Toledo, a Korean celadon vase. But it is a kind of beauty that can also be found in high technology: in aircraft wings, suspension bridges and carbon-fibre-bodied Formula One racing cars.

The idea of formal values growing out of technical discipline in a kind of Darwinian evolution has continually been put forward by theorists and critics. Le Corbusier, for example, filled his polemical book *Vers une architecture* with images of grain silos shown side by side with photographs of the Parthenon, alongside biplanes and motorcars, suggesting that they shared the same pursuit of unadorned simplicity, truth to materials, and the frank expression of the optimum solutions to structural demands. Of course, the reality is rather different. As Le Corbusier would have known, the classical Greeks used a gaudy palette of colours to paint their temples. There is evidence to suggest that he doctored his photographs of grain silos in the Midwest to edit out the decorative flourishes and the historical memories that were used to soften the utilitarianism of their structures in the interests of making his case more forcefully.

F is for

The specific formulation 'Form follows function' became the mantra for modernity in the early part of the twentieth century, in the form of the pseudo-scientific religion of functionalism. The words, near enough, were first coined by the Chicago architect Louis Sullivan. In his 1896 article 'The Tall Office Building Artistically Considered' Sullivan wrote:

> It is the pervading law of all things organic and inorganic, of all things physical and metaphysical, of all things human and all things superhuman, of all true manifestations of the head, of the heart, of the soul, that the life is recognizable in its expression, that form ever follows function. *This is the law*.

Clearly it was a law that left a mark on Sullivan's most famous employee, Frank Lloyd Wright, and its traces are visible in the architect Louis Kahn's mystical injunction to architects to ask of a brick what it wants to be, a perception that shaped his scheme for Bangladesh's Parliament building and the Kimbell Art Museum in Texas.

Using the metaphor of the machine, and the analogy of the scientific method, the modernists purported to eliminate the sentimental and the irrational from their work. They tried to make design as objective a process as possible. They created a language for design characterized by simplified forms and smooth surfaces that seemed to suggest mechanical production. The rhetorical message carried by design became as important as its substance. As a propagandist Le Corbusier had the brilliant insight to describe the house as a machine for living in. With that single sentence he provided the means for architects and designers to posture as engineers and scientists. In the process, he took what had been essentially poetic or metaphorical ideas and made them into the basis for a method of design that brought with it the promise of optimal outcomes. Functionalists made objects that took the proposition of the machine at face value: they believed that an object that appeared rational actually was so.

Futurists, who celebrated the beauty of war, fell in love with the imagery and the rhetoric of the machine, particularly and obscenely so with what they had described as the beauty of the machine gun and the flowers of blood that it caused to blossom. They were somewhat less interested in the efficiency with which machines actually performed.

To ask what is the function of a chair, or a spoon, without thinking about the idea of ritual or of the social hierarchy that objects are used to express, is to take only the narrowest and most literal view of purpose. A better question to ask would require the consideration of a more complex and more detailed set of functional attributes for an object. What is the function of a chair intended for a room to be used by a child is a question that is not likely to have the same answer as the question what is the function of a chair to be used for the negotiating session of a peace treaty, or in a parliament. The function of a spoon intended to be used as a wedding gift is not the same as the function of a spoon designed to be used to measure out a dose of oral penicillin, even if they share the same name and the same basic elements. An understanding of the imperative of price is crucial. To design a chair that is intended to sell for $50 demands an entirely different set of responses and solutions to one designed to sell for $500 or $5,000.

The functions of a sword or of a suit of armour were often not the ostensible ones of combat. They had a more self-conscious purpose as demonstrations of prestige or heritage or authority. Despite the rhetoric of functionalism, close exploration of purpose, and what is sometimes described as ergonomics (the flawed science of usability), is not enough by itself to provide a framework for creating a charismatic object.

This is even more true now than it was in the first decades of the last century, when modernism was still being codified. In what was called the machine age, useful objects still had moving parts that could be either locked into pure sculptural forms to suggest the image of the machine, or put on show as a kind of spectacle. They provided a point of departure for understanding the relationship of each part of a mechanism to the whole.

Since then, the digitalization of almost every product category has stripped away the mechanical attributes of many objects. A typewriter or an adding machine depended on the skilful manipulation of mechanical levers. A laptop takes on the role of a typewriter; a digital camera replaces an analogue camera based on film, and need not depend on moving parts. These artefacts could be said to have the same purpose or function. But they cannot be designed in the same way. Chips and circuit boards do not impact on the form of an object and the configuration of its component parts in the same way that levers, switches and valves do. The priorities, and the underlying processes of designing a digital object, are different from those that shaped its mechanical equivalent. The transition between them is one of the most revealing moments in understanding the nature of an object. Paradoxically, the two may end up looking much like each other because of the visual associations certain forms have with certain artefacts, which have become ideal forms, or archetypes.

The Polaroid SX-70 was the camera that marked the most sophisticated and the most ingenious as well as the most seductive high-water mark of the analogue world. It is a world that, save for such isolated survivors as the mechanical wristwatch, and the more robust category of the automobile and the domestic appliance, is fading away, leaving little behind but nostalgia, as evidenced by the diehard enthusiasts for vinyl record pressings, printed books and negative film on celluloid.

The SX-70, first manufactured in 1972, was designed by Henry Dreyfuss's firm, one of the pioneers of industrial design in America, which thirty-five years earlier had been responsible for streamlining the steam locomotives that hauled the *20th Century Limited* for the New York Central Railroad. The camera was a beautiful object, with an intricate folding mechanism that recalled the bellows lens housings of early models. In its closed position, it had something of the quality of a cigar case, with a brushed-metal finish and leather panels. Pull it open, and the viewfinder clicked into position and the mirrors inside showed you the image through the lens that the Polaroid film, lying flat on the base of the camera, would capture.

Push the button on the front of the machine, and the shutter opened up to deliver a carefully measured dose of light, and then closed again. Seconds later, the film was excreted through the mechanism. As it passed through the camera, the chemicals that would develop and fix the image in less than a minute, contained in a thin pouch running across the bottom of each Polaroid cartridge, were smeared across the film's surface. A wafer-thin paper rectangle was ejected out into the open air, to the accompaniment of a satisfying whoosh. The image started to appear almost at once, and in a matter of seconds the surface of the plasticized paper would go from milky opacity to pin-sharp, full-colour clarity.

Against a background in which photography had been a painfully long-drawn-out process that began with the opening of the cardboard box in which the celluloid film came packaged in a foil wrapper to keep it safe from direct sunlight, and threading the films through the sprockets inside the camera, a Polaroid camera was more than a conjuring trick – it was magic.

A pack of Polaroid film was like a pre-prepared battlefield dressing. It made the process of photography almost instant, and, of course, entirely addictive. To hear the click and the whoosh, to detonate that button, and feel the play of it as you depressed it, and then to see the image materialize, at first like a faint and mysterious echo of the face of Jesus on the Turin shroud, and then to crystallize into a fully realized photograph with depth and colour range, produced an overwhelming urge to see the magic repeated. Yielding to the urge, you had to use more and more of the extremely expensive instant film. Photography had become a temporary epiphany.

This was the closest that analogue technology had ever come to delivering the weightlessness and the dematerialized qualities of digitalization. It removed so many of the technical steps, and the waiting, even though it still depended on physical, chemical and mechanical processes. But it also produced an enormous amount of waste as a by-product of the process – boxes, paper, foil, chemicals – that ended as landfill. Within a decade it was all over. The digital world had triumphed, and it left designers looking for a new way to understand their task.

When digitalization had transformed virtually every product category, it became much harder to maintain the fiction of functionalism. There are precious few moving parts in a laptop and most of the design effort goes into the circuit boards, which remain invisible. These elements are in the hands of people who would not be understood as form-giving designers in the sense that the Bauhaus would have recognized. When you see a fly-through of the inside of an iPhone, you find yourself inside what feels very much like a form of micro-city planning, with urban blocks, boulevards and multilevel circulation routes, but it does not provide an industrial designer who is trying to give the object a form much of a clue as to what kind of object these particular elements are bringing into being. Miniaturization means that the circuits are the least likely element to be the determining factor in shaping an object.

Without these clues, designers fall back on archetypes to find a direction for their work. It is what happened with the camera just before, during and after the digital revolution. The format of the single-lens reflex camera evolved over the years. It was based on the size of the film, on the intricacies of a shutter that needed to be moved aside mechanically to allow silver nitrate film to be exposed to light for precisely the right length of time, and it needed a viewfinder that allowed you to look through the lens to see what the image that was about to be exposed on the film would look like.

How would a new user learn how to operate this intricate and complex piece of machinery if they had never seen one before? He or she would need visual clues to signal which button was the shutter, which lever advanced the film, and, indeed, to suggest what the object was intended to be used for in the first place. Did it look like a camera? Did it communicate anything about where to pick it up, and how to operate it?

The format of the analogue camera became an archetype in order to demonstrate how the new digital cameras worked and to remind us what they did. A camera based on particular mechanical and technical issues came to define what cameras with entirely different technologies would look like. They needed to look like a camera because that is what cameras have always looked like. Photography is no longer based on a chemical process, film, or its exposure to light. It does not depend on shining controlled amounts of light through the celluloid, through another lens and on to photosensitive paper.

The idea of digitalization makes all of these processes fall away. There is no need for a viewfinder when it is possible to use a screen that shows exactly what the receptors in the camera will record when a button is pressed. There is no need for a shutter, although, as we know, every mobile phone in the world has been equipped with the sound of one and, in the case of the first generation iPhone at least, a visual simulacrum too. There is no need for a physical focus process, no need for a lever to advance the film. The image a digital camera captures is instantly transmitted to the photographer's laptop now, to be checked and manipulated.

How were designers to respond to all this? A camera that uses pixels rather than film could have been styled to look like almost anything. At first, some manufacturers, especially those with no previous experience in the field, looked to establish entirely new forms to signal just how much had changed. Some took on the shapes that had once been associated with cine cameras. Other manufacturers ended up with digital cameras that looked like miniature rocket launchers, or telescopes. Luigi Colani proposed cameras that took on the organic form of sea creatures.

And all of these ideas about cameras needed to find new ways to communicate with their users about how to operate them. But very quickly, many digital cameras started to look exactly as single-lens reflex cameras had always done, the same size, the same configuration of controls, because they were communicating what they were doing even if there was no mechanical justification for the message they were projecting. Digitalization allows for a more direct interaction between subject and photographer. It has become more difficult for the camera to serve as a barrier or an alibi.

The camera has just about survived as an object, even as the boundary between moving and still pictures has evaporated. The distinctive form of the television set has not. An object shaped by the need to accommodate a cathode ray tube, firing electrons in a vacuum tube, does not make any sense when the picture is digitized, and so the television was reduced to a flat screen, and all that is left to the designer is to tidy up the edges. It has taken longer to find a way to accommodate flat screens to the domestic environment. Hanging them like pictures on the wall with a dangling power cord is somehow too intrusive.

The impact of digitalization in many areas of technology has been to diminish the traditional role of the designer as a sculptural shape-maker. Design has turned into something that involves a sequence of images on a flat screen, and developing a logical way to move through them.

It is a change that has forced designers to explore other approaches to design, to look at the ways that design can be used to communicate the purpose and the meaning of an object, rather than to treat design primarily as a question of solving mechanical and technical problems.

There is, however, one area of design where the

idea of objective analysis on the functional model has maintained its grip. To ask about how an object can be made and used in ways that will minimize energy consumption and carbon emissions has allowed a new generation to rediscover the moral certainty of functionalism.

In one sense, the issue of green design might be regarded as an almost nostalgic hankering to find a way to approach design as it once was. Rather than focusing on what an object does, and the connection between its moving parts and its operation, the idea of ecology as a generator of form has given designers the chance to analyse energy performance, embodied carbon, and all the rest, with the implied promise that if it is green it will also be good design. It's a reassuringly familiar formulation, but barely an adequate one. It is an approach that still leaves too many questions unanswered. What, for example, about the concept of embedded carbon? Converting the entire world to driving electric cars, if this means replacing every existing car and scrapping the entire petrol distribution network, may make no sense. Soldiering on in thirty-year-old Volkswagens for another five years rather than buying new electric cars may make more sense. If we all had electric cars, we might, provided that the electricity was all generated by nuclear power, be reducing the carbon emissions caused by driving. But achieving an all-electric future would have massive carbon emission implications. Frugal energy consumption and recyclability may be desirable attributes, but they are no more the entire story of design than any other version of functionalism.

When I found myself buying a new laptop every eighteen months and a new mobile phone every six months, and when each new generation product has a power cord you can't use with the last I began to feel queasy about the prospect, even as a non-green. But then I also began to think about what I really had in my hand with a fourth-generation iPhone. This was a replacement for a telephone, a music system, a camera, an emailer, a library and a GPS. Think of all the things that it has done away with: the film, the chemicals to process the film, the paper on which the prints are made, the record players, the vinyl, the factories in which the vinyl is made, the shops in which they are sold, the carbon footprint that visiting that shop entailed. There is no way yet to be definitive. Millions of iPhones are acquired and discarded every year. They have to be fed by the strip mining of lithium needed for their batteries – life expectancy of remaining sources is estimated at another forty years. The toxic by-products of dumping exhausted batteries in landfill are being addressed. But we still simply don't really know enough to understand the balance between the resources consumed by disposability and the resources saved by the versatility of appliances rendered immaterial by digitalization. In the 1960s, the critic Reyner Banham, the pop artists and the architect Peter Cook dreamed of an utterly guilt-free, liberated disposable future, unmonumental and unmaterialistic. It is just possible that Apple and Steve Jobs have given it to us.

is for
GRAND THEFT

A new generation of what we still call video games allows enthusiasts to wallow in blood-splattered gore, but they are also a way for those with gentler interests to listen to music, to communicate, to explore the texture of the city. And in their complex modelling of space, architecture and urban form, they require of their creators both the literary and dramatic imagination of a scriptwriter and also the spatial perspective of an architect. They are also a powerful way to explore what design has become in the ethereal digital world that has supplanted material design.

Never previously having laid a finger on a PlayStation console, or an Xbox, I had to be walked through *Grand Theft Auto IV* by a very polite and infinitely patient member of the Rockstar Games team that designed it. But as an adolescent, I did have a brief, though intense, interest in model railways, which was enough for me to recognize in *GTA IV* the most elaborate train set in the world.

The affluent middle-aged men who are now Rockstar Games freest-spending and most numerous customers are some of the same people who a generation or two ago might have spent days on end in their garden sheds or their attics, surrounded by intricate spaghetti coils of 00-gauge track, trying to run their own railways, moving them to timetables that attempted to match the real world. It's an enthusiasm that still exists, but is mostly the preserve of elderly rock stars of a nostalgic temperament. They build miniature worlds in extraordinary detail, full of interconnecting branch and main lines, passenger, freight and express trains. Period steam locomotives may be electrically powered, but they have connecting rods that move. The lines are controlled with colour light signals that actually work. The landscape is tamed with tunnels and bridges, and populated by architecturally exact recreations of grand terminals and modest country stations.

The digital version involves hours in the game room with a sixty-inch flat screen plugged to an Xbox, pursuing the same kind of pleasures, but with the added attraction that you get to kill people. *GTA* creates a world far more complex than even the most elaborate of train sets. It is, of course, still a world programmed to run on predetermined tracks, but with so many possible alternative routes that it gives the illusion of a system with free will. It is devised with enough cultural ambition to envisage a world in which making the trains run on time is not the only measure of achievement. *GTA* is a game that is capable of asking critical questions about the nature of the world it describes. Imagine a train set that allowed the possibility of cottaging in the station lavatories while changing trains, and you get some of the jolt that Rockstar gave gaming when it launched the *Ballad of Gay Tony* expansion of the *GTA IV* format.

The Manhattan portrayed in *Grand Theft Auto* is stripped down to four boroughs, and it goes by the name of Liberty City. There is no Staten Island – its suburban terrain was judged lacking in dramatic potential – but northern New Jersey is renamed Alderney, suggesting the British origins of Rockstar's founders and a certain dry wit. The game allows you to experience Liberty City from a helicopter, a car, on foot and in the subway, or any combination of them.

Liberty City may lack a third physical dimension, but it has sound and light, and an astonishing level of realism in the way in which it is modelled. It works in accelerated 24-hour cycles, so the city goes from day to night and back again, with digitally controlled traffic adjusting itself to rush hours and quiet periods. Players can marvel at the views, and at the architecture. They can, if they wish, go shopping, cruise around in a car, listening to the live radio station of their choice. And of course they get to kill. They can splatter policemen and FBI agents, professional assassins and innocent bystanders, with a range of impressively detailed weapons, from rocket launchers to AK-47s.

When government departments start talking about investing in what started out as the private concerns of pale young men with ironic stubble and black T-shirts, there is a good chance that we are looking at a once brilliantly successful aspect of Britain's creative industries that is already past its glory days. The official attention suggests that they are on the way either to benign irrelevance, or to being overtaken by Taiwan and South Korea. What is called, somewhat misleadingly now, the video games industry is pretty much such a phenomenon. There are calls for investment in an academy for video-gamers, for tax breaks and new degree courses. Meanwhile, the string of gamers, programmers and designers who set light to the gaming boom across Britain either moved abroad, merged or closed down.

But you can see why the politicians got interested. *Grand Theft Auto IV* sold 3.6 million copies in the first week after its launch at the end of 2009, for which it grossed $500 million for Rockstar Games' American owner, Take Two Interactive. Two years later, it had sold a total of twenty-two million copies. Its predecessor, *GTA III*, which marked the jump into realistic representation, had sold twenty-seven million copies from 2006 when it was launched. Given that Rockstar's first iteration of *Grand Theft Auto*, launched in 1998, sold just 150,000 copies, it's clear that something dramatic had happened to gaming.

Rockstar seemed like the perfect example of the emerging post-industrial economy. There was no need for geographical concentration, for factories or offices. Rockstar worked like a federation of craft guilds: the visuals come from one outpost, the code-writing from another. Because the black-T-shirt wearers, unlike investment bankers, corporate lawyers and footballers, have no apparent interest in Michelin stars, shopping for art with Larry Gagosian, or visiting the theatre, there are Rockstar Games studios in Lincoln and Leeds, as well as in Vienna and San Diego. There are signs now that the explosive growth of video games may have petered out. Rockstar's competitors have announced lay-offs. Rockstar's parent company reported a loss for the financial year 2012, in part because of its trouble launching *Grand Theft Auto V*. But it was also a reflection of the maturity of gaming, and the escalating costs of a production process that can involve hundreds of people working for two and three years at a stretch. When it was finally launched, *Grand Theft Auto V* – set in Los Santos and the surrounding countryside – earned $1 billion in its first three days on sale.

What made *Grand Theft Auto III* and *IV* stand out was that they really lived up to the claim that the video game was a new cultural form: somewhere between the nineteenth-century novel and the spaghetti western. It can certainly be described as a designed artefact, one which invites its users to explore urban and architectural space with a new perspective. Early cinema-goers were terrified by the experience of watching an express train coming straight towards them. *Grand Theft Auto*'s players are well aware that they are in no danger from the helicopter gunships that chase them around the streets of Liberty City. But they play for the sense of an immersive experience that they get, one which takes them much deeper into the picture plane than the conventional cinema can achieve.

The achievements of *Grand Theft* were technical, visual and literary. What made it possible were two British brothers, who may well have had black T-shirts and stubble when they brought Rockstar Games to New York. But Dan Houser had also been to Oxford. And his purchase of what had once been Truman Capote's house in Brooklyn Heights certainly suggests that he is anything but a member of the nerd class.

The explosion of the video-gaming industry reflects many aspects of the early days of Hollywood. It has produced its own share of moral panics to match anything that introduced censorship to the film industry. There have been complaints about nudity, the sex and the violence. Like the novel, and the feature film, gaming needed its own visual and narrative techniques. Rockstar was responsible for creating them.

In Dan Houser, gaming may have found its Wilkie Collins, if not its Charles Dickens. He is a master of a new cultural form, one which has not yet fully evolved and stabilized. Just as the novel required new literary techniques to analyse the life of the mind and the internal monologue, Rockstar played a big part in the evolution from the early era of arcade games, which revolved around zapping relentless ranks of ever-more menacing aliens and spacecraft with a button, into an open game that created a cityscape or, in the case of *Red or Dead Redemption*, a western landscape, which allowed the player to roam at will. It was a landscape that could be experienced from multiple perspectives, rather than only the first-person view of the shooting games that were limited to a labyrinth of interlocking rooms.

Like the novel, which, no sooner had it emerged, also demanded the emergence of a new form of literary criticism, so writing about gaming has moved from the early enthusiasm of the fanzine to more traditional forms of cultural criticism. *The New York Times* described *Grand Theft Auto IV* as 'a thoroughly complete work of social satire disguised as fun; violent, intelligent, profane, endearing, obnoxious, and sly'.

But for an insight into what *GTA IV* really represents, you need to look to more specialist critics, who examine the meta-sources of the genre. Analysis of *GTA IV*, on the one hand, focuses on technical questions. There are issues with frame rates that undermine the naturalism with which space is delineated, and pop-ups, which disrupt the flow of play. There has also been a fascinating discussion of the way in which players interact with the characters that populate *GTA*. The premise of the game is that the better shape you are in physically, and the better your armour, the better your chances of survival. But you also do better if you are part of a loyal posse. That means regular socializing with your gang members. So the game has a friends-management system. If you don't respond to their text messages, they lose interest, and your vulnerability increases.

But the other level of discussion is on the aesthetic and spatial level. 'A bank heist moves from bank to vault to street to subway and back into the street, shooting cops all the way, without a single pause in the action of a single screen. Everything unfolds in the impressively continuous city, without a single seam showing,' was how one gaming critic described the technical tour de force at the heart of *Grand Theft Auto*, sounding remarkably like a film critic talking us through the achievement of a Kubrick or a Hitchcock. It's also how a new generation of architects will approach the process of navigating and designing space.

h

is for
habitat

If Habitat was once the Elizabeth David of the domestic world, established by Terence Conran to rescue the British middle classes from Anaglypta wall finishes and electric fires that did their unimpressive best to impersonate burning logs, Ingvar Kamprad's IKEA is more like Delia Smith. IKEA is cheaper, unavoidable, and ready to take short cuts with half a can of mushroom soup. Its impact has been all but universal, present everywhere from northern Europe to China. Its designs are derived from precedents devised by others, yet it has had far more impact on the way that everyday life is lived than the Bauhaus and the Design Council put together.

Habitat, which for a while became a small part of the IKEA empire, then came close to death, stood for free-range design. IKEA, with its vast supplier factories that each year turn endless acres of Slovakian and Latvian pine forests into self-assembly chipboard shelves, is the battery chicken of home-making – extremely cheap, filling, but not exactly about the subtler flavours, and with worrying implications for the environment.

Habitat, and its founder, had wider cultural ambitions than IKEA. What really makes Conran stand out as a designer is his ability to create a way of life that other people want to live too. Many critics have compared department stores with museums. Conran opened a lot of shops and built a museum. He opened the Boilerhouse Project in the Victoria and Albert Museum's basement, an undertaking that had a very particular idea of what both design and museums should be about. It involved a certain amount of friction; he was pushing museums in directions they didn't necessarily want to take. So much so that Conran once suggested taxidermy for the Victoria and Albert Museum's director at the time, the exquisite Sir Roy Strong: stuffing him, putting him in a glass case and turning him into an exhibit in his own museum, on the grounds that his languid moustache, along with his weakness for brown velvet suits with tulip lapels, made him a valuable period piece in urgent need of preservation.

But Conran himself probably represents a more revealing insight into the shifting tastes of contemporary Britain. He went to France as a student and he wanted everyone to enjoy the heavy white crockery, the enamel coffee pots and the garlic presses that he found there. So he opened a shop to sell them. He got interested in cooking so he opened a restaurant. He designed furniture, but nobody else would sell it, so he started his own shop to do the job. And when he believed that Britain had lost sight of what Design with an upper-case D should be, he set up the Boilerhouse Project to stage a series of exhibitions intended to remind us that design was about mass production and the future rather than silver snuff boxes. It was at this point that Roy Strong got the rough edge of his tongue, shortly after which the Boilerhouse packed its bags and set up as the Design Museum in a Conran-owned building in Southwark.

Conran is no missionary, but making money was never the whole point for him. He discovered design very much in the way that he discovered good food, simply from a sense of curiosity, and, having done so, he wanted everybody to have it. 'Given the choice between something that is well designed, and something that isn't, I've always assumed that people would choose the former,' says Conran.

Conran, who began Habitat in 1964, has done as much as anybody could to shape our dreams of the domestic good life and our attitudes to the things that we use, and the way we live. My kitchen in the Clapham of the early 1980s had a cork-tiled floor which I bought at the big Habitat store in the King's Road. I installed the Habitat kitchen units with pine uprights and melamine surfaces myself. I hung three chrome metal lampshades aligned in a row above the butcher-block table, at which I had four killingly uncomfortable folding red-stained beechwood chairs made in Yugoslavia, with a Gitane-blue durrie on the floor. Every item had come from Habitat. As had the wallpaper, which was brown and cream with an outsize basket-weave pattern.

The twists and turns of Conran's early career are the story of post-war design in Britain. As the country emerged from wartime austerity, the then still stick-thin young Conran was zipping back and forth between his Earl's Court flat and the studio he shared with Eduardo Paolozzi in the East End on his newly acquired Vespa, one of the first imported from Italy. 'He taught me how to make *risotto nero*,' Conran remembers, 'and I taught him how to weld.' He was at the Dome of Discovery for the Festival of Britain. In the 1950s, he officiated over a very stylish espresso machine in his first café, the Soup Kitchen, in his striped shirts and three-inch-wide braces. He opened the first Habitat off the

King's Road just ahead of the Swinging London explosion in the 1960s, by which time he had sprouted sideburns. He defined the middle-class living room in the 1970s with his distinctive blend of cantilevered chrome-plated steel Bauhaus armchairs, modular seating units and whimsical antiques. And in the 1990s, he moved beyond the domestic world to invent the giant restaurant, creating a new version of public life. Conran made restaurants on an industrial scale, big enough to function as a species of street theatre, and triggered a desperate shortage of chefs and waiters in the process. So successful was the Conran approach to restaurants that, for a while, having one suddenly became a must-have status symbol for ambitious provincial cities on the make. Glasgow for one was ready to put public money into persuading Conran to open up there.

Conran is not in the business of creating objects that beat you over the head with their personality; instead he calls his designs 'plain, simple and useful'. They are not aggressively modern, but rely on comfortable, simple materials, especially timber. And many of them are made in the workshop that Conran set up in the grounds of his country house in Berkshire with two young furniture-makers in 1983. They remind you of the ingenuity of the schoolboy Conran, who once made his own potter's wheel and kiln from pieces of an old camshaft. As designs, they are engaging and touchingly English, the product of a magpie eye and a feeling for making things.

Conran style works not because people want to be like him, but because he has a knack of creating a way of life that anybody can buy into, a way of life that includes fresh coffee and holidays in France, going out to unflashy restaurants, and gardening in a stylish manner. It was never about conspicuous consumption; bright new plastic chairs could sit comfortably next to junk-shop finds and the occasional antique. It began as the style of choice of the strapped-for-cash student, the young professional setting up home for the first time, and bit by bit it almost imperceptibly elbowed aside what had gone before to become the signature style of grown-up Britain, a generational shift that had its apotheosis on the night that the Blairs took Bill and Hillary Clinton for dinner at the Pont de la Tour, Conran's Thameside restaurant. And of course it's also taken on some of the aura of a period piece, albeit a period piece that is already the subject of a nostalgic revival.

The world according to Conran is an attempt to make ordinary, banal places a little out of the ordinary. The Habitat catalogues brilliantly encapsulated that world, and made us all feel as if we were putting our noses to the glass to peep in on somebody else's Christmas. Even from the other side of the glass it looks so attainable, not grand, not posh, but comfortable. It's about dreams, of course; France as we would like it to be, not the way it really is, and of family life as it ought to be.

IKEA, born in 1943 when Kamprad was just seventeen, is still a family-owned business, despite an interlocking thicket of holding companies, licences, Dutch-based trusts and foundations, and one that has been far more successful as a business and in its impact on the world than Habitat.

It has 150,000 employees, sales of around £27 billion a year and stores in heading for fifty countries. It is, by any standards, a remarkable company; not least because it has been astonishingly successful by doing things entirely its own way. It turned home furnishing from a cottage industry into a multinational production line. It was brilliant at getting its products reduced to the simplest elements that could fill trucks to capacity, and sourcing production from the cheapest possible suppliers. And it has proved that consumers from Hong Kong to Russia, and Dubai to Wembley, are happy to make their own homes with exactly the same raw materials.

IKEA arrived in Britain in the 1990s, entirely unknown, and it now has eighteen giant stores in the country. It was not just that it made Britain shop for furniture differently: ready to set off for those giant out-of-town blue sheds, and come home with a boot full of flatpack chipboard and an Allen key. It also changed how British homes look. IKEA ignored pretty much all the conventional wisdom about what Britain likes, and how it likes to do things.

Despite Habitat's high-profile success in the 1970s, the vast majority in Britain still took the view that modern design was a piece of chilly good taste of the kind that the well-bred attempted to inflict on those less fortunate than themselves; lingering memories of wartime utility furniture, the tables, chairs and wardrobes designed by the best of Britain's designers to make the most of rationing to help the bombed-out, and newly-married-made simplicity and modernity irretrievably associated with hard times. When they had the chance to choose for themselves, the vast majority of the population looked in the opposite direction. The misconceived attempts of the Design Council to show Britain what good design was all about – log-effect electric fires were bad design, unadorned naked electric bars were good design – did not help.

IKEA's stuff is not just cheap. It is designed intelligently, and it looks as if it belongs to the real world rather than suggesting that it is trying to be something that it is not. IKEA's product range is firmly in the modern design camp. It also comes equipped with names that are easy to mock.

Most companies, if they had a product range that was designed with an entirely different audience in mind, especially one named after an unpronounceable selection of Swedes, Finnish vegetables and Norwegian cities, might consider some sort of modification of how things looked, and even a bit of rebranding.

IKEA's strategy was to go on the offensive. It was not the company that had got things wrong, it was British consumers who needed re-educating and reprogramming. Famously IKEA set out to persuade us to chuck out the chintz, and flock to its checkout tills to ask, perhaps with a little hesitation at first, for the Jerker desk. And then for all those other ranges, called things like the Stiby, the Kubbio and the Knos. Who cares that Moker is a ridiculous name for a desk lamp? It only costs £2.75.

Astonishingly, the strategy worked. Shopping for a new kitchen used to be a once-in-a-lifetime affair. At such low prices, it's become more like buying a new outfit every

Saturday at Top Shop. The IKEA formula was so successful that by the end of the 1990s, when I was living in Glasgow and the company had not yet crossed the border from England, Scotland was so hungry for Klippan shelves and crockery that there were people making a reasonable living by taking orders from customers, driving down to Newcastle to fetch the IKEA product shown in the catalogue, delivering, assembling and installing it.

It's not just nostalgia and the antiques business that IKEA has tried to educate us. The company turned its fire on to the design world too. Its advertising agency in Britain invented Van Den Puup, a designer superstar with Cruella De Vil's wardrobe and the self-deprecating modesty of Philippe Starck. He was the frontman for a remarkably well-funded pressure group called Elite Designers against IKEA. It claimed to be dedicated to stamping out cheap furniture. 'We are,' said its manifesto,

> the elite designers. We design profound and
> beautiful furniture for those with the wealth and
> taste, which is why IKEA makes us furious, livid
> and angry. Do their designs live, breathe and growl?
> Are they born from tears of pain? Do they gently
> touch the bottom of the human soul? Pah, of course
> not. No more than weeds can attract a bee. The big
> blue place is odious. Its affordable design is sick-
> eningly shallow, and we loathe it, even more than
> we loathe football. Please join us in our unquali-
> fied hatred.

It was of course an advertising campaign, but one with a curiously mixed message. IKEA was trying to have it both ways. On the one hand, it was suggesting that designers are time-expired buffoons, monstrous, egotistical figures of fun, a view that can sometimes be hard to disagree with. It is also saying that IKEA does it better and cheaper than the rest; a line that could be understood to mean that it's OK to be taken for a ride, provided that you haven't paid too much for the privilege. Would Top Shop, say, be likely to bite the hands that feed it to run a campaign lampooning Vivienne Westwood and Karl Lagerfeld?

Its catalogue is still devoted to the same message. Design without the designer price is the mantra it keeps repeating. If you are prepared to spend the day in a giant, city-killing, edge-of-town IKEA shed, lining up to wait for your sofa, shelves and kitchen cabinets to show up, and then negotiate self-assembly instructions that are not for the faint-hearted, then you can equip pretty much an entire flat for the price of one upmarket sofa. And provided that you don't start examining how things are made, or worrying about how long upholstery that has been stapled into position is going to last, then it will look pretty good.

IKEA has done a lot for the way that we all live. It has given us cheap, simple kitchens, affordable, comfortable sofas. But it has also played its part in the unravelling of the fabric of our cities, and turned shopping for furniture into a pretty exact facsimile of negotiating Terminal 5 at Heathrow on a bad day.

is for

Imperfect

Perfection may not be easy, but at least it's not hard to understand what it is. Depending on your degree of skill, to a greater or a lesser extent you succeed or you fail to achieve it. It has been a preoccupation of designers ever since they were first asked to work on industrially produced artefacts.

Perfection is what once drove Dieter Rams and now drives Jonathan Ive as they and their teams invest limitless energy in achieving the perfect radius curve, and the perfect finish that shows no marks. The search for perfection is what created the language of modernism, and as such has taken on something of the flavour of a period piece. Imperfection is a more elusive and a more difficult quality to work with, not least because it is harder to measure. It can be an equally positive quality, one that speaks of the more agnostic times that we live in now, when compared with the moral certainties of the 1930s.

Attempting perfection in manufacturing is to know what to aim for in the design of every joint, the creation of every seam, and the shaping of every surface. To find justifications for the positive qualities of imperfection, you cannot blindly commit to a mechanical process or to a template and expect the desired outcome simply through the exercise of skill or persistence or consistency. It demands the exercise of a different kind of judgement.

The pursuit of the perfect is rooted in one of the key issues of the early days of mass production when many components were made using moulds. The process of filling and refilling a mould with hot metal inevitably wears away its sharp lines, degrades its finish, and so diminishes the quality of the copies it can be used to make. In the course of manufacturing, each new example, bit by bit, loses the precision that the mould began with, and results in less and less perfect versions of the original. It is in this phenomenon that the concept of the limited edition has its origins. To make just nine examples of an object, or a print, is to guarantee that each of them will have a certain quality. Conversely, irregularity has been understood as synonymous with the less-than-perfect, and so with the inferior. Mass production has looked to find ways to maintain the perfection of every piece that comes out of the mould.

For a designer the most difficult thing about looking for the positive qualities in imperfection is the demand that it places on them to justify every aesthetic decision they make. It introduces the possibility of subjective as well as objective qualities in design.

The possibility of perfection implies the existence of an original, with the special qualities that implies, to which copies can only aspire. But mass-produced objects are the outcome of industrial processes in which, though there may be a prototype, or prototypes, there is no original on which all subsequent copies are more or less accurately based. There is only the tool, or the idea. There is no single ideal object, with what Walter Benjamin called the 'aura' of art, creating a category of object to distinguish it in an age of mechanical reproduction from the limitless copies. It is the mass-produced nature of the object that is the point of the exercise. It means that every Volkswagen Polo from a particular production run is exactly the same as every other

Polo. Aside from the optional extras, any deviation from the car's specification represents a defect. And to be defective is not the same as to be imperfect. Each car has the same characteristics, the characteristics of the particular model, just as each sheet of paper in a notebook is the same as every other sheet, and every copy of a given edition of a newspaper is identical to every other copy.

It is in many ways a characteristic that is antithetical to the human desire for the distinctive and the individual, the instinctive desire to make our possessions our own. Or the impulse that the carpet weavers of the Muslim world had to build imperfection into their work with loving care as an expression of religious humility in the face of the Almighty.

Interestingly, in the case of a banknote, the guarantee of the genuine and the perfect is in ensuring that each note is not quite the same as every other note; each serial number is unique. Counterfeiting finds this more difficult to deal with than copying detail.

To explore the attractions of imperfection puts the designer in a more exposed position than attempting to achieve perfection. Every step of the design process demands making a decision without, as it were, a safety net. It is the way that Hella Jongerius, one of the more influential designers of her generation, works. She is not an artisan maker, shaping objects one at a time, to a specific brief, for a specific user, each one showing the distinctive mark of the making process, the hand and the countless individual decisions on which it depends. She works within the framework of the industrial system, and all that it has to offer in terms of the potential to spread the costs of tooling across unlimited production runs. She appreciates the way in which our understanding of the material world is informed by our familiarity with the potential of industrial production. But she is also interested in using industrial production with a new level of sophistication. It is not that she wants to use a machine to make an object that looks as if it were made by hand – something that has been a subtext to manufacturing since the beginning of the nineteenth century. Nor is her approach to be understood as a manifestation of the familiar idea of the customized, and perhaps somewhat inauthentic, outcome of multiple options for consumers. The latest incarnation of this is what is described as mass customization. It is a development that is driven by new production techniques that do away with the need for costly tooling, and instead rely on digital printing techniques that build complex forms without moulds or tools, and so remove the purpose and the benefits of uniformity.

When there is no mould, there is no need to make large numbers of identical objects that look exactly the same simply in order to amortize costs over a long production run. When the quality of production can be taken for granted, there is no purpose in pursuing precision or repetition for its own sake. It becomes possible to introduce the potential of variation from a perceived norm into the process. Jongerius loves mixing craft methods with new materials: porcelain vases, finished in spray paint and lacquer; making fabrics that combine felt and wool.

Jongerius explores ways to make something new out of the manufacturing process: so shiny, glossy surfaces can be replaced by lesser degrees of polish. Pure geometry is not the only possible formal language. Pure colour can give way to muddy mixes. Symmetry is not the only option. It's an attitude that she shares with older designers such as Gaetano Pesce, who looked to find ways of working with artisans and workshops to make pieces in series or batches that were not identical but which offered the potential of individual variations instead.

Attempting to exploit the possibilities of imperfection by tinkering with mass-production methods offers the opportunity to soften and domesticate industrially made objects and to give them the charisma of the individual and the original. It is to suggest that a particular vase, glass or chair is not the same as all the others, and so can be understood as distinctively personal, or, to use a word which has more positive connotations than imperfect, to be unique.

Imperfection can be suggested by the traces of the loom, or the process marks required by colour-printing textiles, or the use of upholstery buttons that do not match, or by deconstructing the glass-making process in order to show the marks of the hand.

This is not to be confused with the skill of the craft maker. It is closer in a way to what Rei Kawakubo, the Japanese fashion designer, once described as her continual search to introduce special qualities to the fabrics woven for her garments, even, if necessary, by tampering with the machinery of the looms that made them.

Imperfection is a new take on old ideas. It is the concept of *wabi-sabi*, which still underpins Japanese culture's view of aesthetic quality. *Wabi* is the quality of rusticity; it suggests the potential to find resonance in the accidents of construction. *Sabi* refers to the patina of age and wear. *Wabi-sabi* is the acceptance that perfection is elusive, and that beauty is to be found in its absence. *Wabi-sabi* is a form of the aristocratic preference that many cultures share for the old and weathered set against the vulgarity of the new.

On one level the post-industrial interest in imperfection is a reflection of the cult of imperfection that has its roots in the West in the writings of John Ruskin and William Morris. They railed against the tyranny of the machine, and the straightjacketed perfection that it imposed on the craftsman. Ruskin was equally outspoken in his attacks against the constraining hand of the designer who insisted on a precise and lifeless delineation of every detail, thereby removing any possibility of self-expression by the artisan.

In *The Seven Lamps of Architecture* Ruskin suggested that, in pursuit of imperfection, 'the laying of colour by a mechanical hand, and its toning under a vulgar eye, are far more offensive than rudeness in cutting the stone. The latter is imperfection only; the former deadness or discordance.' He continues later with:

> [H]and-work might always be known from
> machine-work; observing, however, at the same time,
> that it was possible for men to turn themselves into
> machines, and to reduce their labour to the machine

level; but so long as men work *as* men, putting their heart into what they do, and doing their best, it matters not how bad workmen they may be, there will be that in the handling which is above all price: it will be plainly seen that some places have been delighted in more than others – that there have been a pause, and a care about them; and then there will come careless bits, and fast bits; and here the chisel will have struck hard, and there lightly, and anon timidly; and if the man's mind as well as his heart went with his work, all this will be in the right places, and each part will set off the other; and the effect of the whole, as compared with the same design cut by a machine or a lifeless hand, will be like that of poetry well read and deeply felt to that of the same verses jangled by rote . . . it is not coarse cutting, it is not blunt cutting, that is necessarily bad, but it is *cold* cutting – the look of equal trouble everywhere – the smooth, diffused tranquillity of heartless pains – the regularity of a plough in a level field. The chill is more likely, indeed, to show itself in finished work than in any other – men cool and tire as they complete: and if completeness is thought to be vested in polish, and to be attainable by help of sand paper, we may as well give the work to the engine lathe at once.

Ruskin did not escape ridicule. The economist Thorsten Veblen mounted a frontal assault on Ruskin's idea of imperfection in his book *The Theory of the Leisure Class*. 'A limited edition is in effect a guarantee – somewhat crude, it is true – that this book is scarce, and that it therefore is costly and lends pecuniary distinction to its consumer,' he wrote. 'Hence has arisen that exaltation of the defective, of which John Ruskin and William Morris were such eager spokesmen in their time; and on this ground their propaganda of crudity and wasted effort has been taken up and carried forward since their time.'

But Ruskin had many enthusiasts. His essential point was distilled by Charles Rennie Mackintosh (from an observation by the architect J D Sedding) in his characteristic font: 'There is hope in honest error; none in the icy perfections of the mere stylist.' The same idea was repeated much later, in the 1970s, by Christopher Alexander, semi-mystical architect. His advice to the designer, as he writes in his essay 'The Perfection of Imperfection', was: 'To get wholeness you must try instead to strive for *this* kind of perfection, where things that don't matter are left rough and unimportant and the things that really matter are given deep attention. This is a perfection that seems imperfect. But it is a far deeper thing.'

Now that we live in a world where we are close to the point when we will all be able to download the digital specifications that will allow us to print a door handle or a spare part on a three-dimensional printer, the characteristics of perfection and imperfection are qualities that require another reassessment.

When there is no tool needed to make an object,

then it is no longer credible to continue to depend on the intellectual equipment developed to deal with mass production. Designers used to create shapes that could be formed using factory tools, things that could be made by moulding metal, or pushing molten plastic through tubes. The shapes and tools created a visual language for design that designers worked in. It creates a vocabulary of finishes. That is a vocabulary that is based on the past. We are in the middle of creating a new one. And it is the changing idea of the relationship between perfection and imperfection that will define it.

J IS
FOR JIM
NATURE

Philippe Starck is not a designer that the contemporary generation of design students shows much interest in. They look at Apple's Jonathan Ive, or the more radical approach of open-source design. Hacking, additive manufacturing, as 3D printing is now called, and critical design make Starck look dated, if not irrelevant.

For all his blithe claims to have been motivated by ecology long before green became fashionable, and still is, now that it is not, he is identified, if he is identified at all, with that moment in the 1980s when the cult of the designer celebrity was born. He built his career as much on his own force of personality as with the objects that he has designed. He relies on colour, sensuous styling and an impressive way with hotel lobbies.

The ease with which he could come up with a philosophy of nursery-rhyme simplicity for every new product, from chairs with three legs to toothbrushes apparently inspired by Brâncuşi's sculpture, meant that, once the initial charm had worn off, Starck came to be seen as the personification of the glib. And yet, perhaps enough time has passed since François Mitterrand hired him to redecorate the president's private office at the Élysée Palace to look at Starck with more distance, both as designer and as a phenomenon.

Born in 1949, Starck is like a knowing reincarnation of another celebrated French-born designer, Raymond Loewy. It was Loewy, with his natural gift for self-publicity, who created the prototype for professional designer as heroic form-giver. He managed to have himself photographed cross-legged, crisp white handkerchief in his pocket, perched on a shelf, in a reconstruction of his studio inside the Metropolitan Museum in New York, and to make the cover of *Time* magazine at the centre of a universe of things he had designed. There is an unforgettable image of Loewy lolling casually at the front end of a massive steam locomotive that he turned into an enormous streamlined bullet for the Pennsylvania Railroad. He wears a soft felt trilby, neatly trimmed moustache, and an immaculately tailored suit, apparently effortlessly in command of the immensely powerful mechanical monster on which he is balanced.

Starck does not go in for hand-made suits. In his early days, he looked rumpled and sported stubble that never quite turned into a beard. But he had an eye for publicity every bit as developed as Loewy's, and a similar line in cracker-barrel philosophizing. Loewy was always claiming to have streamlined the sales curve with his MAYA formula – the 'most advanced, yet acceptable' solution. Starck will tell everybody who will listen that he believes not in design that is beautiful, but in design that is good.

But Starck's way with words should not distract from his real achievements. Perhaps more significant than his commission to decorate an imperial presidency was when the Thomson consumer electronics company, newly nationalized by the French government, brought in Starck in a last-ditch attempt to stave off the inevitable collapse of European television manufacturing. In 1994, just as the cathode ray tube was facing extinction, Starck produced a series of remarkable objects for the various brands that Thomson owned.

There was little chance of competing on price, or with innovative technology. But Thomson were prepared to allow Starck to rethink the language of electronic objects, in both materials and shape. The most memorable of them was produced under the SABA brand. Starck called the portable tv Jim Nature – one of his more irritating affectations is to use characters from Philip K. Dick science-fiction novels to provide the names for his objects. Jim Nature's case is partly moulded chipboard and partly injection-moulded plastic. The carrying handle is a strip of fabric. Using wood for the case is a memory of the early days of television. Like the radios, television sets were treated as pieces of furniture at first, to be domesticated by cabinetwork.

Jim Nature is simultaneously looking to the past and, with its tight curves and a back that is designed just as carefully as the front, to the future. The messages sent by the materials are deliberately mixed. Wood could be understood as a signal both of luxury, like a walnut dashboard on a car, or of economy of means: chipboard has a suggestion of utility. And given the way that television over the previous decade had avoided the use of once conventional wood, Starck was able to make an utterly distinctive object.

The television set was one of the most charismatic objects of the twentieth century. It was found in almost every home. The technology on which it depended has become obsolete. The social behaviour it encouraged, as a kind of surrogate fireplace, has vanished. The particular form of media that it encapsulated, broadcasting by a few networks and national broadcasters, which created massive audiences for a restricted range of content that was consumed simultaneously by entire nations, has gone.

Jim Nature stands at the end of a line of self-consciously designed TV sets, one that began in Italy in the 1960s with Marco Zanuso and Richard Sapper's work for Brionvega, the Algol, and Black, the minimal acrylic black cube, and saw Sony's Trinitron technology applied to the Profeel range of monitors. And Starck's contribution to close this sequence is the one that has the most to tell us about how design can be used as a language that goes beyond formal perfection.

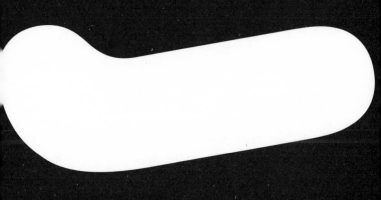

is for
JUMBO

Of all the objects that can be understood to be a piece of design, none is more complex than an aircraft. Not exactly mass-produced but made in their hundreds and occasionally thousands, the aircraft has to face the supreme challenge of leaving the ground safely, carrying passengers long distances at an acceptable degree of discomfort, and then landing again. It needs to be fabricated and funded in such a way as to meet the needs of the air-travel industry, which is notoriously caught between boom and bust. A modern aircraft might not be quite as big as an ocean liner, but it has a larger scale than a lot of architecture. And building it stretches the capacities of the industrial system to its limits.

The impact of aircraft on the way that the world works has been profound at every level. Mass air travel has transformed migration flows, the relationship of one city with another, and the nature of the modern economy. The form of the aircraft has worked its way into our visual consciousness at every level. Harley Earl, first head of styling at General Motors, ushered in the era of high-rise tail fins for the car industry – and came up with a Cadillac with an acknowledged debt to a Lockheed P-38 Lightning fighter. The profiled aluminium hulls of pre-war Junkers transport planes inspired architects and engineers such as Jean Prouvé. The plywood construction of the Second World War aircraft helped to underpin the technical development of Charles Eames's furniture. The first-generation Comet, the first jet airliner, made by De Havilland, had sculptural elegance. With great engineering finesse the engines were made an integral part of the wing. It had a beauty that Brâncuşi would have appreciated. It was part of a succession of aircraft which helped to create a visual language that reflected, and was reflected by, the contemporary world. The extraordinary beauty of the wings of the Second World War fighter, the Spitfire, the amazing watershed represented by the Stealth Bomber were both landmarks, not only in aeronautical history. They affected the design of cars and furniture, clothes and domestic appliances.

But it is the Boeing 747, known in its early days as the jumbo, that has the most powerful visual presence, and which can be said to be the aircraft that has had the single biggest impact on the world. When the Boeing 747 made its first public appearance on 30 September 1968, it was the largest passenger jet the world had ever seen. The first version could take 450 passengers, more than twice as many as its largest predecessor. The later, bigger versions ended up carrying more than 600 people. It did not actually fly for another four months, or reach airline service with Pan Am until January 1970. But from the moment that the swelling whale snout and the aluminium alloy body of the *City of Everett*, tail number N7470, first emerged from a hangar door in Seattle, it was clear that the modern world had a new icon on its hands. There was nothing else like it. A double-deck passenger airliner had been speculated about; here was one for real. It was not just another airliner. Its shape made it instantly recognizable; it was the jumbo, with a silhouette which identified it as a type that was all its own. What was not so immediately obvious was that the plane would also turn out to be one of the most successful airliners ever built. Still in production thirty-five years later, Boeing delivered the 1,000th 747 to Singapore Airlines in September 1993. There have been another 400 built since then: bigger, faster, smarter but still basically with the same ingredients as the original N7470, even after the introduction of the curious swept-up wing tips and the stretched upper deck of the later versions.

The Boeing 747 was not the only aircraft that attempted to define the new category of wide-body, or twin-aisle jet. It was developed just ahead of rival products from Lockheed and McDonnell Douglas in a titanic struggle for domination of the market for big passenger jets that would eventually force both Boeing's rivals out of the business. The starting point was military research. The US funded tenders from three aircraft builders for heavy-lift aircraft and troop transports that offered the potential to be developed for civilian use. Lockheed built the Tristar and McDonnell Douglas was responsible for the DC-10. Both went for more modest three-engine alternatives to Boeing's bolder, and costly, four-engine version. Lockheed produced an integrated design that built its third engine into the tail plane. The DC-10 was more blunt about the way its engines were distributed. Its third engine did not sit on the hull like the Lockheed, but was lashed, in an apparently ad hoc way, to the tail. It looked unstable, and the aesthetic prejudice was reinforced tragically when a DC-10 lost an engine on take-off and crashed, killing all on board. The Boeing 747 became more than a commercial necessity for airlines flying heavily trafficked routes. For the more insecure politicians and tycoons, owning a jumbo or two became an essential trophy for a while, one to go with the fleet of armoured Mercedes cars and the crop of mirror-glass skyscrapers in their home towns.

Its sheer size gave the first jumbo an extraordinary presence, towering over pygmy ground vehicles swarming across the tarmac to greet it, like Lilliputians trying to lasso Gulliver, on that long-ago day in Seattle. The front view is as impassive and intimidating as Mount Rushmore. The four engines hang from pylons that are like the flying buttresses on a Gothic cathedral. In fact they are the genetic inheritance from the B-52, Boeing's nuclear bomber. Boeing had built the American strategic bomber fleet, and with it came the expertise to hang jet engines from pylons slung beneath the aircraft wing, which was essential for the jumbo. The tail towers over the hull, like a ski jump. All this and it moves too. Initially the shock of seeing one of these remarkable machines flying overhead would bring people running into the street for a glimpse. It was like watching an office block sailing through the clouds.

Wandering around on the ground beneath a Boeing 747 induces a curious sense of vertigo. You lose the sense of scale and proportion. This is a vehicle, a man-made object capable of hurtling down a runway at speeds of more than 200 miles an hour and lifting off into the air. Yet it has the character of a piece of the landscape. Even its wheels are bigger than a man, though from a distance, they seem tinier than the castors on a wheeled office chair.

The wide body and the upper deck was the chance for the realization of those schoolboy fantasies of the 1950s about what air travel could be like one day. In the early 1970s, there really were pianos and cocktail bars in the skies as the airlines struggled to find entertaining ways to deal with overcapacity. All that vanished in the age of mass intercontinental air travel, when the planes filled up and 600 people found themselves crammed into conditions not that dissimilar from the lower decks of a nineteenth-century migrant ship. The only saving grace was that the experience did not last as long as crossing the Atlantic by sea. Yet even now, there is still a moment of release from the pressures of the outside world when the cabin door swings shut on the first leg of the flight to Australia, with twelve guaranteed interruption-free hours all the way to Singapore.

The jumbo is an airliner with an architectural interior rather than a cabin. It is made up of infinite loop corridors and a sequence of rooms each with a different character. It is in an entirely different league from the pencil-slim, claustrophobic flying cigar tubes that previously represented the airliner. Not so surprisingly, when Norman Foster was asked by the BBC to make a film about his favourite piece of twentieth-century architecture, he was able to devote it entirely to the jumbo jet without even a hint of having his tongue in his cheek.

The 747 is one of those very rare industrially made objects that acquire an authentic personality of their own. They are made in factories and represent cold commercial logic and painstaking engineering calculations, but, nevertheless, like a VW or a Bakelite phone, they have an identity. The Boeing's eulogy came from an architect, Norman Foster, in a film. The Citroën DS got Roland Barthes and an essay.

At the same time, the 747 is a technical phenomenon whose impact on the course of social history has been enormous. Its capacity ushered in the age of mass air travel, which the 707 had only hinted at. Its economies of scale slashed the cost per seat of flying the Atlantic. For most Europeans, air travel had previously been limited to the Mediterranean. The jumbo put Florida and Thailand within reach. It accelerated the convergence of the world's cities and transformed the nature of migration. Perhaps even more far reaching in its long-term impact on the cultural perspective of the world was the way in which affordable air travel made migration reversible and permeable. If it took four weeks and a year's salary to sail from Sicily to Australia, then family ties and cultural connections were broken by migration. But now Britons born of Pakistani or Jamaican descent can fly to Rawalpindi or Kingston for the weekend, the connections and presumption of identity are very different.

The jumbo is an object of real beauty, and that is almost enough to forgive it the noise and the pollution that it produces. Only the name itself is curiously inelegant. And it spawned British Aerospace's 146, an even less elegant, diminutive, four-engine regional jet that was a compromised coda to the long history of British-built airliners, and which was dubbed the jumbolino by one Swiss airline.

The jumbo was the starting point for a series of

further developments that gradually expanded the original format by extending what began as a bubble behind the flight deck further and further back along the hull. It was a strategy that was taken to its ultimate conclusion by Boeing's nemesis, the A380. Airbus Industrie created what became the world's largest passenger aircraft by taking the idea of the upper deck and extending it down the entire length of the hull, leaving Boeing in its dust. Creating it was an extraordinary achievement: with wings built in England – reflecting an expertise that goes all the way back to the Spitfire – a fuselage made in Germany, and final assembly in France, where it was necessary to widen roads and create new bridges to allow the components to reach their destination, it took a positively pharaonic approach. The big Airbus was an undertaking on the scale of the building of Stonehenge, or Notre-Dame. Half shark, half whale, the A380 looks too large and too ungainly to climb into the air. Inside it has a grand staircase that feels like something out of a Busby Berkeley production. It is big and it is an extraordinary engineering project. It lacks the presence and the charisma of the original 747 wide body, not because of any failing in the abilities of the design and engineering teams that made it possible, but perhaps because of the fundamentals of aerodynamics. An aircraft of one category has the potential to provide a gainly elegance, but step up a collar size or two, and a line has been crossed, and it is no longer possible to have charisma.

IS FOR KAPLICKÝ

When you are writing about architecture for a living, you feel a certain obligation to put what little money you have where your pen is. And so it was that I asked Jan Kaplický to remodel a flat inside a white-stucco terraced tenement in London's Maida Vale for me. I was at the *Sunday Times*; he had just been made redundant by Norman Foster, who was going through one of his periodic downturns.

Kaplický and I had talked every so often for years, and it was clear to me that he was an architect like no other. He was born in Czechoslovakia, and had been educated behind the Iron Curtain. But what he was fascinated by was the future. He loved the idea of designing robotic space-station buildings, demountable houses for helicopter pilots, and nose-cone shelters that could be buried on a beach or a mountaintop. I wasn't expecting to get anything like that. But there was always something new that he was becoming enthusiastic about.

Kaplický was once asked to choose an artefact to be photographed with from an exhibition about tools at the Design Museum. He picked a Bren gun, designed in Brno, in what is now the Czech Republic, and made in Enfield in England. He was always looking for ways to reconcile the two worlds in which he lived. In Britain, he talked to me about Tatra limousines, the curiously reptilian Czech ancestors of the Volkswagen, the Villa Müller in Prague, designed by Adolf Loos, Czechoslovak military fortifications from the Second World War, and showed me the pictures that he brought with him of the handful of projects that he had built before he left Prague in 1968, when he fled the arrival of Soviet tanks. These were designs that would be startling in their freshness in any context. In what we thought we knew of life in the countries of the Warsaw Pact, they were extraordinary.

Kaplický lived a life fractured by the tragedies of the twentieth century. He was a baby when Czechoslovakia fell to the invasion of Hitler's army and the young republic's brave experiment in modernity was extinguished. And he was a child when Czechoslovak democracy was destroyed once more by the Soviet Union in 1948. By 1968, just as he was beginning to make his way as an independent architect, the Soviet Union's tanks arrived in Wenceslas Square.

He had already been to America by this time. He had even seen the work of Charles Eames and Buckminster Fuller at first hand, albeit in Russia. Kaplický had seen the American National Exhibition in Moscow, designed by George Nelson with an installation by Charles and Ray Eames, during which Khrushchev had the famous kitchen debate with Richard Nixon. Kaplický made his way to London in 1968, but not before he had painted, in careful Cyrillic, a sign on a wall at the National Museum in Prague, inviting the Russian neighbours to go back to where they had come from, and checking with his mother that he had got the grammar right.

The first time that I saw the inside of Loos's Villa Müller was for Jan's funeral. He died the day that his daughter, Johanka, was born in Prague. A few days later, his family and a few friends gathered to say goodbye to him inside the villa. He had been married there and, sixty years earlier, he had played with the Müller children in the villa's garden when he was growing up in Prague in the 1940s.

Kaplický was a Czech, and Loos was a German-speaking Bohemian. But in terms of their architectural output and general demeanour they have a certain amount in common. They were both polemicists, even if Loos believed that it was his duty to celebrate the sober, and the appropriate, and Kaplický was convinced that architecture that was not, in some sense, shocking or abrasive or outrageously sensuous was not worth thinking about.

London in the 1960s put Kaplický at the centre of an architectural world which he had only previously glimpsed through a keyhole of smuggled copies of *Vogue* and *Life*. Once he got there, he had a habit of being in the right place at the right time. He is in the group photographs of the Renzo Piano and Richard Rogers team that won the competition to build the Pompidou Centre in Paris. He went on to work for Norman Foster, on the early stages of the Hong Kong and Shanghai Bank.

He had a flat that was decorated with a photographic image of a hamburger that took up a whole wall, and an aluminium dining table that was full of holes and looked as if it had been borrowed from a Wellington bomber.

But Kaplický was living in another world, all this time. He was living in the world as it ought to be rather than the world as it is in reality, a world in which architecture was not the messy, muddy business that it actually is but in which he could design robot-built orbiting space stations, in which emergency shelters could be helicoptered into position slung from beneath the belly of a Chinook. A vision that he could only sustain by an unquenchable optimism that he could take the rest of us with him into a one-piece Neoprene-lined solar-powered rocket ride to the future; an optimism that sometimes he could not understand why we were conspiring to stop him from sharing with us.

With his friend David Nixon he started Future Systems, a name that suggests a corporation staffed by hundreds. It was sustained mainly by Kaplický's determination, and the exquisitely beautiful drawings that he made. Elegant ink lines that recall, perhaps, the precision of his mother's work as an illustrator.

Future Systems became more than a dream when Kaplický set up his own studio. Job One was my flat, a spaceship trapped and tethered inside a nineteenth-century London terraced house. He borrowed builders from his fellow Czech exile the architect Eva Jiřičná to make it happen. He created a series of aluminium-skinned platforms that stopped short of the walls, and what he called a culinary workstation – a T-shaped kitchen unit with a fibreglass top. If you put anything hot on the fibreglass, you risked a domestic version of the China syndrome.

Kaplický was able to turn some of his constant stream of ideas into physical reality. Others stayed as dreams that inspired others, among which were the design for the National Library of France in Paris, a glass canyon split by a footbridge across the Seine, and a brilliant scheme for the Parthenon Museum in Athens.

Finally there were big things to build with Amanda

Levete: his department store for Selfridges in Birmingham, the press box at Lord's Cricket Ground in London. And then he won a competition to design the National Library in Prague and was also asked to design a concert hall in České Budějovice; both were projects that attracted a great deal of attention, but were unrealized.

His architecture was always a celebration of beauty. He found aesthetic inspiration in the wing of an aircraft, the curved blade of a helicopter rotor, in the legs of a lunar lander, in a metal dress by Paco Rabanne, in the curves of a human body, and they are all there in his architecture, showing us another way to understand the world around us.

K is for Kitchen

In the early twentieth century the middle-class kitchen was at the front line of a particularly bitter variety of class warfare, carried out for the most part in conditions every bit as constricted as those endured by the sappers digging under the trenches of the Somme. It was a conflict between maids, expected to remain mute and invisible in the background of the intricate domestic arrangements of the families that they worked for, and their scarcely less constrained employers, for whom every act of daily life was carried out with a spectator present. Every creak of the stair, every cry from another room, had an audience on both sides of the social divide silently registering the significance of what they were unwilling parties to hearing or seeing.

The scale of a country house had allowed for a social campaign of movement and manoeuvre with back stairs, green baize doors and servant's halls mitigating the claustrophobic aspects of domesticity. But a suburban kitchen crammed the combatants toe to toe in territory in which every square inch was contested.

The kitchen, whatever its size, was a kind of buffer zone. It was like the boiler room of a ship, populated by crew rather than passengers. With a few exceptions, its design was pragmatic and utilitarian rather than an aesthetic statement. But this variety of simplicity had a growing appeal. Terence Conran, largely responsible for the look of the aspiring British home for the last quarter of the twentieth century, recalls his schooldays in a Norman Shaw house, where it was the below-stairs world of kitchens with long deal tables, open fires and plain walls that he found much more appealing than the grander rooms on the upper floors. The kitchen was the route through which electrical and mechanical appliances started filtering into the home. Given the association of machinery with work, it was a sensitive process. Throughout the nineteenth century, those who could afford to kept work and home entirely separate. To be able to do so was a reflection of social status. Early wireless sets and gramophones were camouflaged as furniture for fear that in their raw state they would compromise the domesticity of the home. The kitchen was the most mechanized part of the home, the place in which order and method were seen as desirable.

The contemporary kitchen is the product of the mingling of these two worlds that came when domesticity flooded through the bulkhead to colonize what had once been no-man's-land. The kitchen has become the symbolic centre of the home in a way that it never used to be, a domestic shrine to the idea of family life and conviviality. But it is also a place in which the conspicuous celebration of efficiency has acquired a symbolic value.

If Conran helped to make the kitchen a fashionable alternative to the living room, Margarethe Schütte-Lihotzky, a Viennese architect, and a lifelong revolutionary socialist, is paradoxically responsible for its underlying organizational principles. In the late 1920s, Schütte-Lihotzky combined egalitarianism with logic and devised the Frankfurt kitchen, a concept that has a claim to be understood as the mother of all fitted kitchens. As many as 8,000 examples were installed in the blocks of flats built for Frankfurt's workers by the city. She was influenced by the theories of Taylorism, named for Frederick Taylor, the American inventor of the time-and-motion study, and by his determination to lay the production line out so efficiently that the worker became an integral part of it. She went on to work on the plan for the city of Magnitogorsk for Stalin, and on schools for Fidel Castro.

Schütte-Lihotzky lived long enough to celebrate her one hundredth birthday in 1997 in the atrium of the Museum für Angewandte Kunst, Vienna's version of the Victoria and Albert Museum. Soviet and Cuban flags flew in tribute to her unflinching radicalism and the work that she had done in both countries. Waiters in white gloves dispensed *Sekt* and *Sachertorte*, while Schütte-Lihotzky took to the floor to dance a waltz.

In 1916, Schütte-Lihotzky had been one of the first women to study architecture at the Vienna Academy of Applied Art, in a building that still stands next door to the museum. While most of her year were enthusiastically pursuing the decorative style of the secessionists, Schütte–Lihotzky was more interested in functionalism. Her student projects showed that she could draw beautifully, but she wanted to find ways of using architecture to deal with the everyday questions of survival. She later claimed that 'What attracted me to architecture was the very concrete task of serving the people.'

The First World War triggered a traumatic social upheaval in post-imperial Vienna. The city was struggling to accommodate a flood of refugees. Schütte-Lihotzky worked on a number of emergency schemes to help them cope with life in the burgeoning shanty towns and camps springing up around the edges of the city, and the epidemics that came with them. She spent her evenings, after classes, touring squatter shacks, working with their inhabitants to install running water and electricity. It was at the height of the influenza epidemic that killed twenty million people in 1918 – including both Egon Schiele and Gustav Klimt. Schütte-Lihotzky was spared influenza but contracted tuberculosis. The epidemic clearly played an important part in impressing on the early modern movement pioneers the urgency of making hygiene an essential part of their programme.

After graduating, she worked on designing social housing projects for Adolf Loos, a man whom she remembered as 'charming, but too ready to drop everything to go down to the Riviera' to be able to make it in the serious world of public housing.

She had met Ernst May, the German architect who was building pioneering social housing in Frankfurt, by chance while she was standing in for Loos, who was due to give May a tour of some newly built flats. She ended up being offered a job with May's team in Frankfurt, and later followed him into exile in the Soviet Union. For five years in the late 1920s, she produced a series of standardized kitchens to be installed throughout Frankfurt's new social housing.

Schütte-Lihotzky's designs had to work within the constraints of minimal-space standards in which every inch counted. Her kitchens were characterized by neat rows of storage bins and racks and work surfaces designed to be easy to clean. When I was a child in Acton in the 1950s, our kitchen was a scullery just big enough for two people to stand up in, with a gas oven, a sink and no refrigerator, in a disorganized version of Schütte-Lihotzky's galley.

Her built-in units give the impression of a sense of purpose. She designed a prefabricated concrete basin for one version of the kitchen to keep costs down. Given the need to cram everything into the smallest possible space, washing was combined with cooking in some cases, and she designed bathtubs that came with a lid so that they could provide an extra work surface when not in use. She used wide, sliding doors which connected the kitchen to the living room, to allow mothers to keep an eye on their children. She was equally practical and businesslike about planning. She persuaded Frankfurt to drop its scheme to accommodate single women in hostels; instead, they were assigned accommodation integrated with family housing. Rather than putting working women in a ghetto, it made more sense to give them accommodation close to that of families. It would allow those women who weren't working to earn a little money from washing or cleaning or child-minding for their neighbours.

Margarethe moved from Germany to the Soviet Union in 1930 with Ernst May and his team of architects to plan settlements for Stalin's Great Utopia. When purges and show trials made life impossible there, she left, and, after brief stays in London and Paris, ended up in Istanbul, where she joined a group of anti-fascist exiles.

Kitchen

In 1940, she volunteered to return to Austria to work against the Nazis, but was caught by the Gestapo almost at once and sentenced to fifteen years in a labour camp. Liberated in 1945, she worked in East Germany and in Cuba, as well as in Austria, designing social housing, nursery schools, children's furniture and exhibition systems.

It is not for designing any single house that she will be remembered, but for the radical approach she brought to understanding how ordinary people related to life in the homes that architects designed. She was one of the first to insist on the responsibility that architects must have to their real clients: not the government bureaucracy responsible for the brief and the budget for social housing but the people who would live in it. For the first time, Schütte-Lihotzky made this the centre of an architect's vision. That the logic and discipline she brought to the design of the kitchen should become the starting point for the worktop, the built-in sink and the spice rack is one of the great ironies. There was not much space in the Frankfurt kitchen for sipping orange juice and eating bircher muesli on leisurely Sunday mornings. But it is precisely the combination of the domestic ideal and Schütte-Lihotzky's celebration of efficiency that has made the kitchen the centre of the domestic world. And, as a result, it is the place in which the affluent can be persuaded to invest in more travertine floors, limed-oak storage units and stainless steel worktops per square inch than anywhere else in the home, even as the customs of shared meals and preparation of food atrophy. The kitchen is where they can live out their dreams of

Provençal farm houses, or wood-lined Scandinavian cabins, or cook to the precision of a Michelin-starred restaurant. There are domestic kitchens that have preparation kitchens attached to them. One for the staff, and one for their employers to eat in against a background of temperature-controlled cabinets for wine, ice available on tap, and the kind of hotplates that depend on magnetic resonance. It is now even possible to purchase from Electrolux a domestic version of the laboratory equipment that Ferran Adrià used at El Bulli – provided you have the means to afford the £250,000 price.

Despite Schütte-Lihotzky's devotion to the proletariat, it is the kitchen that has become the greatest domestic class-signifier of them all. What you eat, where and when you eat, and how and who prepares it provide the most intimate portrait of any individual. The elite are fascinated by the world of the lumpen, where shared meals, if they take place at all, are consumed on the sofa, without the benefit of crockery, glassware, or much in the way of cutlery. They look on in wonder when food is consumed by the underclass while they are in motion on the street, and when the dining table and mealtimes no longer exist. But they themselves fret anxiously over their own food rituals. Is it worse to be catered for by bright young things who do it for a living than to rely on the part-prepared offerings of the supermarket? If the purpose of fashion really is to measure class distinctions, it is at its most effective in the kitchen, which is still full of social anxiety about shifts in taste.

K

is for

KRIER

Léon Krier has spent most of his career attempting to divert the course of the architectural mainstream away from modernity. And yet his ideas, deeply reactionary to some, iconoclastic but fundamentally optimistic to others, have done as much to illuminate those aspects of the modern world that he detests as to provide an alternative to them.

He does not look much like an architect. Most of the species now dress in the dominant, if somewhat dated, all-black Yohji Yamamoto manner. Krier, by contrast, wears a lot of linen, and he has the wire-frame glasses, broad-brimmed headgear and neck stock that are conventionally associated with minor characters in Merchant Ivory cinema adaptations of the classics. He keeps his hair in what might best be described as a bird's nest and has a vaguely clerical air about him. But despite the mild manner, an architect he is, with a violent edge to his polemics, and one who has had an impact far beyond the few, but growing number, of designs that he has actually built. Krier gives a fundamentalist tone to his theoretical pronouncements that might be seen to suggest both a Marxist past and the passion of a convert. His two greatest enemies are consumerism and modernism, characterized by the generic contemporary city lost in a wasteland of business parks, and endless suburbs punctuated by aggressively exhibitionistic landmarks. He celebrates the humility of the traditional city, a world of robust, handsome, but unpretentious streets, enhanced by the occasional, judiciously placed monument in classical style. He believes with perhaps unjustified optimism that there is nothing to stop us from building places with the qualities of the centres of Oxford, Prague or Ljubljana.

It is a measure of the extent of his skill as a polemicist that he has made his position the official architectural policy of the next king of England, as well as of the mayor of Rome. Robert Stern, once a board member of the Disney Corporation, now Dean of Yale University's School of Architecture, is the author of the introduction to Krier's most recent book and the architect of the presidential library of George Bush the Younger in Texas. And Krier has disciples everywhere from Florida to Romania. He is the father of what his American followers like to call the New Urbanism: of which the Prince of Wales's development project at Poundbury outside Dorchester, is the prime British example. In argument, Krier takes no prisoners, and apparently accepts no compromises.

He certainly has no fear of unfashionable causes. He has written at length of his most dubious architectural hero, Albert Speer, whom he purports to see as the last great hope of classical urbanism. Speer in Krier's eyes was the tragic victim of Nuremburg, incarcerated in Spandau because he was guilty of a passion for Doric columns. The far more destructive talent of Werner von Braun, author of the flying bomb, was judged useful enough to have him whisked to comfortable exile in the US to oversee a research project that would eventually bring the world the cruise missile and the predator drone.

> Speer's projects continue, not unlike sex for the
> virgin, to be the object of pseudo-embarrassment
> for architects ... the inability to deal with the
> problem today in an intelligent manner reveals
> nothing about National Socialist architecture, but
> tells us a great deal about the moral depravity of a
> profession which, on the one hand claims against
> all odds that modernist architecture is better than
> it looks, and on the other, that Nazi architecture is
> profoundly bad, however good it may look.

When he was young, Léon Krier argued that it was the melancholy duty of every architect of principle to give up any idea of building at all. 'A responsible architect cannot possibly build today ... Building can only mean a greater or smaller degree of collaboration in a civilized society's process of self-destruction.' To do so, he suggested, would be to take part in the crime of the century, that is to say, the destruction of the traditional European city. 'I can only make Architecture,' he said in the 1970s, 'because I do not build. I do not build because I am an Architect.'

But Krier has decided that the time is now right to engage with the world, and offer a set of prescriptions that, if followed, might indeed offer a solution to all that self-destruction. 'After years of failed promises and experiments, the critical situation of the suburbs leaves us little choice but to seek practical solutions. These are, in fact, readily available, but it is evident that a modernist bias harbouring ideological and psychological blockages causes traditional solutions to be ignored, discarded, and even discredited.'

This is, then, apparently, not just a Krier who has changed his mind about tactics but also a Krier who is attempting to present a less unremitting fury about the world around him. But Krier, even when he is being conciliatory, flavours his words with invective. His opponents are guilty, he says, of 'unjustifiable nonsense'. Even if they are concerned with nothing more controversial than street lighting, regulations that Krier takes objection to are 'insane'. Naturally, 'the idea of replacing the world's rich panoply of traditional architecture by a single international style is dangerously insane', an observation which, given that it would be all but impossible to find anyone who would suggest such a thing, seems a little redundant. However, it is possible to see a certain family resemblance between the languid village hall in Florida designed by Krier and his work on the Italian town of Alexandria.

Krier set out to provide a primer for the New Urbanism. 'The lack of clarity in the vocabulary, the mixing-up of terms, and the extensive use of meaningless professional jargon stand in the way of clear architectural and environmental thinking . . . I shall now define some of the main concepts and notions.' Pay attention at the back: 'The terms "modern" and "modernist" are regularly confused. The former has a chronological meaning . . . the latter is an ideological designation,' he points out, to demonstrate that he is no hopeless reactionary but is perfectly ready to accept fast cars, and to deftly sketch in a silver-hulled, four-turbo prop-engine Super

Constellation in the skies over his scheme for the completion of Washington, rendered in the grandest classical manner, a style that President Lindbergh would have warmed to as he took over the country in Philip Roth's *The Plot Against America*.

Krier believes in typology. We know what a church looks like, so we don't need to invent one every time a new one is built. We are perfectly capable of developing new typologies, as and when required: railway stations, for example, and even, belatedly, airports; Krier approves of Charles de Gaulle airport's latest departure gates, and César Pelli's work at Washington.

What Krier hates is innovation for the sake of innovation – although so did Mies van der Rohe, who always wanted to design good buildings rather than interesting ones. 'In traditional cultures, invention, innovation, and discovery are the means to modernize proven and practical systems of living, thinking, planning, building, representing . . . They are the means to an end. They aim to conceive, realize, and conserve a solid, durable, practical, beautiful, humane world.' Krier finds the antithesis in modernist cultures. In them, 'invention, innovation, and discovery are transcendental ends . . . For traditional cultures, imitation is a way of producing objects that are similar but unique.' Krier understands that 'Traditional architecture comprises two complementary disciplines: vernacular building, on the one hand, classical or monumental architecture, on the other.'

Alongside Krier's definitions, he has shrewd observations to make: you get more architecture out of low buildings that have high ceilings than you do from high buildings with low ceilings. And he offers firm guidelines on how to achieve the right balance of public and private space in a city. More than 70 per cent public is too much, less than 25 per cent is too little. What makes his prescriptions palatable is that he embellishes them with lacerating, sometimes hauntingly beautiful, drawings. These are occasionally dazzlingly witty – in a manner that recalls the great nineteenth-century champion of the true principles of Pointed or Christian architecture, August Welby Pugin, in his *Contrasts* phase – rendered with the calligraphic style of *Barbar the Elephant*, and with a format that owes quite a bit to Le Corbusier in his polemical tract *Vers une architecture*. Things that Krier/Le Corbusier disapprove of are crossed out with big Xs. When they have something IMPORTANT to say, they burst into capital letters. And indeed this continuing relationship with Le Corbusier suggests that personal psychology may be important to understanding Krier's career.

Krier, who was born and brought up in Luxembourg, describes an early family visit to Le Corbusier's Unité d'Habitation in Marseilles. As he tells it, the adolescent Krier had fallen in love with images that he had seen of Le Corbusier's work. But when he finally got to see Marseilles for himself, he was horrified by the streaked concrete madhouse that he found. What was meant to be a transcendent experience turned into a betrayal. Krier calls it a defining moment. Clearly it is the sense of betrayal that has driven his animus for modernism. He even publishes a touching attempt to redeem his fallen Lucifer. Decades after his visit to Marseilles, he set one of his student classes at Yale the task of redesigning Le Corbusier's gleaming white house, the Villa Savoye, retaining the energy of its plan and composition, but using traditional materials and techniques.

Whatever did or did not happen in Marseilles, it did not stop Krier from going to London in 1968 to work for James Stirling for six years. Often described as the foremost British architect of the twentieth century, Stirling was not somebody who appealed to the Prince of Wales. Indeed the greatest enthusiasts for the prince's position on architecture at Cambridge did all they could to get the Stirling-designed History Faculty Library demolished. And though Stirling's development at No. 1 Poultry clearly shares many of Krier's compositional techniques, the prince denounced it in terms almost as intemperate as those he used for the Mies van der Rohe glass stump for which it was substituted. Krier's deft pen-and-ink drawings were used to powerful effect while he was with Stirling. In the corner of his perspectives of the Olivetti Training Centre, Krier placed Stirling's bulky figure in a representation of one of the Thomas Hope chairs that his employer collected. Krier played a significant part in the competition design Stirling submitted for the centre of Derby. They didn't win, but the project would have included a sweeping semicircular galleria, and advocated retaining the classical façade of the town's existing assembly rooms, but turning it into a piece of flat stage scenery, and tilting it at a 45-degree angle. Krier also put together a monograph of Stirling's complete works, in a style closely modelled on Le Corbusier's own *Oeuvre complète*. Clearly Krier's change of heart did not come at once. Indeed, in the

1970s, he even confessed himself to have been moved more than he had expected by a visit to Norman Foster's intricate steel-and-aluminium aircraft-hangar-cum-Greek-temple that is the Sainsbury Centre at the University of East Anglia.

After Krier had left Stirling, he started teaching at the Architectural Association, the private design school in London that during the 1970s served as a kind of unofficial opposition to the lacklustre world of mainstream British architecture. He developed a contempt for his chosen profession, which came close to that of Rem Koolhaas – another architect with a Le Corbusier fixation, who also happened to be teaching at the AA at the time. While Krier came to believe that no respectable architect could build anything with a clear conscience, Koolhaas ridiculed what he took as the sentimentality and impotence of architects whose only response to the tidal wave of business parks and mega-malls overwhelming the globe was to retreat into an autistic obsession with the precision with which doors could be fitted into walls, or the width of the gap between a floorboard and the plaster wall that floated above it. Koolhaas seemed to be busy trashing the very possibility of architecture, on his way towards the exit. Neither he nor Krier seemed much interested in the physical, material possibilities of architecture. The difference between them was that while Krier had acquired the same kind of horror as William Morris for the modern world, Koolhaas innoculated himself from it by embracing the nightmarish vision of what he characterized as 'junk space', the soft underbelly of shopping malls, giant sheds and airport terminals.

They both taught Zaha Hadid while they were at

the AA. Rather than build, Krier conducted a two-decade-long guerilla war against modern planning and architecture. He tried to create the basis for cities that had their roots in the traditions of the past.

Both Koolhaas and Krier have changed their stance since then. Koolhaas met Miuccia Prada, and the director of the Chinese state television company, while Krier joined the court of the Prince of Wales. The world, Krier thinks, is ready to listen to him now. Clearly he believes that he has succeeded in turning the tide. Krier suggests that with one more heave it will all be over. He claims he has won the argument on city planning. All that is left is to banish plate-glass skyscrapers, and the exhibitionism of the current crop of architectural stars.

> Modernism represents the negation of all that makes architecture useful: no roofs, no load-bearing walls, no columns, no arches, no vertical windows, no streets, no squares, no privacy, no grandeur, no decoration, no craftsmen, no history, no tradition. Surely the next step must be to negate these negations.

> In fact for several years now neo-modernists have had to admit that there is no true substitute for the traditional fabric of streets and squares. Nevertheless, they continue to reject traditional architecture with the same obsolete arguments that yesterday compelled them to reject traditional urbanism.

Krier takes no prisoners in his assault on modernists, but there is surprisingly little to choose between his idea of lively streets and animated public spaces, and those of Richard Rogers, with his passionate championing of pavement cafés and galleria.

Krier has found himself working for a range of clients: for the developers of Seaside, the utopian holiday resort on the coast of Florida; for the Prince of Wales, for whom he prepared a master plan for the new township of Poundbury. He planned new towns in Italy and Romania; worked for Lord Rothschild; and for Sir Stuart Lipton, who commissioned him to replan Spitalfields Market. And even, to declare an interest, for me. In a previous incarnation as editor at *Blueprint* magazine, contributing editor Dan Cruikshank and I asked Krier to replan London's South Bank. He suggested concealing the National Theatre behind a swathe of palladian façades – and was the first planner to use the word 'quarter', a term that has subsequently become a developer's favourite.

Part of Krier's obsession with the work of Speer could be seen as provocation, but demonstrating that there is no necessary connection between classicism and authoritarian regimes is one thing. Campaigning to save Speer's street lights from what Krier called the brutal demolition of the only substantial part of Speer's scheme to build Germania is quite another.

To draw attention to his sympathy for Nazi architecture, which Krier now minimizes, cannot, of course, discredit all his prescriptions. As he points out, Mies van der Rohe did everything that he could to secure the commission to build the new Reichsbank for Hitler, and produced a design for a Brussels pavilion, in the same reduced glass-and-steel manner of its Barcelona predecessor except for the eagle and swastika insignia that he proposed to put on its flat roof. Yet nobody would rationally claim that Mies was a Nazi, or that the Seagram tower is an example of Nazi architecture.

But Krier's enthusiasm for Speer's vile plan to transform Berlin, for Hitler, with vast triumphal boulevards and a monstrous great hall is perhaps evidence of a certain naivety or unworldliness, which persists in his attitudes. On page 18 of Krier's *The Architecture of Community*, there is a drawing by him of three heads, supposedly displaying the idealized and harmonious racial characteristics of a European, an African and an Asian, separate but equal over the legend 'TRUE PLURALISM'. It shares the page with another image, of a face made up of a violent blend of all three racial characteristics, and the message 'FALSE PLURALISM'. Can such a sophisticated polemicist really be unaware of the possible dubious misreadings that are inherent in these images?

The Prince of Wales has attracted a whole cloud of architectural advisers. Most of them have been discarded as inconveniently interested in self-publicity, one after the other. Krier is no lightweight, and, far from being dumped, the word is that he had to be pressurized not to resign from the Poundbury project in despair at the watering-down of his guiding principles.

Krier's designs are vigorous and inventive. He is light

years ahead of the feeble neo-Palladianism of Quinlan Terry, let alone the heavy-handed Robert Adam, or John Simpson, or even his own brother, Rob Krier, also an architect.

His designs take traditional elements and reassemble them in new and unfamiliar ways. Their impact comes not from the fact that they evoke something that they are not. It is in the vigour and energy of what they are, in the quality of the physical experiences that they offer and the intelligence which comes from his imaginative manipulation of the elements of architecture.

Seaside, the holiday resort in Florida, was planned by two of Krier's disciples: Andrés Duany and Elizabeth Plater-Zyberk. It was, as the setting for *The Truman Show*, a gift to those who see it as a whimsical exercise in nostalgia, which is of no relevance to the world as it really is.

Though you would never guess it from Krier, the way that our cities look and work is hardly the exclusive result of decisions made by architects. They are the product of economic and political systems, of population growth, of wealth and poverty, of transport systems and highway engineers. These are rarely the targets of Krier or his patrons. It is a narrow view that serves to reinforce the architect's own sense of self-importance, which appears to underlie the psychological make-up of all architects, not just the modernists. The militant humility of Krier is perhaps no humility at all.

is for

LOGO

The logotype is the contemporary means by which complex meanings and identities can be distilled into graphic symbols. It has its roots in a process that pre-dates written phonetic languages. The early scripts, cuneiform, Egyptian hieroglyphs or Chinese characters, began as systems of pictograms, which have a strong claim to be regarded as the ancestors of the logotype. Some signs are designed to be understood only by initiates. Others look for universal recognition.

While Christianity was still a persecuted religion, its followers used the sign of the fish to communicate their shared faith to other believers. When Christianity got going in earnest, the cross emerged as one of the most enduring symbols that there has ever been. It is one with such extra-ordinary power that it has come to be understood not only as a symbol for the Christian religion but as a physical embodiment of it.

This is very like what the most ambitious brand managers aspire to achieve. A few have managed it. The Coca-Cola bottle is both a logo and a product. With Levi jeans, you wear the logo. This is the graphic designer's version of transubstantiation. The Coke bottle prepares you for what the contents will taste like. The massive investment over many decades in advertising pre-programmes the emotional triggers. Drink Coca-Cola and play your part in making the world a more peaceful place, in making a festive family Christmas, in being modern. With Coke and Levis, the key has been a single-minded focus on the essence of the product, and a robust and easily identifiable logo, or set of trademarks. It's not just the bottle, and the can, it's the script, and its association with the colour red. With Levis, it's the name, the way it is written – which has been modernized over the years much more freely than Coca-Cola – the patch label, the copper rivet and the tag on the back pocket.

But it is not just quality and a strong identity that makes a logo. The financial stakes are high enough now for the legal system to become closely involved where logos are concerned. When London started planning for the Olympics of 2012, a number of remarkable pieces of legislation were enacted in the UK Parliament. Laws were passed to allow tax exemptions not just for visiting athletes but also for all official sponsors too. There were measures to outlaw what was termed as ambush marketing, but which in other circumstances might be called freedom of speech. An outrageous set of rules was put in place to prevent the use not only of the Olympic rings, but also of the words 'Olympic', 'London' and '2012', in any permutation, without the consent of the International Olympic Committee and the London Organizing Committee of the Olympic Games.

An early casualty of these new laws was the author of a children's book with a title that fell foul of the rules. LOCOG's fearsome legal team went into action to try to stop publication. This was followed by the Brazil Olympic Organizing Committee trying to have a book they disapproved of pulped, because it had the word 'Olympic' in the title, a word they claimed to have the right to prevent anybody else from using. This was a preposterous idea, but the fact that it was entertained even for a moment shows the over-reaching power of the Olympic 'family', as they call themselves.

The Olympic rings have become a logo, and the new laws were an intimidating display of the extent to which the ownership of a logo has led to the privatization of certain words, and even of some meanings.

If a group of elderly men of questionable ethical standards, who fly the world in six-star luxury, can claim ownership of a word, can they, or those who claim to act on their behalf, also stop you from using the word not only on the cover of a book but inside a newspaper too? As I discovered myself, they could certainly threaten to take you to court to stop you using it as an exhibition title. And if you wanted to make the Olympics the subject matter of an exhibition, they were equally well equipped with the means to stop you. LOCOG claims the copyright for every design that they have commissioned; so don't try to show the architecture of a stadium or an Olympic mascot or even a poster without their approval. And do not expect that the approval will be granted easily: these are privileges reserved for the commercial sponsors, even if their donations are just a fraction of what has gone into the staging of a games from a national government. It is the IOC and the organizing committees that benefit most directly from the commercial sponsors, and their commercial interests come first.

The embrace of the logo by commerce over the last two centuries has made logo design into an industry if not a science. Its adepts get uncomfortable about outsiders who gloss over the differences between marks and brands, between logos and corporate identities. But this is to split hairs about what can only be understood as a kind of alchemy. It is one that has astonishing values attached to it. When Ford needed a financial bailout at the end of 2006, the company mortgaged, among its other assets, its blue oval trademark in exchange for a $23.5 billion loan.

Names may change, but logos linger. British Airways has at various times been called the British Overseas Airways Corporation, British Airways and plain British. It is now once more called British Airways, but is owned by something called the International Airlines Group. When the airline decided that to be inextricably associated with the national identity of the United Kingdom was off-putting to its international customers, it dumped the union flag and a single style applied to the hulls of all its aircraft in favour of multiple identities. It invited a number of artists from all over the world to come up with motifs that were used to ensure that no two aircraft were identical. Then it changed its mind again, not least because of a notorious incident involving Margaret Thatcher, when she descended on the British Airways stand at a Conservative Party conference and used her handkerchief to suppress what critics described as the ethnic tail fin on a model of a BA jet. But whatever the name of the company, the speed bird has been painted somewhere on the hull of its aircraft for all of the last seventy years, even if in recent incarnations it has been made to look more like Nike's swoosh than the elegant device that goes back to the 1930s.

This vaccilation is the sign of a corporation that does not know what it is. Coca-Cola, on the other hand, has never flinched. It may be an ugly American, but it is still an American, and not shy of admitting it, even if the logo has been rendered in Thai, Mandarin, Hebrew, Arabic and Cyrillic scripts.

Corporations are as susceptible to fashion in the way that they choose to name themselves as the rest of us are when we come to look for the names that we give our children. Twenty-five years ago, there were very few companies with names that ended in 'ia'. Now, despite the abject and costly failure of the attempt to rename Britain's Royal Mail as Consignia, it's hard to find any corporation with a name that doesn't sound as if it is the product of a computer programme. There is a generation of deliberately synthetic-sounding brand names that do all that they can to filter out every trace of a linguistic inflection and any specific meaning. They are placeless, being designed to be inoffensive in any language, and to have no immediately obvious connections to any particular country. But often they drop hints about their origins. Consignia was meant to be a subliminal reference to the idea of insignia, and so brought with it a faded memory of the crown that distinguished the Royal Mail, and perhaps also the idea of the trustworthiness of the postal service to which we consigned our most precious messages. As was pointed out when the Post Office revealed just how much its rebranding project had cost, no brand could have carried more implicit value than that of the Royal Mail, a brand that the company already owned all the rights to, with no further payment necessary.

The company that provides my pension plan used to be called the Norwich Union. Now it is Aviva. Capita was once a sideline of the Chartered Institute of Public Finance and Accountancy. Accenture grew out of Arthur Anderson Consulting; Ivensys was once the British Tyre & Rubber Company.

Previous fashions in brand names included the fondness of computer, technology and communication companies for naming themselves after varieties of fruit: Apple, of course, but also Apricot, Tangerine, Orange and BlackBerry.

Logos have similar trajectories. In the first half of the twentieth century, they still owed a lot to heraldry. In the second half of the century, modernism pushed them towards abstraction, as in the case of the double arrow with which British Railways supplanted the rampant clutching a wheel lion that had once been emblazoned on the side of every locomotive, in a deliberate attempt to suggest that rail travel was the equal of the drip-dry modernity of air travel. British Rail has vanished, but the double arrow lingers on as the generic sign of rail travel rather than of any specific provider. The geometric abstractions of the mid-twentieth century have been replaced by rather less assertive identities. Hard-edged geometry and abstract symbols have given way to softer, more representational symbolism.

It is at points of crisis – marriage, divorce, birth and death – that the logo becomes most visible. It is the subject of half-measures, or else of radical surgery.

It is the logos that are now counted as among the most valuable which cost the least to create in the first place. The Coke brand, Ford itself, Nike and Apple were all graphic devices originally created with remarkably little ceremony, and for very little investment. As they have matured, and the more valuable they have become, the more money has been poured into the hands of consultants charged with nurturing them. The most powerful examples have remained all but identical despite endless and costly creative effort. It is a narcissistic process, a corporate version of psychotherapy, which ends in endless navel-gazing, and very little resolution.

IS FOR
MANIFESTO

For an architect aiming to make a mark, a manifesto is not quite the essential prop that it once was. Agnosticism about modernism in the 1970s called into question the sense of certainty required to deliver a convincing example of the genre, with all its prescriptions and its certainties. However, it is a form which shows signs of flickering back into life. Some architects, and a few designers, are once again feeling the need to express themselves through words as well as objects and buildings. They feel the need to underpin their work with the intellectual ballast that serves to dignify what otherwise might be regarded as the frivolous indulgence of shape-making with the rigour of theory.

There is a far from clear distinction between the self-promotional intentions of such projects, and the genuine contributions that they may or may not make to an understanding of the dilemmas that face design.

Of all the aesthetic manifestos of the 1920s, none got more attention than Le Corbusier's 40,000-word epistle *Vers une architecture*, or as its first translation into English called it, *Towards a New Architecture*. Published in 1923, it was an extended version of a series of articles that he had written for his own magazine, *L'Esprit nouveau*, and then repackaged as a book.

Its impact was instant and incendiary. It provoked a mutiny at the architecture school at the École des Beaux-Arts. In Rome the book was removed from the library of the university's architecture faculty. It galvanized a new generation of architects and designers from Scotland to Japan. And eighty years later, it was still goading commentators into paroxysms of fury. Simon Jenkins, the Chairman of the National Trust and former editor of *The Times*, was so provoked by the Victoria and Albert Museum's exhibition on modernism that, in reviewing it, he claimed that 'the cruel brutalism of Le Corbusier must have caused more human misery than any other in history'.

As a graphic composition, *Vers une architecture* was remarkable. Le Corbusier's enthusiasm for ocean liners, aircraft, concrete grain silos and fast cars was visible on almost every page. I still have the copy I read in my last year at school. It was an edition from 1967, but had hardly changed since the first English printing of 1931. It was like a prayer book, and there has never been much appetite for tampering with a sacred text.

Le Corbusier put an image of a Farman Goliath biplane next to a photograph of Notre-Dame. He reproduced a collage of the Paris Opera House, Notre-Dame and the Arc de Triomphe shown against the silhouette of a Cunard liner, the *Aquitania*. It was a shocking juxtaposition, an embrace of the modern industrial world that seemed to be saying something powerful, though elusive, about scale, cities and progress. The impact of the images was somewhat undermined by the foggy quality of the reproduction, which made some of the plates barely comprehensible.

Le Corbusier's arguments were less nuanced to read than the book was to look at. It was shot through with a series of deliberately shocking slogans that set out to provoke the architectural profession into coming to terms with the impact of industrialization, and, perhaps even more, to attract attention to the author. Le Corbusier had no doubt about what architecture was not. 'The styles of Louis XIV, XV, XVI, or Gothic, are to architecture what a feather is on a woman's head, they are pretty sometimes, but not always, and nothing more.'

And he knew equally clearly what it was. 'Architecture,' he wrote 'is the masterful, correct and magnificent play of volumes brought together in light.' This of course is a quite traditional conception of architecture as a material and sculptural process; one that Le Corbusier's own Villa Savoye, hoisted off the ground on a double file of pilotis, had in common with the Doric temples of Paestum.

The most didactic and famous of all his slogans sounded more radical: 'A house is a machine for living,' he once suggested. In an acid review of *Vers une architecture* for *The Times*, the English classicist Sir Edwin Lutyens was moved to dismiss it out of hand: 'To be a home a house cannot be a machine.' Lutyens claimed that 'The logic of a French mind may make a Le Corbusier villa, or even a Versailles, but never a Hampton Court.' To Lutyens, Le Corbusier's architecture was 'for robots without eyes, for eyes that have no vision cannot be educated to see'.

Le Corbusier presented himself as a tough-minded technocrat, ready to look his times in the eye unflinchingly.

> A great era has just begun. There exists a new spirit. Industry, invading like a river that rolls to its destiny, brings us new tools adapted to this new era animated by a new spirit. The law of economy

necessarily governs our actions. Only through it are our conceptions viable. The problem of the house is a problem of the era, social equilibrium depends on it today. The first obligation of architecture in an era of renewal is to bring about a revision of values, a revision of the constitutive elements of the house.

Mass production is based on analysis and experimentation. Heavy industry should turn its attention to building and standardize the elements of the house.

We must create a mass-production state of mind. If we wrest from our hearts and minds static conceptions of the house and consider the question from a critical and objective point of view we will come to the house tool, the mass-production house, that is healthy, morally too, and beautiful.

The two most influential architects of the first decade of the twenty-first century, Rem Koolhaas and Jacques Herzog, are both ready to measure themselves against Le Corbusier. Koolhaas gives the impression that he believes he is the reincarnation of Le Corbusier, while Herzog, with the self-confidence of a man who lives in Basel but who has built an Olympic stadium in Beijing, is capable of slyly suggesting that Le Corbusier is over-rated. Koolhaas has clearly learned a lesson from the way that Le Corbusier established his reputation through his books. And perhaps that is why, despite building so much more, Herzog, who has written less, remains somewhat in Koolhaas's shadow.

No architect since Le Corbusier has published so many words as Rem Koolhaas. He is responsible for a torrent of books, which suggests that Koolhaas is more interested in polemics than he is in actively building architecture. It was only after a screen-writing interlude, and a spell as a journalist that notoriously preceded his architectural studies, that he finally went to the Architectural Association in London. It was a school that he claimed to have selected as an alternative to his only Dutch option, the Technical University of Delft, where, as he put it, he would have learned how to design hospitals for the Viet Cong.

Even then, Koolhaas began his career as an architect not by designing a building, but by writing a book. It was not the usual kind of architect's book, full of glossy colour pictures of the author's work and tributes from friendly critics; rather, it was a book of ideas. *Delirious New York*, as it was called, purported to be a retrospective manifesto, an account of how New York became the embodiment of what Koolhaas describes as 'the culture of congestion'. Since, by this time, architects no longer believed in the rhetorical ambition required to make a manifesto, given the disastrous outcomes that most of them had had, Koolhaas's position rested on a carefully nuanced ambiguity poised on the edge of satire. It was a brilliant move, instantly establishing Koolhaas as an intimidating intellectual presence on the architectural landscape when there was nothing to show for what his vision of the architecture of the contemporary world might physically be like.

A second book followed, as thick as a brick. It went by the name *S, M, L, XL*, a suitably banal taxonomy with which to organize an account of his work. By now, Koolhaas had actually started an architectural practice that seemed to offer at least the possibility of building something. This time, the space was found to publish some resolutely unglossy pictures of Koolhaas's buildings. He had built a couple of houses, an exhibition centre close to the TGV station in Lille, a dance theatre in The Hague, an art gallery in Rotterdam. But it was even less of a conventional architectural monograph than *Delirious New York*. Koolhaas's work was depicted in its pages as a series of raw cut-and-paste collages and screen grabs, rather than in airbrushed perfection. Maybe there wasn't much else to show.

Alongside the buildings portrayed in a multilayered collage were many other distractingly engaging images and narratives – a fantastic history of Mies's Barcelona Pavilion, Japanese pornography, the Berlin Wall – as well as diagrams recording the time that Koolhaas himself had spent in the hotel rooms of the world. Clearly the intention was to signal that Koolhaas's career was about something more important than mere architecture. The book did as much as or more than his architecture to make Koolhaas's name inevitably linked with every new project involving the requisite high-octane mix of fashion and celebrity.

In *The Harvard Design School Guide to Shopping*,

Koolhaas's next substantial book, he comes across a lot like Savonarola in a Prada suit. *Shopping* is a lacerating mixture of Koolhaas's contempt for his contemporaries and what sounds very much like self-loathing. Here he is on minimalism: 'a self-righteous crime; it does not signify beauty but guilt'.

According to Koolhaas, the phenomenon of shopping has swallowed the world, making museums and malls and hotels all part of a single chaotic whole. He set his doctoral students at Harvard to work on a three-year study of shopping and concluded: 'The best metaphor for shopping is that of a dying animal – a dying elephant that in its death struggle becomes completely wild and uncontrollable.' He paints a picture of the realities facing architecture that is so profoundly, disturbingly, apocalyptically bleak that the only rational response is professional suicide. We have, he writes, just witnessed nothing less than the final extinction of architecture.

> In the twentieth century architecture disappeared. The built product of modernization is not modern architecture, but junk space. Although its individual parts are the outcome of brilliant inventions, lucidly planned by human intelligence, boosted by infinite computation, their sum spells the end of enlightenment, its resurrection as farce, a low-grade purgatory.

Despite his bottomless pessimism about architecture, Koolhaas just can't bring himself to give it up. For all the shock-jock violence of his denunciations of the complacency and corruption of consumerism, he wraps himself energetically in its air-conditioned and scented embrace. Koolhaas's design for Prada's store in SoHo was carved out of the heart of what was once New York's downtown Guggenheim Museum, breaching the final frontier between culture and commerce. He accepted a commission from Condé Nast to become a creative consultant to the publisher of the world's glossiest magazines.

But no matter how pessimistic he is, Koolhaas has succeeded in achieving buildings of genuine power. And their impact is often in the way that they critique the work of other architects. Halfway up the razor-sharp cascade of metal steps that forms a spectacular approach to the main auditorium of Porto's new concert hall, the Casa da Música, is a curious pair of red crushed-velvet armchairs. They seem to belong to another time and place, translated through a wormhole in the space–time continuum direct from the disco era into Rem Koolhaas's soaring structure. They were designed by an obscure Portuguese architect in the 1970s. And Koolhaas chose to have them made up from the original drawings especially for use in his building because, as he put it: 'It liberated us from the need to imagine more than was necessary.'

Koolhaas's comment is not quite as profound as it sounds at first hearing, but is a sharp elbow in the ribs for those of his peers still unliberated and uncool enough to want to design their own sofas. He has contempt for the obvious and for architects who try too hard to be 'interesting' or 'inventive'.

Speaking of Porto's auditorium, with its risk-taking use of two glass walls, he writes off the entire architectural profession in the manner of Harrison Ford dispatching a scimitar-wielding opponent with a single shot from his revolver: 'The ideal acoustic form for a concert hall is a shoe box. And we have seen a lot of architects trying to make shoe boxes interesting, or to design interesting shoe boxes. We got rid of the shoe box.'

By accepting commissions from the retailers and the museums about which he is so savage in print, he hints that he is engaged in attempting subversion from within. But, willingly or not, he has become so thoroughly part of what he denounces so passionately that he can no longer be considered a neutral observer, still less an oppositional figure. And in this murky territory, Koolhaas has found the perfectly ambiguous vehicle for his words. *Shopping* is published by Taschen, alongside their art and architecture books. They are the deadpan purveyors of over-the-counter hard-core pornography. Shortly after *Shopping* was launched at Tate Modern in London (an institution that he excoriates at some length), Koolhaas was hired to extend Los Angeles's sprawling twenty-acre County Museum of Art. In the manner of General Westmoreland's strategy for saving Vietnam from itself, his scheme started by demolishing it. The museum's director at the time, Andrea Rich, called Koolhaas 'the most influential architect of his generation' and 'the perfect partner to help LACMA create the museum of the future'. Koolhaas was fired after six months.

But to Koolhaas, 'Museums are monasteries,

inflated to the scale of department stores.' They are, he writes, 'sanctimonious junk space' and 'there is no aura sturdier than holiness'. While coyly not bringing himself to name the Tate, he rails against museums where 'no sequence is too absurd, trivial, meaningless or insulting'.

Museums are places 'where curators plot hangings and unexpected encounters in a donor-plate labyrinth with the finesse of the retailer'. Lingerie becomes 'nude/action/ body', cosmetics is 'history/memory/society'. Finally, with withering scorn for his one-time collaborators Herzog & de Meuron, who built Tate Modern, he describes a museum where 'all paintings based on black grids are herded together in a single white room, and large spiders in the humungous conversion offer delirium for the masses, and the more un-treated the oak, the larger the profit centre.' Such an astrin-gent way with words may help to explain why Koolhaas has managed to lose more than one job with almost as much speed as he has attracted so many others.

Koolhaas's onslaught on the Tate seems like over-compensation, even pique. There was talk of a joint submis-sion for the Tate Modern competition before Herzog & de Meuron won the contest to build it alone. And later, Herzog and Koolhaas worked on a plan for a hotel in New York for Ian Schrager, which was torpedoed by Koolhaas's way of breezily antagonizing his client.

Herzog loyally declined to take on the project on his own. Their relationship was a symbiosis. Restless, gifted but erratic, Koolhaas holds the architectural world in thrall. It responds by treating him as its great thinker, although to judge by the meagre intellectual nourishment offered by 'Koolworld', the issue of *Wired* magazine that he guest edited, that reputation may be difficult to sustain when overexposed. Herzog, on the other hand, is subtler and calmer, the one who cares about building and who knows how to draw.

Between them, they have transformed architectural debate – Koolhaas by trying to get people to take in an urban landscape that is changing with dizzying speed; Herzog by inventing a dazzling series of building types and ways of building that sustain a whole school of followers.

There is another way in which Koolhaas's Le Corbusier fixation manifests itself. Le Corbusier, despite earning a French state funeral and a place on Swiss banknotes, saw himself as a perpetual outsider and a tragic victim: abused by mindless clients, his designs stolen, his ideas ignored. Koolhaas has the same monkey on his back. He documents in loving detail the projects on which he has lavished so much care and effort only to reveal that they have been abandoned by his clients. It's what happened to his plan for the massive MGM Studios building in Los Angeles, to the Whitney extension in New York, to the City Hall in The Hague. And in the case of the China television headquarters in Beijing, there was a real tragedy. A firework display, for the Chinese New Year, detonated just before the building was completed and set it on fire, killing an undisclosed number of people, overshadowing what might have been the crowning building of Koolhaas's career. It also contributed to an acrimonious professional divorce: his Beijing resident partner Ole Scheeren left, suggesting that the CCTV building was his design as much as it was his employer's.

Koolhaas has a morbid fascination for precision in everything except his buildings. He revels in tabulated information, dates, graphs, maps, bar charts and raw data of all kinds. When Miuccia Prada took a group of journalists to the opening of her store on Rodeo Drive in Los Angeles, Koolhaas showed me the top floor next to the VIP area, where the walls are plastered with statistics.

Later that year, I went to see Koolhaas's exhibition *Content*, at Berlin's National Gallery, staged to mark the opening of the new Dutch embassy he built in the city, which was filled with even more numbers. There was a chart about European immigration; another compared the 800 euros that a Dutch backpacker will typically spend trekking around Machu Picchu to the 4,000 euros a Peruvian illegal immigrant must find to have himself smuggled into Spain. He listed the annual income of every major museum in the world and the average age of the inhabitants of the largest cities – and a head-spinning level of random detail about almost everything else you could think of.

Venturing past these statistics, you found an effigy of the architect himself, in the form of an artwork by Tony Oursler. A doll, impaled on a steel rod, emerged from the middle of a pile of discarded and broken models. Its miniature black shirt and its grey striped trousers, just like Koolhaas's, were clearly from Prada. A digital projection of the architect's face played over the doll's blank white head, and if you listened carefully, you could catch snatches of him reading from one of his essays. It could almost have been a lament for all the dead projects in the show.

Koolhaas took me to his taxi and we set off to see the embassy he had designed. When we passed over into what was once East Berlin, he told me, while carefully studying my expression, how proud he was that the Netherlands had chosen a site for their embassy in what was the DDR, a part of the city that was suffused with a spirit of friendship, as he portrayed it. A spirit of friendship that people were prepared to risk death to escape from, I suggested. 'You ex-Communists, you are all the same,' he told me.

When we got there, it was hard to avoid noticing that the carpets that the staff had put down to mop the flood of water had turned the entrance lobby into a trip hazard.

A year later, Koolhaas, very sensibly as it turned out, refused to take part in the Ground Zero competition, fulminating against America's attempt to create a massive monument to self-pity on a Stalinist scale.

The subtext to all his words is that Koolhaas, once more following in the unsentimental austerity of Le Corbusier, is the toughest kid on the block. While most of his fellow professionals wring their hands in horror about theme parks and urban sprawl, he suggests that he looks the world in the eye and deals with it on its own terms. Talking of the chaos of Lagos, Koolhaas says: 'What I thought would be depressing was powerful, inspiring and brutal.'

'Brutal', in Koolhaas's vocabulary, is a term of enthusiasm. Koolhaas is trying to prove that the well-intentioned architects who tried to tame the contemporary city with pedestrian precincts and conservation got it all disastrously wrong. They should have been trying to intensify the city's intrinsic qualities, not neuter them.

What is amazing is that you can draw a genealogy between Jane Jacobs and Disney. Since the Sixties, the most well-meaning brains in our profession have contributed to this final, terminal condition of shopping.

The effort to preserve the street, the hostility to the car, the hostility to all those elements that were the inevitable elements of the twentieth century – all of this has somehow created the space for this preservation, and, in the name of preservation, the conversion of entire areas in the centre of the city to fundamentally anti-urban conditions. This ought to make everyone weep. Nobody could have guessed that the twentieth century could end on a Faustian bargain with a mouse.

M IS
FOR
MUS
EUM

The Guggenheim Museum on Fifth Avenue is the capital of a quixotic, cultural empire that stretches all the way from New York to the banks of the Ibaizabal river in Bilbao and the Grand Canal in Venice. It is the Guggenheim's work with Frank Gehry that has gone furthest in turning the museum into the most flamboyant building type of the first two decades of the twenty-first century. With the massive publicity that the Bilbao building attracted, museums around the world have had no choice but to follow in its footsteps, and to erect ever-more attention-seeking structures.

The Guggenheim is constantly trying and failing to go a lot further. There are, or were, Guggenheim outposts and dependencies in Berlin, SoHo and Las Vegas. The museum dreamed of building more fiefdoms, in among other places, Salzburg and Vienna, St Petersburg, Paris, Abu Dhabi, Rio, Hong Kong and Macao, Taichung, Helsinki and Monterrey. To date, none of them have been realized. Its plans for a massive new museum in Manhattan designed by Frank Gehry were abandoned a decade ago. The Abu Dhabi Guggenheim has been on hold, restarted and delayed, while a referendum in Helsinki rejected the mayor's plans to build one in Finland.

It's an outrageously ambitious strategy, one that has transformed the world's perceptions of what constitutes a museum. No longer is a museum primarily seen as a place to care for precious artefacts. Nor is it a national treasure house. The most successful museums have become a focus for entertainment, urban renewal and spectacle. Success is judged by size: by the number of visitors – anything less than five million a year excludes you from the first division – and the Guggenheim can't achieve that even counting all its outposts.

The current incarnation of the Guggenheim is the work of former director Thomas Krens; it is one that has both dazzled ambitious politicians looking to repeat the perceived success of the Bilbao outpost and attracted the scorn of other museums. The Pompidou Centre's director, Alfred Pacquement, asked about the Guggenheim by a Hong Kong journalist was reported by the *South China Morning Post* to have said 'A museum is not a Coca-Cola factory, you can't have museum branches everywhere in the world.' His curator, Alain Sayag, who was supposed to be cooperating with Krens on a scheme for a huge new cultural complex in Hong Kong, went so far as to suggest, 'The Pompidou and the Guggenheim are on different levels. We are world class, they are second class.' He was being more than usually frank. Museums complain about each other as a matter of course in private, but rarely in front of an audience. He was also being unfair. The Guggenheim has done as much as any institution to reinvent the nature of the modern museum with its attempts to build a global network. Whether that model will actually work has yet to be determined, but the Guggenheim is far from being alone among the museums that want to try it. That is why the Pompidou's director and his chief curator were forced to eat their words by their own museum's president, and ultimately by the French government, which insisted that they sign a partnership agreement to make a joint bid for a potentially lucrative deal, setting up a new cultural institution in Hong Kong. In the end, the whole scheme collapsed: Hong Kong's government decided to keep the development of the West Kowloon cultural district under its own control.

The Guggenheim is a particularly gaudy example of museum egotism and of rampant monument building, but it serves to illustrate how these character traits shape to a greater or lesser extent the development of every museum. They are institutions fuelled by a mix of ambition and wealth, the product of constant infighting between trustees, directors and architects, fractured by the competing impulses of collecting, and showmanship. It's a battle that reveals its traces in every architecturally exhibitionistic new wing, every gallery named for a benefactor, and every new trophy acquisition for a collection.

The Guggenheim has not always been so ambitious or so imperial in its vision as it was at the turn of the millennium. According to Thomas Krens' inaccurate account, the Guggenheim Museum was the product of an anything but accidental meeting one morning in 1927 in a Parisian hotel. Hilla Rebay, a striking woman in her late thirties, the daughter of a baron with a modest reputation as a painter, spent three days camped out in the lobby, waiting for a chance to talk to Solomon Guggenheim. Rebay had fallen on hard times during the debauching of the Weimar Republic's currency, and was reduced to making a living as an illustrator and a somewhat conventional portraitist. She chose one of the richest men in America, already married and well past middle age, as her escape route out of Europe. Krens suggested to me that Rebay got Guggenheim's name from the passenger lists for the transatlantic sailings published in the newspapers, along with his hotel; and waited for a chance to ambush him. Krens told me, over profiteroles after a long lunch with his trustees in his favourite restaurant in Bilbao, that their meeting had been 'like that scene from *Basic Instinct* when Sharon Stone uncrosses her legs'. There are other versions of this first meeting. By one account it did not take place until Rebay arrived in New York with a letter of introduction to Guggenheim. Another claims that Rebay met Guggenheim's wife, Irene, first, introduced by mutual friends while she was on holiday in America. The *New York Times*' unflattering obituary suggests that it was in Berlin.

The curators of the Guggenheim's own Rebay retrospective say that there is nothing in her letters to suggest that she and Guggenheim were ever lovers. What is not in dispute is that Rebay persuaded Solomon Guggenheim to commission her to paint his portrait, and then took command of his chequebook to become his adviser on art. Guggenheim switched from Rembrandt and Fragonard to collecting work by Kandinsky, Klee and, particularly, Rudolf Bauer, who certainly had been Rebay's lover. He even started to buy paintings by Rebay herself. By 1939, the Guggenheim collection included 215 works by Bauer, 103 by Kandinsky and thirteen by Rebay.

The question of how to show this work in public concerned Guggenheim almost from the start. Rebay was a self-absorbed egotist, but she was also a missionary zealot, convinced of her duty to bring the gospel of non-objective art to the masses. Alfred Barr's slightly earlier experiment at the Museum of Modern Art in New York left mainstream modernism already accounted for, so Rebay offered her own expressionist take on contemporary art. Guggenheim's canvasses first went on show at his suite in the Plaza Hotel, until the Museum of Non-Objective Art acquired what had been a showroom on the Upper East Side as a temporary home. Rebay insisted that Guggenheim's paintings were exhibited in galleries with carpeted floors and in which music was played in order to get visitors in the right frame of mind. Shortly before Solomon Guggenheim's death, Rebay persuaded him to hire Frank Lloyd Wright to design a permanent museum on Fifth Avenue.

Solomon Guggenheim was not the only Guggenheim with a taste for art. His niece Peggy began collecting in the 1920s when she lived in Paris. Peggy was the daughter of Solomon's not-quite-as-wealthy brother Benjamin. He died a heroic death on the *Titanic*, spending his last hours helping women and children into the lifeboats, then changing into evening dress to meet his fate. Peggy Guggenheim went through a succession of artist lovers and husbands, the most distinguished of which was Max Ernst. She married him so he could qualify for an American visa that allowed him to escape the Nazis. But she also had a well-developed eye for art. It brought her into bitter conflict with Rebay. Their clash of wills came to a head in Rebay's reply to Peggy's letter to Solomon offering him her collection for his own museum. Gracelessly brushing the offer aside, Rebay claimed that 'we do not buy from dealers', and abused Peggy for cheapening the family name.

Peggy called Rebay a 'Nazi witch' to her face. Rebay threatened to have Max Ernst deported if she ever used the words again. In fact it was Rebay herself who had trouble from the US immigration authorities, after falling out with Bauer. At Rebay's bidding, Solomon Guggenheim had ransomed Bauer from the Nazis and set him up with a Connecticut estate in Westport and a housekeeper. But when an ungrateful Bauer married his housekeeper, Rebay began stalking him. Bauer called the police, claiming that she was a German spy. The resulting FBI investigation kept her confined to Connecticut, but revealed nothing more incriminating than a humiliating hoard of black-market sugar and coffee.

Rebay's connections ranged from Hans Arp to Jackson Pollock, who worked for her as a carpenter. Added to Guggenheim's money, these relationships created one of the world's great collections for the Guggenheim Foundation. Rebay's private eccentricities spilled out in public. In her view, Bauer was by far Kandinsky's superior as an artist and so she gave him pride of place in the museum, while Klee and Mondrian were kept in store. Rebay was even discovered attempting to repaint one of the canvasses in the collection during an exhibition.

In Frank Lloyd Wright, Rebay found an architect with an ego as well developed as her own. Wright eventually submitted to Rebay's constant urging that he and his third wife, Olgivanna, have their teeth extracted, in search of the spiritual health that she believed only drastic dental surgery would bring. But Olgivanna rejected Rebay's suggestions that their daughter submit to the same treatment. 'We have sacrificed enough for this commission,' she told her husband. Wright was ruthless in his determination to build the museum that he wanted, turning to Robert Moses, New York's autocratic municipal power broker and his cousin by marriage, for help in finding a site for the museum and overturning the restrictions of the building code that his design contravened.

It was only after Solomon Guggenheim's death that the trustees of the museum finally mustered the determination to prise Rebay out of her office. Harry Guggenheim took over Solomon's role, and hired James Johnson Sweeney, who had recently left the Museum of Modern Art following a row with the director.

There have been just six directors in the history of the Guggenheim Museum and they have not, by and large, held each other in much regard. Rebay was particularly unflattering about Sweeney, a poet with a private income – and a one-time collaborator of James Joyce. Or, as Rebay put it, 'a corset salesman, who got himself fired by the Museum of Modern Art'.

Wright was well over eighty when he designed the Guggenheim's famous sour-cream-coloured spiral, and created one of the twentieth century's most recognizable architectural landmarks. The building was, in his eyes, far more important than the art that it would contain, and the design had little to do with the specifics of the commission, or the site. Why should he care about the client, at this late stage in his career? He had no interest in compromise. The commission was a chance to get something off his chest. Wright had already sketched out a similar-looking form ten years before and described it as 'an automobile objective'. The Guggenheim was the chance to build it. But he was not going to get things all his own way.

Sweeney was perhaps the first museum director to have had to tackle a modernist architect head-on and insist on some measure of response to the brief. Many have followed. He battered Frank Lloyd Wright to a draw, then, when he and Harry Guggenheim could no longer stand each other, he moved to Houston and did the same with the building that Mies van der Rohe had designed for the city's Museum of Fine Art. Sweeney invented the white-walled minimalist museum, the very opposite of the kind of space that Wright and Rebay wanted. Sweeney despaired of Wright's spiralling, sloping walls as a place in which to show serious art. Every attempt that Sweeney made to persuade Wright to modify the building to make it a little more fit for purpose was ignored. Wright responded by trying to have Sweeney, whom he described as 'a picture hanger', fired, even offering to find a replacement himself who could bring well-connected funders to the museum. Wright said that Sweeney was responsible for a 'malicious campaign to paint the museum white, thereby destroying its organic unity'.

In the end, Sweeney had to wait until after Wright's death to devise a system of rods and cables to display flat rectangular canvasses on curved sloping walls. Even then,

Robert Motherwell, Willem de Kooning and nineteen other New York artists, signed a petition questioning the building's suitability as a setting for showing their work. 'We shall be compelled to paint to suit Mr Wright's architecture', claimed one signature to the letter to the Guggenheim's trustees.

Sweeney's successor, Thomas Messer, devoted a great deal of effort to ensuring that Peggy Guggenheim's collection came under the control of the museum on her death. He managed to snatch it away from the Tate in London, to which she had at one time promised it. Thanks to the Italian tax laws, she could never afford to take it back to America from her Venetian palazzo. It had become an essential part of the cultural landscape in Italy, and so was born the idea of the Guggenheim as a multinational museum.

Thomas Krens learned several important lessons from his predecessor's time as director. The first was to ensure that he would never let himself be dominated by the trustees nominally in control of the museum's destiny, as Messer had been. Second, that there was nothing to stop him selling off large parts of the collection to pay for his expansionist policies. Added to this, Krens brought to the job a thick skin, a gift for self-promotion and an obsession with monumental architecture.

When Krens arrived, the Guggenheim was so short of money that he was reduced to agreeing a $54.9 million bond to pay for the restoration of Wright's building, and the construction of a new wing to provide a more sympathetic space to show the collection. Shortly afterwards, Krens sold three paintings, a Modigliani for $10 million,

Kandinsky's *Fugue*, sold to the Swiss dealer Ernst Beyeler for $20.9 million, and Chagall's *Birthday*, an image endlessly reproduced as the best-selling postcard in the Guggenheim shop. Krens used most of the money to acquire Panza di Biuma's holdings of conceptual and minimal art, including work by Donald Judd and Dan Flavin. It was a bold move but one that horrified some critics at the time, who claimed the museum was surrendering to what would turn out to be a short-lived art fad for minimalism. Others were simply envious that they hadn't spotted the opportunity.

Krens's next step made him, and the Guggenheim, internationally famous in a way that it had not been since Wright's sensational building in New York opened. Krens discovered that it was possible to franchise the museum's name. First, after a false start in Salzburg, came Bilbao, then Berlin and finally Las Vegas, flattering Basque politicians, German bankers and Nevada casino owners into funding his expansion plans. A whole new architectural category was born overnight: the museum as visitor attraction. By this time the Guggenheim had long since stopped being a museum of non-objective art. Nor was it a museum of conceptual art. It was ready to show anything from Brazilian Baroque to Armani and motocycles.

Each new project was more flamboyant than the last. In Rio, the French architect Jean Nouvel designed a Brazilian Guggenheim Museum that would have been mainly underwater. It was budgeted at $250 million, and Krens unwisely claimed in public that it would bring the Guggenheim $40 million in fees. His vainglory provoked an outcry in the city from those who saw the proposed museum as either a piece of cultural imperialism or a frivolous waste of money, or both. The Rio courts ruled the deal illegal and blocked the signing of an agreement to build the museum. A similar project with Taiwan got as far as Zaha Hadid designing a museum. The plan was to build it in the provincial city of Taichung, which has no international airport, in the hope of attracting more tourists. The city council overruled its mayor and refused to pay for it.

This was a problem for the Guggenheim. Krens needed the fees from Rio and Taichung to keep afloat. The cash crisis resulting from their cancellation demonstrated in the most painful way that his economic model of constant expansion didn't work. Krens had gambled that a worldwide network of museums would allow him to spread exhibition costs across his increasingly restive colonial subjects in Berlin and Bilbao and wherever else he planted the Guggenheim flag. He could make the most of the revenue from ticket sales for exhibitions that could reach much larger audiences, but touring the kind of crowd-pleasing shows needed to pack in audiences and balance budgets does not work that way. A museum is not the same as a publisher packaging international co-editions to boost print runs and bring down costs. Lenders don't like lengthy tours, and the savings from shared costs turned out to be far smaller than Krens had assumed. Despite all its frantic activity, the Guggenheim could not generate enough revenue to stabilize its budget. It was forced into a continual search for new sources of cash.

In seventeen years at the Guggenheim, Krens turned a modestly scaled museum – with an endowment and a collection a fraction of the size of much less-well-known institutions – into a global art circus, positioned conceptually somewhere between a casino and a department store. Opening the Bilbao Guggenheim netted the museum a $20 million fee from the Basque government, but the Guggenheim was forced to draw on its endowment fund to meet its New York running costs in 2001 and 2002, and it sold another $14 million worth of its art holdings to help pay its bills. In the boom years, the Guggenheim was being compared with Enron. Krens even presided over the costly launch of the website guggenheim.com. With *Martha Stewart Living* magazine's former homes editor to help, the website was meant to make the museum rich.

The opening of a Guggenheim in a Las Vegas casino represented a collision between high and popular culture that seemed beyond parody to many. Krens talked about building yet more franchises in Tokyo, Guadalajara, St Petersburg and Edinburgh, but his ability to defy the laws of gravity could not last for ever. The Las Vegas Guggenheim, in its Rem Koolhaas-designed rusty steel box in the bowels of the Venetian casino, opened and shut after a humiliatingly short life. A huge, new, Gehry-designed Guggenheim in New York was cancelled. Even Bilbao saw a decline in its visitor numbers. In New York, the Guggenheim's curators couldn't afford to mount their exhibitions programme as planned, and Krens seemed too focused on how to find the money for the next big architectural model to ship to the Far East to tempt a new partner into yet another new Guggenheim.

When Krens unsuccessfully asked Charles Saatchi for several million dollars in cash to put on a show of his Chapmans and his Hirsts in New York, the world got to hear about it. When Krens did indeed manage to collect $15 million from Giorgio Armani as the price of exhibiting his clothes on the Guggenheim's spiral, he was roundly condemned for surrendering the museum's dignity, even though the Metropolitan had got away with a similar deal with Ralph Lauren, perhaps because it didn't look so needy.

Of course it came to nothing, but the Guggenheim is still working on a stop-and-start plan to open in a Gehry building in Abu Dhabi. Krens, meanwhile, was last seen as a member of a consortium that termed itself as the cultural equivalent of a private equity fund, touting its prospectus in Moscow hotel lobbies, and with more success in China, offering to commission iconic buildings, acquire key artworks, or curate blockbuster exhibitions. Hilla Rebay might have recognized the glint in his eye.

N IS FOR NATIONAL IDENTITY

The techniques by which identity is manufactured, and which constitute a key aspect of the practice of design, have always fascinated me. I can remember wondering why the 1,000-dinar note in what was once called Yugoslavia, where I spent summers as a child, came with an image of a steelworker, in cap and overalls, posed in front of a blast furnace on one side, and a cluster of burning torches and red stars on the other. In Britain, as I had already noticed, money was signified by representations of eighteenth-century notables with whiskers and sizeable wigs, along with portraits of the queen.

A couple of decades later, just at the time that Yugoslavia was degenerating into blood-soaked chaos, I organized an exhibition in Copenhagen that was about the way design is used to construct a national identity. I tried to chart the ways in which Croatia and Slovenia were redesigning themselves as new nations. The Slovenes were happy to help, lending us the material we needed on the handsome new toller currency that they were working on even before the war started. My German assistant told me that she had a much tougher time in Zagreb looking for similar help on the kuna that the Croats had devised to look as much like the Deutschmark as possible. Anonymous security sources wanted to look into my origins before any cooperation could be considered.

National identity was the same subject that I was billed to discuss at Belgrade's first-ever design festival in 2007, taking me back to a city I had not seen in twenty-five years. The hotel and the hulking conference centre wrapped around it, where the festival was based, were the high-water mark of Marshal Tito's Yugoslavia. They were finished in 1979, in time to allow Belgrade to host one of those innumerable non-aligned summits that seemed so important at the time, no matter how endlessly inconclusive they were. The building was a showcase, designed to let the country look the developed world in the eye. The architect got the chance to do a tour of convention centres all around the West, and learned enough to design a huge glass-skinned box with an uncomfortable resemblance to a giant fan heater. He used it to scoop up all the bits and pieces from the brief: shops and restaurants as well as the auditorium. It was hardly beautiful, but with one bound a notionally Communist state had introduced those of its people with access to hard currency to five-star hotels and shopping malls, even if none of the international chains which usually populated them were allowed into the country.

Inside the complex, you can still believe the illusion of Tito's Yugoslavia for a moment. Nothing has been touched since the flawed leader opened it. The orange-and-lime-green colour scheme has faded now but is still intact. The Pompidou Centre-style exposed duct work still snakes through the structure. A mirage of a state that claimed to have been built on brotherhood and unity, but required the apparatus of an all-pervasive secret police to function, still lingers here. It seems progressive, competent and modern. But the mirage quickly evaporates once you get outside. The approach roads are potholed and across from the hotel's taxi rank is an encampment of ragpickers and their horse-drawn carts.

Under the chandeliers in the hotel lobby is a little onion-domed church built from plasterboard, complete with fake icons and ersatz revolutionary posters. It is there to provide the mood music for the Rasputin Café that serves coffee here, a theme in somewhat questionable taste given that this is where the homicidal Serbian warlord Arkan was shot dead by three attackers armed with Heckler & Koch machine guns.

Even now, identity is not an entirely comfortable subject to bring up in Belgrade. The cable channel on the TV in my room at the InterContinental played a continuous loop of films celebrating Serbia's armies, marching to victory in the Balkan wars of 1912, with a stream of text messages of support for Karadžić and Mladić rolling out at the bottom of the screen. I scratched whole paragraphs from the talk I had planned to give.

Architecture had played its part in the lead-up to the conflict in Yugoslavia, but going into too much detail in this particular setting didn't seem like a good idea. The Croats and the Serbs engaged in a bout of competitive church-building in order to lay claim to disputed areas. It was immediately visible which side was which. The Roman Catholic Croats built demonstratively modern churches, in concrete and glass. The Orthodox Serbs built equally demonstrative Byzantine domed 'traditional' structures in stone and tile. The message was not just about which community an area belonged to. The Croat churches seemed to be suggesting that they belonged to a state looking West rather than East. That openness to the new might also be understood as part of a programme to use culture in a deliberate effort to create a distinctive identity. Such a use of architectural style can be described as a kind of cultural nationalism, a tactic with which both the Croats and the Serbs were familiar. All the Marxist states were inculcated with the political uses of culture.

Once the wars of Yugoslav succession had started, the obverse side of this policy was the deliberate targeting for destruction of the architectural landmarks of the peoples that the Serb extremists were trying to destroy. After the other warring parties in the former Yugoslavia joined in, the Croats and Bosnian Muslims and the Kosovans engaged in round upon round of mutual destruction. Minarets in Bosnia were blown up by the Serbs. Mostar's medieval bridge was destroyed by Croats. The national library in Sarajevo, with its collection of precious books going back centuries, was obliterated by Bosnian Serbs. I took the view that this was not the time or the place to bring any of this up, and stuck instead to architectural politics well away from the Balkans.

I delivered my speech, suitably toned down. Afterwards I met a wistful architect who talked about the sense of isolation here. 'My worst student is the one who is doing the best, building houses with balustrades for the nouveau riche.'

From my taxi window on the way back to the airport I saw the Hotel Yugoslavia, huge, modern and empty. Its current owners have no interest in running it; all that they wanted was the casino licence that came with it. Next door is the equally massive, and equally empty, former home of the Federal Government of Yugoslavia, built in a fit of modernization in the 1980s, with nobody left inside it to govern a country that has ceased to exist.

There is yet another memorial to a dead Yugoslavia just outside the airport: a glass bubble that houses the Aircraft Museum. Outside it, the ground is littered with rank upon rank of elderly helicopters and enough trainers to equip a squadron. The once-glossy glass skin is decayed and stained. But the building is still open, and I find myself touring a collection of immaculately restored aircraft. They tell a political, as well as a technological, story. It starts with a string-and-wood biplane of 1912, from the Austro-Hungarian empire. Then comes a Messerschmitt, representing the military aid given to the pro-German Royal Yugoslav government just ahead of the country's entry into the Second World War in 1941. It is one of the planes that fought against the invading axis powers in the desperate, ill-fated defence of Belgrade that lasted just nine days, when anti-Nazi officers seized power. In the next gallery, there is a Spitfire, used to give the Partisans air support. Then there is an American Thunderbolt: a reflection of Cold War realities. Tito may have been a Communist, but he was also Stalin's enemy, and so America and Britain equipped the Yugoslav Air Force in order to deter the Soviet Union from extending its dominion to the Adriatic Sea. The last group of exhibits is more disturbing: a Tomahawk land-attack missile shot down near Kraljevo in March 1999. One of the three fins has snapped off, and the guidance system has been removed, most likely sold to the Chinese government. The

missile carries the stencilled message next to the manufacturer's name 'Caution, warranty void if equipment misused.'
Next to it is the tail fin and canopy of an F-16 shot down
outside Belgrade. There is a painted eagle on the distressed
fin, camouflage blistering, carbon-fibre components unravelling. The number of missions flown is signified by a neat
row of bombs painted beneath the registration number.
Also on show is the General Electric M61 Vulcan six-barrel
cannon salvaged from the crash, with a bent-nosed round
still in the chamber. A predator drone, landing gear in place,
hangs from the ceiling. In a glass case is the canopy from
an F-117A stealth jet, the name 'Capt Ken "Wizz" Dwelle'
painted underneath the escape hatch. These are difficult
things to look at.

When the F-16 was in the air over the skies of
Serbia, I was in Glasgow worrying about design exhibitions. In the few moments that I did think about Belgrade,
I believed that bombing was the only way for NATO to
stop a bloodbath in Kosovo. Now I know a bit more about
what it would have felt like to be on the ground, waiting for
the bombs, an experience faced by two of my uncles, their
wives and my cousins. And it posed a question of identity
far sharper than anything I had experienced in Scotland.

'As a prominent Englishman, working in Scotland,
have you ever experienced any examples of racial prejudice?'
It was the kind of question to which there is no right answer.
It was put to me on the telephone by a reporter from the
Scotsman the morning after the country had voted for a de-
volved parliament of its own in Edinburgh. I didn't know

whether to be flattered by the attention or, in some kind of subtle way, mildly humiliated. Was I being told that I didn't belong? Certainly it made me realize how much people judge who or what you are by how you sound rather than what you say. And in Glasgow, where I was halfway through my time as director of the city's Year of Architecture and Design programme, there is no doubt that, despite having a name which most English people, never mind Scots, need a certain amount of coaching to pronounce, I did sound pretty English.

Clearly an accent is an essential part of anybody's identity. And mine is the product of growing up in London in the 1950s and 1960s with parents who didn't speak English to each other at home. Couldn't the man from the *Scotsman* pick up on the fact that I belonged to a very specific subset of Londoners, or its Glaswegian equivalent, just by the way I sounded on the phone? My accent is the product of a constant diet of the BBC Home Service between the ages of one and five. Back before it was called Radio 4, the Home Service relayed the authentic sound of received pronunciation in the incarnation of Daphne Oxenford booming out of a beige plastic wireless set to invite me to listen with mother every afternoon. 'Are you sitting comfortably?' Daphne would ask. 'Then I'll begin.'

I didn't, I was told afterwards, say anything much until I was three or so, but when I did begin to speak it all came in a rush. I was fluent in the English of the BBC, as well as my parents' native Serbo-Croat. Heaven knows how they must have felt at producing an offspring whose ever so slightly snotty version of English would have made them feel how acutely foreign they were becoming to me every time I opened my mouth. But in fact I had no idea that they had an accent that was different from mine, or that they had a command of English that was anything but perfect, until I was well into my first pair of long trousers. I realized then, for the first time, that when other people used the word 'aunt' it did not rhyme with 'count'. And I hadn't understood that parents could get embarrassed about these things until I tried correcting my mother. I used English to blend as much as I could into a suburban London that still had milk bottles delivered every morning on a horse-drawn float steered by a man in peaked cap. It was a London in which the red trolleybus that ran past the end of my street disappeared one day to be replaced by a new kind of bus that didn't have sticks protruding from its roof. I didn't know it at the time, but the Second World War was still close enough for the sugar and tea to be stored in recycled cream-coloured tin cans embellished with a royal crown and the initials of George VI. They had originally contained the powdered milk ration that wartime nursing mothers were entitled to.

We lived in a modest semi-detached house on a quiet suburban street where coal was delivered every autumn, poured one sack at a time by a muscled man in a flat cap into the cellar through a hole in the pavement with a cast-iron lid. For a minute or two, the whole street filled with the acrid sweet tang of anthracite.

Since I became an adult, I've been back to see the house a couple of times, trying to remember the thrill of anticipation I felt on summer Thursday mornings when I would get up at seven o'clock to sit on the bottom step of the stairs, waiting for a glimpse of the paper-delivery boy through the stained-glass panel in the door, so I could snatch up the latest copy of the *Eagle*. The *Eagle* was a worthily up-market comic designed for middle-class boys, which came on china-clay-coated paper rather than downmarket news-print. It introduced me to the special pleasures of opening a magazine reeking of fresh ink. The big attraction was the chance to catch up on the latest episode of the adventures of Dan Dare, in *Pilot of the Future*. Frank Hampson's exquisitely detailed visions of the city of the future, in which Dare and his faithful batman, Digby, battled the evil Mekon and his Treens, were modelled on Frank Lloyd Wright's version of urbanism. The strip may even have got me started on the path that culminated in my studying architecture.

The west London of the 1950s was still a place in which the most exotic sight was the delicatessen on the high street, where melancholy Polish refugees would stock up on pickled cucumbers from a pine barrel by the door. I was more interested in the local drapery store, which had an amazing contraption to whiz my mother's change to her by way of an overhead system of electrically driven containers that shot back and forth from a central till.

I never really understood how my parents would have seen their lives in London. But eleven-year-olds, especially ones who spend most of their time withdrawing into the world of books and the radio, don't on the whole spend much time thinking about what life feels like for other people.

For a while, my father worked for the BBC World

Service, reading the news in front of one of those big old microphones hanging on coiled springs in a metal circle. I would occasionally be taken to the studio, deep in Bush House's bowels, to watch him at work through the glass wall of the control room. He had an upright typewriter at home to write his bulletins, which he would pound away on with two fingers, using carbons, and smoking Player's Navy Cut, like something out of *The Front Page*. That was when he developed the discreet attention-demanding cough that I realize to my dismay I have inherited. He didn't have a fedora, but in his drawer one day I found his pass for the press gallery for the Nuremberg War Crimes trials. I was proud of him. Not as proud as if he had been English, of course. Somehow being a journalist in a language nobody else could understand had the same relationship to the real thing as the Bulgarian Riviera has to Saint-Tropez. And I was not as proud as if it had been a real job, rather than simply the occasional shift to help out while he worked sporadically on ill-fated plans to make a fortune, successively by getting big in non-stick frying pans, holiday lets and DIY.

It hadn't always been like this. After the war, he and my mother had lived well on his salary as a foreign correspondent for Tanjug, Belgrade's state-run news agency, and the extras from the slush fund he hinted he was operating for Tito's government to try to win friends and influence people. There was a mansion flat in Kensington, nannies, and private schools for my two elder brothers. He had a regular table at the Gay Hussar, and holidays in France. Later, a lot later, I found a picture of my father sitting next to Marshal Tito himself, interpreting for some group of visiting British politicians.

My world in Acton felt secure and solid compared to the unknown, anxious uncertainties of the world my parents had left behind. The Balkans would intrude only occasionally with the arrival of one or other of my grand-mothers, dressed from head to foot in black. We would collect them from Victoria station, accompanied by the ter-rifying crescendo of a departing steam engine. My grand-mothers would arrive with, to my eyes, embarrassing gifts: a whole roast suckling pig wrapped in brown paper, boxes of sugary cakes, and alien vegetables. And they stayed just long enough to get on everybody's nerves. My mother's mother, however, was equipped with the highly prized skill of making apple strudel, a process that involved taking over the kitchen table and laboriously stretching pastry in thin sheets right across it.

At first the Balkans seemed a scary and threatening place that was overshadowing my childhood. I was too young to understand that the Second World War had ended years earlier, but I still associated the country with violence. From this distance the memories seem like a presentiment of what had not yet happened. By the time I was ten, I had started shut-tling back and forth every summer between these two worlds. It involved a two-day journey that started at Victoria, with a ride on the boat train to Dover, and ended on the stone jetty of the village harbour in Montenegro that my father's mother still lived in. Self-contained English schoolboys, in Clark's sandals, find it hard to adjust to emotionally demonstrative village life infested by moustachioed aunts who are going to give you a hug no matter how much you shrink away.

For my parents, both citizens of countries that had ceased to exist before they started school, who then owed allegiance to another state that also vanished, and who became citizens of yet another state when they eventually secured British nationality, the questions of identity and belonging were constant issues. For year after year they had to have their passports stamped by the Home Office in London with the precious words 'Granted leave to remain'.

Understanding that made me realize for the first time how their experiences have coloured my own preoccupation with understanding how buildings and everyday objects shape our sense of who we are. It made me see, beyond the narrow world of design, just a little of what it must feel like now to be an asylum seeker; a member of a more visible migrant community caught between identities.

My father was never a very organized man. Though he had trouble forgetting about certain things, he certainly wasn't good at keeping anything. When he died, he had no more than a few shopping bags full of carbon-copy typescripts, a lot of books and some old clothes with which to make something like sense out of the eighty-three years of the life that he had lived with varying degrees of success. If he had been more careful, he could have left behind a six-thick stack of passports, each from a different nation.

When my grandmother Draga (meaning 'dearest' in English) married my grandfather Jovo Sudjic, who had emigrated to America from the little Adriatic town of

Petrovac (accessible at that time only by boat or donkey track), she went to live with him in Bisbee, Arizona. It was a copper-mining town which, in the first decade of the twentieth century, was full of Eastern Europeans looking for work and a more secure life.

My grandmother had two children, my father, Miša, and my uncle, who died in infancy and is buried in Arizona. My grandfather, a clerk in a dry-goods store, succumbed to influenza shortly afterwards on a trip back home. Draga decided to stay in the security of her family home, with my father, and her American passport. Montenegro's coast in 1912 was still a province of the Austro-Hungarian empire. During the course of the First World War, its borders shifted back and forth, but by the time of the Armistice, the Kingdom of Montenegro was ready to sink into the newly formed Kingdom of Yugoslavia. When Italy and Germany invaded Yugoslavia in 1941, Montenegro was reconstituted as a puppet kingdom. Tito in turn declared the formation of the Federal People's Republic of Yugoslavia, of which the Socialist Republic of Montenegro was a constituent state. A decade later, my father had moved permanently to London and was in the process of swapping identities, no longer Yugoslav but British. Before he died, the Yugoslav state of which he had once been extravagantly proud had dissolved into bloody anarchy.

It is a stack of passports that never existed. In 1912, the United States of America did not expect many of its citizens to have passports. Miša travelled on his mother's documents. But I have always tried to imagine them. At

332

the bottom of the pile would be a folded and creased sheet of paper with a red paper seal fixed to one side, beneath the outstretched wings of an engraved American eagle. The Austro-Hungarian passport at the turn of the century was an eight-inch-by-nine-inch rectangle of paper. On the front was Austria's double eagle, the emperor's insignia, and a physical description of the bearer. On the obverse were detailed instructions for travellers negotiating the various imperial provinces.

I did get to see my father's passport from the People's Republic of Yugoslavia. It was a maroon-covered cardboard booklet, with the burning torches and star insignia on the cover. It was replaced by the dark navy-blue cover with gold embossed lions and unicorns that characterized pre-European Union Great Britain.

It's a ghostly collection that has always made me regard the whole idea of national identity as somehow provisional and yet also utterly compelling. And every kind of design is still put to work to achieve these ends.

IS FOR

ORNAMENT

Ornament is anything but superficial. It's a deadly serious business: the means with which cultures and individuals define themselves. Tattoos, camouflage, acanthus leaves and graffiti all qualify as ornament.

So did the pattern on the pages of the newly emerged state of Slovenia's passports in 1992. Rather than using the conventional pastiche of a nineteenth-century banknote engraving employed by most passport designers to deter counterfeiters, Miljenko Licul took an ordnance survey contour map of Mount Triglav, the highest peak in the new country, tore it into fragments and made it the basis of a collage. It was ornament in the sense that a nineteenth-century critic would have recognized it. Even though it was disruptive of the design language traditionally associated with its purpose, it was a decorative scheme that referred to its national roots for inspiration.

Over the centuries, style (which is the signature of a visual language) has mostly been defined by ornament. What made the nineteenth century different from any previous period in history was the emergence of a need to rethink that connection. Ornament was once the way that individual craftsmen could make their personal contribution to a larger idea. Machines put an end to that personal link.

For some critics, creating a new underpinning for ornament became a vitally important issue. Without it, the modern world could not be entirely defined, or entirely complete. For others, the end of handwork was the chance for modernity to define itself, not with the right kind of ornament but with no ornament at all.

Owen Jones, one of the key figures behind the Great Exhibition of 1851 and the establishment of the Victoria and Albert Museum, produced a definitive encyclopaedia on the subject, entitled *The Grammar of Ornament*. He formulated the idea that, as he put it, 'Construction should be decorated. Decoration should never be purposely constructed.' In other words, function, while it comes first, must be properly dressed if it is to achieve basic standards of good manners. But decoration for the sake of decoration is, in itself, even more unseemly that its complete absence.

More than a century later, in the 1970s, when Richard Rogers and Renzo Piano, the architects of the Pompidou Centre in Paris, chose to paint the pipes that were left exposed on the side of the building that erupted into the Paris streetscape they were following, most likely unconsciously, Owen Jones's ideas.

The puritanical streak that runs through contemporary architecture moved them to try to find a functional alibi for the colour scheme that they chose. They adopted the conventional rendering system used by engineers: water-carrying pipes are green, electricity cables are yellow, and so on. To render these ducts and pipes in this way serves no practical purpose. It is as wilful as painting flowers or clouds on them, but it mitigates the appearance of being subjective and sentimental. It could be called decorated construction.

Owen Jones's most accomplished protégé, Christopher Dresser, perhaps the world's first industrial designer in the modern sense, argued in a lecture delivered to the Royal Society of Arts in 1871 that 'true ornamentation is

of purely mental origin, and consists of symbolized imagination only. Ornamentalism is not only fine art . . . it is high
art . . . even a higher art than that practised by the pictorial
artist, as it is of wholly of mental origin.' He was saying that
decoration had moved out of the realm of the crafts, and had
become an intellectual concept rather than a subjective one.
Dresser, who had studied botany as well as design, looked
for analogies with nature to provide him with intellectual
ammunition. It is a position that had a historical aspect: the
architectural orders have a strong botanical content, from
acanthus leaves to papyrus. But botany and natural forms
also seemed to offer an important lesson for contemporary
design. Dresser suggested that there was nothing superfluous in nature, where everything is beautiful, and everything
has a simplicity of form and a clear function. He tried to
apply the same principle to design.

Dresser had a number of roles: working as a designer, as a consultant to manufacturers, as a critic and as a
teacher. He declared that 'as an ornamentalist, I have much
the largest practice in the kingdom', and produced designs
for wallpaper, textiles, stained glass, ceramics and metalware.

Dresser was a remarkably inventive designer, who
worked in a wide variety of media and had an impressive
formal range. His ceramic, glass and metal domestic objects
were startlingly original. They seemed to have no connection to any historical period nor, in many cases, any obvious
connection to natural forms. The teapot that he designed
for the Birmingham manufacturer James Dixon, in 1879,

had no applied decoration of any kind; it was an exercise in pure geometric form that would have looked new sixty years later and still seems bold today. Dresser was one of a number of people who were looking to find specifically modern forms of ornament. Gottfried Semper, exiled temporarily to London in 1850 and 1851, set about formulating his architectural theories there. And in Vienna Josef Hoffmann and Adolf Loos engaged in a somewhat one-sided debate about ornament. Both came from Moravia, went to the same schools, and moved to Vienna at about the same time. They had much more in common than the violence of Loos's polemics would suggest. At first, Loos had to confess a certain difficulty with writing about Hoffmann. In 1898, he claimed: 'I am utterly opposed to the direction being taken today by young artists, and not only in Vienna. For me tradition is everything – the free reign of the imagination takes second place. Here we have an artist with an exuberant imagination who can successfully attack the old traditions, and even I have to admit that it works.'

But when Hoffmann established the Wiener Werkstätte, an enterprise that Loos characterized as making work for the daughters of the rich, the gloves really came off. The bitterness that Loos showed towards Hoffmann may have had more to do with the sharpness of professional jealousy than a genuine ideological gulf.

Loos was certainly the more gifted writer of the two. But perhaps it was his very brilliance with words that overshadowed a better understanding of his meaning. His most famous text, *Ornament and Crime*, is a more nuanced and subtle argument about the nature of contemporary visual culture than the bald but attention-grabbing headline would suggest. The piece needs to be understood against the background of the cultural politics of Vienna, a city which Otto Wagner, a supporter of both Loos and Hoffmann, had rebuilt. Hoffmann was better at securing work, Loos was the more effective, and the more brutal, of polemicists: the Rem Koolhaas to Hoffmann's Norman Foster, perhaps.

Much of *Ornament and Crime* is not the full-frontal assault on applied decoration that the title suggests. The battle for simplicity, as the text claims, had already been won. It had historical inevitability on its side. In fact it's a critique of Josef Hoffmann and Koloman Moser's Wiener Werkstätte, the company that they set up to manufacture tiny numbers of exquisite objects in a contemporary manner, and their rediscovery of ornament. Their manifesto claimed that:

> The immeasurable harm caused in the realm of arts and crafts by shoddy mass production on the one hand, and mindless imitation of old styles on the other, has swept through the entire world like a huge flood. We have lost touch with the culture of our forebears and we are tossed about by a thousand contradictory whims and demands. In most cases the machine has replaced the hand and the businessman has taken the craftsman's place. It would be madness to swim against this current.

> Usefulness is our first requirement and our strength
> has to lie in good proportions and materials well
> handled. We will seek to decorate but without any
> compulsion to do so and certainly not at any cost.
> The work of the art craftsman is to be measured
> by the same yardstick as that of the painter and
> the sculptor.

Loos was just as much a believer in usefulness, good proportions and materials well handled. But Hoffmann's view of decoration as a kind of art gave Loos an opening in which to slip in his assassin's stiletto.

Loos claimed to have brought the world a vitally important message. 'The evolution of culture is synonymous with the removal of ornament from utilitarian objects.' He had brought the gospel to set men free, and then, as Loos saw it, up popped Hoffmann attempting to reinvent ornament for the modern world by pretending that it was art. Loos clearly had a problem with decoration. Talking about food, he suggested: 'The show dishes of past centuries, which employ all kinds of ornaments to make the peacocks and pheasants and lobsters look more tasty, have exactly the opposite effect on me . . . I am horrified when I go through a cookery exhibition and think I am meant to eat these stuffed carcasses. I eat roast beef.'

But he was not unaware of what he was demanding of his contemporaries. Loos was asking them to give up the attempt to make their own mark on history, to make their own style. Ornament, for them, meant style. Modern style, he was saying, is the obligation to make no style at all.

> We have outgrown it. We are at the stage when we prefer a plain cigarette case to an ornamented one. If I want to eat gingerbread, I choose one that is quite smooth and not a piece representing a heart or a baby or a rider and which is covered all over in ornament. Ornament does not heighten my joy in life, or the joy in life of any cultivated person.

In the Loos view, his opponents based their case on ersatz spiritual values and fake art.

It wasn't just Hoffmann that Loos was targeting. The Belgian architect van de Velde was the subject of the mockery of Loos's essay 'The Poor Little Rich Man'.

A tattoo is an ornament; only criminals and degenerates wear tattoos; therefore ornament is a sign of criminality is the sledgehammer-subtle thrust of his case against applied ornament. But there is much more to Loos's ideas about decoration than the headlines would suggest. Mass production changed everything for Loos. It means that 'ornament is no longer organically linked with our culture. It is no longer an expression of us.'

He suggests that mass production makes design democratic, and asserts the economic case, both for the consumer and the worker. 'Ornament is no longer a natural product of our culture, as a result, the work of the ornamenter is no longer adequately remunerated. Ornamented plates are expensive, the white crockery from which a modern man likes to eat is cheap,' he suggests, not entirely accurately. Simplicity has turned out, in the version developed for the minimalist taste of the twenty-first century, to be anything but cheap.

Loos was prescient enough to use political arguments to support his position. Ornament was not so much an aesthetic crime as an economic one, he states in *Ornament and Crime*: 'The enormous damage and devastation caused in aesthetic development by the revival of ornament would be easily made light of, for no one, not even the power of the state, can halt mankind's evolution . . . But it is a crime against the national economy that it should result in a waste of human labour.' Loos claims that he is not a ruthless puritan, attempting to take away the simple pleasures of the craftsman. At one point in the essay he says: 'I am preaching to the aristocrat, not the revolutionary. The aristocrat among atheists will lift his hat passing a church. The aristocrat of taste well understands the old lady who crochets her wonderful things with glass beads and silk, the aristocrat lets them be, the revolutionary would say it's all nonsense.'

It's designers he has in his sights. They, like he, have higher outlets for their inspirations, craftsmen do not. So, as Loos put it: '[A]nyone who goes to the *Ninth Symphony* and then sits down and designs a wallpaper pattern is either a confidence trickster or a degenerate . . . Beethoven's symphonies would never have been written by a man who had to walk about in silk, satin, and lace. Anyone who goes around in a velvet coat today is not an artist but a buffoon or a house painter.'

There is another, much more pragmatic interpretation of decoration than Jones or Loos put forward. It is to find a functional justification for its application. Decoration and ornament are devices that have always been used to conceal the imperfections of workmanship and manufacturing. In traditional building practice, it is the joints between different surfaces and materials that are embellished to hide any construction defects. When a plaster wall meets a wooden floor, the two materials will have been installed by different people who have different skills. To make the bottom edge of a coat of plaster exactly straight for the whole length of the wall is as difficult for the plasterer as it is for the joiner installing the floorboards to ensure that every plank of wood ends up aligned exactly with every other plank, to provide a perfectly smooth and even surface. Applied decoration accepts this level of imperfection. It gives enough latitude for it not to matter because the uneven gap between plaster and wood is hidden by a more or less ornate skirting board. A cornice does the same job at the point at which the ceiling meets the top of a wall. Drawing attention to skirtings and cornices by decorating them makes it apparent that they are the result of a deliberate aesthetic decision, not a random afterthought. The way that a keyhole fits into a door, or a light switch sits on a wall, requires a similar consideration of how the work to accommodate them will actually be done.

It is, given enough skill, possible to do without a skirting board. They are visually intrusive, and so in the context of the art gallery, and later the domestic interior, came the idea of the shadow gap. To avoid a background element that distracts from looking at art, either on the wall, or on the floor, the skirting is omitted altogether. Instead the plaster is made with great care to stop just short of the floor. And the floorboards with equal care appear to disappear in an even line under the plaster. Conceptually both vertical and horizontal planes are uninterrupted. There is no decorated skirting detail. But it could be argued that the almost invisible shadow gap is in itself a kind of ornament. It is certainly as punishingly hard to get right as the most accomplished of decorative flourishes.

The sign of modernity has become as complete an absence of applied ornament as possible. Pattern is permitted only if it comes from the inherent nature of materials, such as the onyx and travertine that Mies van der Rohe used for the Barcelona Pavilion, or the rust of Corten steel on the exterior of a skyscraper.

The motor industry works in the same pragmatic way as a builder. The details of how the components are put together is designed to make it easier to build a car, rather than more difficult. They smooth over the visual imperfections of the manufacturing process rather than draw attention to them. Look at the windscreen of an average Ford, for example, and you will very likely see a pattern of dots printed on the glass around its edges. The dots are there to make the inevitably uneven line of the gasket that makes the watertight gap between the glass and the metal of the car body into which it is fitted look less obvious.

The dots have no practical purpose, but they have become part of a car's ornamental scheme. Most cars no longer have a self-consciously decorative hood ornament, but the complex curves of a car body have also taken on a decorative role. These are shapes that appeal in part because they are difficult to do (and so have become the signifiers of quality) but also because of how they look. The arrays of lights and the back and front of a vehicle are also elements that the designer has to work with, along with the radiator grille, the door handles and the applied graphics. Car designers call them jewellery.

For contemporary mass-produced domestic appliances, decoration is almost exclusively based on functional alibis. It comes in the way that it is used in Dyson vacuum cleaners and to introduce a dash of colour in the citrus-coloured generation of iBooks from Apple.

It is, though not in a way that he would have welcomed, the vindication of Adolf Loos. Ornament is not art. But it may also be responsible for another phenomenon that he would have been even less enthusiastic about – the way that we decorate our utilitarian possessions after they have left the factory. We keep our smartphones in leopard-skin plastic sleeves, we attach plastic figurines to the handles of our suitcases and we cover them in stickers. It is as if we tattoo our possessions as well as ourselves. It is perhaps a measure of the continuing hunger for ornamentation that people have to make their mark on their possessions and their surroundings.

P IS FOR POSTMODERN

What distinguished Charles Jencks's best-known book, *The Language of Post-Modern Architecture*, first published in 1977, was the violence of its traffic-stopping first sentence. 'Modern Architecture died in St Louis, Missouri, on July 15, 1972, at 3.32 p.m. (or thereabouts) when the infamous Pruitt-Igoe scheme, or rather several of its slab blocks, were given the final *coup de grâce* by dynamite.' This was not the first attempt to abolish modernism and all its works in the name of what has come to be called postmodernism. A decade earlier, the architects Robert Venturi and Denise Scott Brown (who later went on to design Britain's most visible piece of postmodernism, the National Gallery extension), had written *Complexity and Contradiction*, a book dedicated to the proposition that less, rather than being more, as Mies van der Rohe used to suggest, was in fact a bore. They took, gently enough, to decorating their buildings in pastels and floral prints, incorporating fragments of historical detail and quotations from past architectural styles, and toured Las Vegas to learn from Ceasar's Palace.

Little more than half a lifetime after modernism had consolidated itself as the style that was going to end all styles, Jencks went a lot further than Venturi and Scott Brown and declared modern architecture to be dead on arrival. It was a pronouncement that said as much about the ambition of the man who made it as it does about modernity.

Jencks claimed that the fact that 'many so-called modern architects still go around practising a trade as if it were alive can be taken as one of the great curiosities of our age, like the monarchy giving life-prolonging drugs to the

Royal Company of Archers.' Who knows what even more excitable a conclusion he would have come to if he could have known that another huge complex, also designed by the architect of the Pruitt-Igoe, was one day going to suffer a far more tragic end. Minoru Yamasaki was responsible for the World Trade Center in New York. Jencks's glee over the destruction of Pruitt-Igoe, which was, as he put it, 'finally put out of its misery, Boom Boom Boom', certainly has a more troubling resonance now than it did when he wrote the words.

What did it matter, as Jencks later admitted, that he had made up the killer detail that pinned the time of the blast down to the precise minute? According to William Ramroth's account, *Planning for Disaster*, Jencks got both the date and the time wrong. Or even that Yamasaki, a Japanese American with a taste for florid appliqué Gothic ornament, was not, strictly speaking, a modernist at all. Or that, contrary to the newspaper version, Pruitt-Igoe had never won an architectural award and that, as revisionist historians led by Katharine Bristol suggest, the decline of the project had more to do with the absence of fathers living with their families on the estate than with the modern movement. Never mind any of the nuances, the dynamiting was an unforgettable image that allowed Jencks to make his authentically breathtaking declaration that was intended to mark the end of something big. Jencks was just as interested in trying to start something he sincerely hoped could turn out to be equally big, something that he called postmodernism, and which he presented as his own invention. In

Jencks's eyes, if not in everybody's, postmodernism meant design with the wit, the emotions and the history that modernism had rejected, put back into the mix. It was permissive rather than prescriptive, ambiguous rather than clear, catholic in its tastes more than it was Calvinist.

But for those who did not see it in the same way as Jencks, postmodernism was an even bleaker choice than modernism. It was not so much a break with the recent past as it was a further development of it. Postmodernism was modernism plus French literary theory.

What Jencks did not do with any conviction was to define exactly what constituted modernism, or, for that matter, postmodernism. But those omissions did nothing to lessen the impact of his book. Was postmodernism in design questioning capitalism? Yes, said many of its early advocates; but it quickly became synonymous with overconsumption, with Michael Graves's bombastic corporate architecture, and with red plastic birds attached to the spout of an Alessi kettle.

So confidently and so matter-of-factly to write off architectural modernism as dead, and then to dance without a hint of regret on its grave, suggested an overwhelming finality. This was not like saying that art deco was old-fashioned, or to claim that pink was the new black. Nobody ever saw the jazz age as anything more than an amusing, but passing, fashion. Nobody mourned the end of art nouveau. But to be a modernist was not merely about making things look fashionably up to date. It was to have a point of view about everything from music to psychoanalysis. It was to take a moral stand about the 'honest' use of materials, and to believe in the designer's duty to build a better world with the aid of flat roofs and an absence of capital letters. Certainly no other adjective was applied with such promiscuous abandon to almost everything, or is still able to evoke a very particular way of seeing the world. Modern art, modern architecture, modern jazz, modern movement, modern life, these are signals to suggest the way that the world was meant to be. 'Modernist' isn't the same as 'modernism'. One can be equated with the contemporary, the other has come to mean a very particular creative approach, one that has alternately fascinated and repelled us.

Since before the First World War, 'modern', a word carved in steel and concrete, with such apparently unarguable clarity in an impeccably severe sans serif font, had a power like no other adjective used to denote a cultural movement. Setting aside the rhetoric of the demands of the spirit of the age, about new ways of seeing space, 'modern' meant boiling down every complex shape into its constituent forms: cubes, cones and spheres. It involved using non-traditional materials and techniques. But to mean anything of substance, modernity demanded putting those tactics to work to create a new way of life. Modernity was about a new way of seeing the world, not just a new way of seeing space.

Jencks's book didn't bury modernism all by itself. As a movement, it has had all kinds of challenges, from its friends as well as its declared foes. You might equally well argue that 'modern' died on the day in 1929 that Alfred Barr and the Rockefeller family captured it through the skilful deployment of their all-conquering money trap and stored it safely away in their vault, New York's Museum of Modern Art, where it could do no more damage. By doing so, they had turned a turbulent social and cultural force into an aesthetic category.

If modernism was dead after it had done so much to shape every detail of our everyday lives for so long, from the cars that we drove to the art in the galleries and museums, and the typography of our postage stamps to the division of our cities into functional zones, which separated houses from shops and offices from factories and transport from schools, what is left to provide us with a compass for understanding the world?

After modernism had been declared dead, architects began to build apartment complexes that looked like Roman amphitheatres and aqueducts. They decorated their façades with fragments of classical columns, and used a lot more colour. It wasn't only architecture that was transformed, product design and typography and even car design followed a similar course.

Robert Venturi and Denise Scott Brown's range of furniture for Knoll, designed in 1984, took the form of some highly selective quotations of decorative styles, including Chippendale, Sheraton, Empire and Art Deco, and applied them to moulded plywood. That Knoll was a design-conscious company which had established its reputation by manufacturing Mies van der Rohe's Barcelona chair made the sting of their apostasy all the stronger. Their detractors saw this as little more than a cartoon, a travesty of the authentic original. For Robert Venturi, less might have been a bore. But Knoll kept Venturi and Scott Brown's designs in production for no more than four years, suggesting that people could tire of excess as quickly as they did of restraint.

With rather more originality, Daniel Weil deconstructed the language of consumer electronics. He made a radio that dispensed with a conventional rigid case in favour of a see-through plastic bag, inside which the circuit boards were decorated and clearly visible alongside random fragments of cloth.

For a brief moment, the postmodern idea spread everywhere, matching the explosive eruption of art nouveau at the turn of the twentieth century. Typography became militantly illegible. Cars turned playful. This eruption of disorder served to enrage the more inflexible of architects and designers. Harry Seidler, once a student of Walter Gropius at Harvard, who later moved to Sydney to become one of the founding fathers of Australian modernism, ill-advisedly suggested in his old age that postmodernism was the architectural equivalent of AIDS.

Paul Rand, who played a part in American graphic design very close to Seidler's in shaping Australian architecture, producing corporate identities for Steve Jobs as well as for IBM and Enron, was dismayed by what he called a 'collage of confusion and chaos, swaying between high tech and low art, and wrapped in a cloak of arrogance'. He was, of course, talking about postmodernism, and what he called its

squiggles, pixels, doodles, dingbats, ziggurats;
boudoir colors: turquoise, peach, pea green, and
lavender; corny woodcuts on moody browns and
russets; Art Deco rip-offs, high gloss finishes, sleazy
textures; tiny color photos surrounded by acres
of white space; indecipherable, zany typography
with miles of leading; text in all caps (despite
indisputable proof that lowercase letters are more
readable); omnipresent, decorative letter spaced
caps; visually annotated typography and revivalist
caps and small caps; pseudo-Dada and Futurist
collages; and whatever 'special effects' a computer
makes possible. These *inspirational decorations* are,
apparently, convenient stand-ins for real ideas and
genuine skills.

Both Seidler and Rand were responding to a sense that
they, and the ideas they believed in, were under threat.
They saw themselves as stranded by a retreating historical
tide, and believed that their successors were doing their
best to commit patricide on them. The Harvard of the early
1960s in which Jencks had studied was still a place in which
Gropius's influence was pervasive. A decade later the first of
the postmodernists were determined to take their revenge.

For a moment in the 1970s and the 1980s, 'modern'
really did seem to be dead. Architects went through a kind
of collective nervous breakdown. Under the lash of the
Prince of Wales, who (with singular lack of taste and judgement) famously suggested that, 'say what you like about the

Luftwaffe, they did less damage to London than Britain's modern architects', they sheltered under the alibi of a vernacular style, or even a kind of classicism. The ambition to build a sunlit new world that had driven modernism for so long had apparently evaporated.

And then postmodernism withered and died away so quickly that it looked as if Rand's and Seidler's scorn might have been right all along. Michael Graves, perhaps the most celebrated of the architectural postmodernists, saw his reputation go through a particularly sharp decline. What had seemed witty and provocative quickly became frivolous, excessive and indulgent. In the 1980s, Jencks, in his film *Kings of Infinite Space*, described Graves as the most significant American architect since Frank Lloyd Wright. Then, after the world took in the spectacle of Graves's vast hotel in Florida for Disney, topped by gigantic representations of swans, it was almost impossible to find anybody prepared to admit that they had ever been a postmodernist. After that, hiring Graves to build a museum or a company HQ became an admission of being terminally out of touch rather than daringly innovative.

By the time the Victoria and Albert Museum got around to its retrospective on postmodernism, forty years later, it was a moment in design history that seemed as though it had well and truly passed. The virus had been made safe, fit to reappear in its defanged, deactivated form.

If investigating the moment that modernism did or did not die is problematic, working out its origins is also not without its difficulties. Putting modernity down to Walter

Gropius's Bauhaus manifesto from 1919, with its expressionist woodcut cover and its William Morris-influenced ideas about the unity of all the arts, design and architecture, or even to Adolf Loos's writings in the Vienna newspapers in the years after 1900, is to miss the impact of the industrialization of the previous 200 years, of the enlightenment and the invention of the scientific method. Modernism was used in a derogatory sense as early as 1737, when Jonathan Swift branded those who abused contemporary language as 'modernists'.

The critic and architectural historian Joseph Rykwert takes an imaginative leap, claiming, convincingly, that 'modern', as it relates to design, is a concept that begins at least 250 years ago, with the separation of architecture from what were once called the other arts. It is now, he says, a divorce; one which he clearly regrets in that he finds most of what we build now either too banal to discuss or else somehow too empty to notice. But from his acid view of the direction that both art and architecture have taken, you could be forgiven for assuming that he does not believe things would have been much better if the two parties had decided to stay together for the sake of the children.

Rykwert looks back to the days before modernity, whose origins he puts back to a point shortly before the Adam Brothers got going with their eighteenth-century drawing rooms ornamented with plaster swags extruded on an industrial scale, and their mass-produced door furniture. There was, he suggests, a shared public realm then, as well as a shared public culture. As Rykwert sees it, this was a time when artists would have never dreamed of canning their own faeces, an act which seems to have earned Piero Manzoni the unyielding contempt of Rykwert. It was also a time when an architect could have expected to have been consulted about the placing of 500 feet of rusting steel in front of one of his buildings in the name of sculpture. It was a time before the world of advertising and graffiti transformed our cities by hollowing them out of any more complex layers of meaning. This last sounds like a misplaced confidence in the authenticity of pre-industrial cities.

If modernity had its origins in the Enlightenment, modernism, with which it should not be confused, began to be formulated around the time of the First World War, and its first and most energetic period came to a close twenty years later, though it was to spawn a second generation of modernists in the 1960s. It was shaped by such developments in painting as the geometry of purism. Le Corbusier's architecture was a response to the spatial explorations of cubism. It was influenced by cultural innovation in many different fields, from James Joyce's literary experiments to Sigmund Freud's psychoanalysis.

Early histories of modernism concentrated on Western Europe. But it went much further than that. Its roots were not just in Paris, where Le Corbusier settled, but also in Weimar, where Walter Gropius opened the Bauhaus, the art school that established the language of modern design, and in the Vienna of Adolf Loos. It had an early impact in Glasgow and Prague, Budapest and Helsinki. For a short period between the two wars, Czechoslovakia saw itself as a proudly and self-consciously modern state. After the expulsion of the Hapsburgs, the Czech kings were reburied in Prague's Saint Vitus Cathedral in a new, and radically untraditional, catafalque. The Bata family commissioned an entire new industrial city, in which Tomáš Bata's own office was a glass-walled elevator that allowed him to move from department to department.

What distinguished modernism was its vociferous rejection of history, tradition and precedent. Gropius, Le Corbusier and Ludwig Mies van der Rohe, the godfathers of the movement, were driven by the urge to design every chair and teacup as if no such thing had ever been done before. They had a messianic obsession with the idea of the machine, coupled with a tendency to equate design with morality. They believed that decoration was reprehensible because it hid the unadorned truth they professed to find in modern materials. Modernists used the house as a battering ram in their onslaught on conventional ideas, if not necessarily on how domestic life should be lived, then at least on how it should look. White walls, bare ceilings, glass walls and chromed steel fixtures were in themselves an emblem of newness. There was a view that objects should at least be made to look as if they were machines, or made by machines, even if they were actually the product of laborious handcraft. The hard-line technocrat Buckminster Fuller was scornful of the kind of functionalism that confined itself to how the kitchen taps looked, but showed not the slightest interest in the plumbing and water mains on which they depend.

Modernist designers were narcissistic enough to redesign themselves in the spirit of their obsessions. They were forever coming up with simplified, 'rational' new garments, or adopting those thick black-rimmed spectacles in perfect circles, to blink photogenically at the camera. Vladimir Tatlin's 1923 design for standard 'worker's' clothing, with detachable flannelette lining and wide sleeves 'to prevent the accumulation of sweat', was typical. The uniform is completed by a flat cap and boots. Alexander Rodchenko was equally interested in radical 'constructivist' clothing. This was the kind of thing that drew satire, as well as persecution, from the Nazis.

Modernism has defined our tastes to a remarkable degree. Without it, there would be no built-in kitchens, and no loft living. The schools and hospitals of the rich world would look very different. Without modernism, Britain's contemporary domestic landscape would be an entirely different place. We would not have Jock Kinneir and Margaret Calvert's elegantly rational road signs, or the double-arrow logotype with which British Rail displaced the heraldry of its predecessor, British Railways.

Britain is a country that is deeply ambivalent about its place in the modern world. The nation that made the first Industrial Revolution had been so horrified by the experience that it embraced the nostalgic cult of the country cottage like no other culture. It's an ambivalence that lingers. Britain, after all, is the country in which Sir Reginald Bloomfield, president of the Royal Institute of British Architects in the inter-war years, could describe what he insisted on calling 'modernismus' as an alien plot. And it was a country in which the director of the Tate in the 1930s refused to certify Picasso's work as art for the purposes of avoiding import tax.

The British response to the startling eruption of smooth-skinned modernist boxy white concrete houses such as Mendelsohn and Chermayeff's Chelsea house in the 1930s, and its Gropius-and-Fry-designed neighbour on Old Church Street, was encapsulated by Evelyn Waugh's sinisterly comic invention, the fish-eyed Walter Gropius figure Professor Otto Silenus in *A Handful of Dust*. Silenus is discovered by Margot Beste-Chetwynde 'in the pages of a progressive Hungarian quarterly' and is hired to replace the Gothic Revival family home 'with something clean and square'. 'The problem of architecture as I see it,' says Silenus, 'is the problem of all art; the elimination of the human element from the consideration of form.'

It was only when modernism was domesticated in a pincer movement by Terence Conran and Paul Smith that Britain really took to it. And modern lite is now to be found in every branch of IKEA and Pizza Express.

If modernism was dead, and postmodernism was manifestly even deader, what was left to Charles Jencks but to look for another alternative. According to Jencks, 'the New Paradigm' is the next big thing for architecture. It is the aesthetic theory he has put forward in an attempt to make sense of the wave of buildings that looked like blobs of oil, desert dune landscapes and train wrecks that rolled across the Western world at the start of the twenty-first century. Jencks brewed up a blend of ideas on the edge of science and mysticism taken from the fields of number theory, and new thinking about biology, geology, astrophysics and Gaia.

Given that we now understand the nature of the universe differently from how we saw it fifty years ago, why should we cling to the right angle when we build, when nature has different ways of organizing itself? This, according to Jencks, is the idea that unites the shattered fragments of Daniel Libeskind's Imperial War Museum in Salford, Frank Gehry's sculptural shape-making in Bilbao and Zaha Hadid's opera house in Guangzhou, even if it sounds a lot like the same counter-cultural primal soup from which Jencks's original big idea, postmodernism, had emerged. And underneath Jencks's passions you sense he is driven by that anxious quest every critic experiences, the search to find objective reasons to justify what remain the unquantifiable, unjustifiable subjective questions of taste. At heart, Jencks loves curves and lime-green paint more than glass boxes and white walls. If you don't share his tastes, it's hard to subscribe to his view of the significance of postmodernity.

is for

Q W E R T Y

What you write inevitably is shaped by how you write it, or, perhaps, as anybody who has ever used predictive text will know, what you write it with. It is possible to write a book without the use of a keyboard, with a pen or a pencil, and by dictation, to a human or a mechanical recorder. The specific procedure will certainly be reflected in the result. Texts that have been dictated have qualities that are recognizably different to those written with a keyboard, just as telling the time through the analogue hands of a watch rather than a digital readout, or driving on the left-hand side of the road rather than the right, requires a different kind of response from the brain. It is not just the keyboard that is a tool in the communication process. It's the alphabet, and it's grammatical structure too. If the keyboard does eventually disappear, then the act of writing itself might follow. Voice recognition challenges the grip of a primarily literary culture. If there is no longer a need for us to write in order to communicate, then how much longer will we still need to read? Technology will have had the effect of pushing us back to a pre-literate culture in which the storytellers and the sagas would set the pattern for memory.

Linguistic theory suggests that language may shape us as much as we shape it. One American academic economist has drawn a correlation between those countries that save the most as a percentage of GDP, and the grammatical structure of their language. His theory is that the more sharply defined the use of future tense in a language, the less likely that culture is to save. He speculated that those languages which are more vague in their use of the future tense see planning ahead as much more a part of the present.

Jack Kerouac claimed that it took him just three weeks to write *On the Road*, using a single roll, 120 feet long, made of sheets of tracing paper that he had pasted together with Sellotape before starting. Clearly *he* believed that his raw materials, and the ways in which he used them, could shape his writing, and what he had to say, as much as a grammatical structure. He wanted to avoid the disruption of being forced to stop typing, even if only for long enough to feed a new sheet of paper into his typewriter after every 220 words. In much the same way, he wanted to avoid the conventional marks of paragraph and chapter breaks. In part, it's what gave the book its grain and structure.

Kerouac treated writing as a kind of performance work that took its pace and rhythm not from the mechanical constraints of the medium but from the spontaneity of the flow of his words. He wanted to free his writing from the machinery on which it depended. Kerouac was redesigning the process of writing. For a designer too, the way in which a machine is controlled and understood is the crucial part of the design process.

Kerouac ended up with what looks like a contemporary version of the Dead Sea scrolls; each letter is very slightly indented into the surface of the manuscript, its outline smudged and blurred where ink from the typewriter ribbon has seeped into the imperceptibly torn fibres of the paper.

The indentations that mark the beginning of a

paragraph, the commas and full stops that punctuate sentences, are the conventions of a literary form. Feeding sheets into the machine is an unintended consequence of the process of typing. It impacts on the content as well as the form of writing, just as recording technology shapes music. The six-tracks-a-side album was the product of wax pressing, and lost its power as a format when digital downloading took over from the record store.

But if Kerouac managed to sidestep one of the technical constraints of the format he worked in, he accepted a more fundamental intrusion between his mind as it formed words, and his attempts to record and crystallize them. He used the QWERTY keyboard as the route between his fingers and the paper, or rather between his brain and the paper. The relationship between the two is indirect. The skill with which his fingers manipulate the keyboard does not in itself reflect the quality of his words, in the way that a pianist's musical performance would do.

Just as a steering wheel is not the only method of controlling a car, so the QWERTY keyboard is not the only kind of interface that allows a writer to work. Early automobiles used tillers. Contemporary Formula One cars have something more like the joystick of an aircraft studded with electrically operated buttons through which the driver can impose his will on the speed and course taken by his vehicle.

Before Apple got involved, Mobile phones had a different, and far less agile, keyboard that required a varying number of keystrokes to produce the desired result. And this in turn is very different from the dial of the traditional Bakelite telephone.

To be useful, every machine needs to be able to communicate. Some machines communicate only with their controllers and at just the most basic level, through the on/off switch. Others need to address a wider audience in more complex ways: a cash machine through its screen and its keyboard, or an airport through its arrival and departure boards. The dial, the rocker switch, even, in the case of the Bang & Olufsen Beolit 707 portable radio, a slide-rule-like tuning device on tiny ball bearings were the increasingly elegant means by which mankind could be encouraged to imagine itself in command of the mechanical and digital worlds.

Designers began to realize the scope that these routes into the soul of a machine had, either for equipping their users with a sense of just how much was at stake, or simply as playful gestures with which to amuse them. A pistol grip could be used not just to pull the trigger on a handgun, but also for a portable vacuum cleaner, or a watering can designed to appeal to users anxious about their virility.

Mario Bellini, the designer who did more than anybody to create the image of modern Italy in the 1960s, designed a bright-yellow plastic adding machine, the Divisumma, in which he went to infinite pains to maximize the tactile qualities of the keyboard. He made each key into a rounded button, stretching a soft rubber membrane over the whole surface. He somewhat coarsened the effect at his lectures by interspersing close-up photographs of the machine in profile, a single Michelangelo digit reaching out to depress one of the keys with the image of a nipple.

The QWERTY keyboard used to be the most effective way to communicate with and control a machine, until Steve Jobs teamed it with a screen and a mouse – what used to be called the graphic user interface. Jobs created not simply the window through which the computer could be coaxed, haltingly, to explain itself to the user, but the place in which the user could work directly with the machine. The click-and-point mouse was not Jobs's idea, he took it from Xerox's Paolo Alto research lab – which itself relied on earlier studies. Jobs saw a prototype, had his engineers tinker with it, and then made it cheaply enough for it to be both useful and usable.

I wrote my first book on a manual typewriter. It was an ancient upright Imperial, as heavy as a washing machine. Inside its glossy black frame, finished, like a grand piano, with the maker's name picked out in gold foil, like the masthead of a newspaper, was the type basket. The gunmetal-grey keys were greased to allow them to slide easily across each other, but every so often they would stick anyway and had to be prised apart by hand, a procedure that left ink on your hands. The space bar had fractured, and was held together with a makeshift splint.

The move from journalistic sprinting to completing a 100,000-word marathon meant pushing through a barrier of pain. The Imperial made the experience seem like a special kind of torture, both physical and mental, one that left two of my fingers sore and sometimes a little bloody from the continual pounding that came from spending several months bashing circular keys on the end of mechanical levers.

The essential nature of a typewriter is that almost everything moves relative to everything else, the keys, the paper, the roller on which the paper is fed into the machine. It is only the spot at which the keys hit the paper that stays in the same place. And it is what shapes the act of writing using a typewriter.

Finishing each line required pushing the carriage back to the starting gate and twisting the roller to move the paper up by the requisite amount. There was a chrome-finished lever to allow you, when everything was working properly, to make the whole operation in one sweeping move back to the beginning of the next line, with the paper moved up enough to get the right spacing. Just in case you kept typing past the end of the paper, there was a bell to remind you when to stop.

It was a remarkably intricate, mechanically ingenious way of making marks on paper and it was easy to understand because it replicated almost exactly the act of making marks on paper, one letter at a time, with a pen. It was a machine that was manipulated in much the same way as the tool which it replaced. But it was also an utterly unforgiving process. The chances of an untrained typist hitting the wrong key were high, and it was equally likely that something would go wrong with the lever arm, and you would find yourself typing a new line far too close to the last one. With so much potential for getting things wrong, and just a bottle of correcting fluid, or the x key to put them right, it had the effect of making every stroke a carefully considered decision. It was not just a question of the physical process of transcribing thought. A manual keyboard was an essential aspect of the process of writing. It shaped and slowed the creative act. The process of marking out each word had to be approached with almost the same kind of caution exercised by a stone carver setting about cutting a letter with a chisel in a stone slab. There was a compulsion to make every line and every page perfect, annotating drafts by hand in ink, and constantly typing and retyping, to achieve a page untroubled by crossings-out or mistakes. Achieving this demanded a sustained bout of physical labour. And that made sustaining an idea or a creative flow difficult.

Writing long hand, with pen and ink, used to be physically easier, more fluent and, at least for me, quicker, but there never seemed to be enough objectivity. It's a skill that has gradually atrophied. Until I can see the words with the distance that comes from having them typewritten in front of you, then it is hard to measure their impact. And there is little incentive to complete half-sentences and half-finished thoughts until they can be judged and weighed by print that has been removed from the subjectivity of handwriting.

My first job was at the Architectural Press in Queen Anne's Gate, London, accommodated in a pair of eighteenth-century redbrick houses. There was a private pub in the basement, the Bride of Denmark, equipped with a stuffed lion, a bar and skittles salvaged from blitzed gin palaces during the Second World War by the staff of the *Architectural Review*, which had numbered John Betjeman and Nikolaus Pevsner. I was there at the end of the 1970s, and even then, assistant editors were still expected to produce their copy long hand, have it typed by the editorial secretary, send it to the printers for typesetting, and edit the copy on galley proofs. I was impertinent enough to insist on having a typewriter brought into the office so that, with my two-fingered typing skills, I could, hesitantly, cut out at least one stage in the process. It felt very contemporary even if the personal computer was already on the horizon.

When I wrote my first book the electric typewriter was already well established. IBM had launched the Selectric twenty years earlier which, with its golf ball and its transistorized circuitry, seemed the last word in technology as applied to the writer's craft. In fact it was just the first halting step in what came to be known as word processing, an activity that sounded more applicable to the industrial scale of envelope addressing and invoice raising than writing a book people might actually want to read. The golf ball, when it became interchangeable, allowed a choice of fonts for the first time.

Eliot Noyes was trained as an architect by Walter Gropius at Harvard, then became a curator at the Museum of Modern Art before he moved to run the IBM design programme. He gave the electric typewriter a delicately sculpted form that seemed just as much of a glimpse of another world as the new Citroën DS 19 had in the 1950s. And he introduced colour to the world of the office machine. The

Selectric came in taupe, dirty pink and avocado, colours that were as sharp as Noyes himself, with his brushcut hair and his mohair suits.

The Selectric did away with the mechanical levers that the typewriter had depended on ever since it was first patented in the 1870s, the last link to the underlying reason for the layout of the typewriter keyboard and its sequence of four top-row vowels. The QWERTY keyboard was not, as is often suggested, devised to slow down typists in case the early machines turned out to be too fragile to withstand the pounding that agile hands could give them. In fact the keys were positioned in such a way that typists could work quickly without the mechanical levers inside the machine jamming. Letters that were likely to be used in sequence, such as q and u or p and t, were placed as far apart as possible so as to keep the levers that connect the key with the letter from jamming together as one went down and the next came up. It's a layout that produced a sequence of letters that has no apparent logic, and yet is based on what were impeccable functional principles. It was as if the machine were revealing an underlying personality, independent of its human designers.

The Selectric's spinning golf ball did away with the need for all that. But its keyboard retained the same layout, and it still made for a far-from-seamless relationship between creative impulse and print. Once you switched the Selectric on, there was the continuous noise of the machine idling its gears, ready to spring into semi-robotic action like a swarm of mechanical cicadas. A less elaborate mechanical solution was the daisy wheel. It was a gradual sidestep towards the digital and away from analogue, and it began to allow for the production of cleaner, tidier, more polished finished pages. Correcting fluid and Tipp-Ex were supplanted by dry paper, and in the 1970s the typewriter took another hesitant step into the digital world. Typewriters began to acquire memories: a phrase, then a line, then a paragraph could be input to ensure that everything was letter-perfect before it was printed out with the daisy wheel.

For Kerouac all this tinkering would no doubt have seemed an even more frustrating delay than feeding his machine with a new sheet of paper every 220 words. In fact it was on the way towards the frictionless interaction between the intellect and the printed word that he had searched for.

The QWERTY keyboard is an archetype that, for all the attempts to dethrone it, remains firmly in command of the format. Its longevity is not simply a result of the difficulty of retraining everybody who has ever learned to touch-type. Despite the claims of superior performance and logic from alternative layouts, nothing has yet been devised that can deliver enough to justify such a massive change. Witness the halting efforts on smartphones, palm devices and voice recognition. Attempts to reconfigure the keyboard in supposedly more rational ways are as doomed to failure as attempts to substitute Esperanto for English as a universally understood language, and are equally cranky. As a control panel, which is what the keyboard in substance is, QWERTY has the enormous advantage of being intuitive. Hit the key, and you see what you are going to get. The only nuance on a typewriter was upper or lower case, a smattering of symbols and, in a few cases, colour. Multicoloured ribbons made it possible to choose between red and black. Copies were made by inserting an unpleasantly sticky sheet of carbon on to the roller between the regular pieces of paper and hammering the keys hard enough to make a legible impression through two or three layers. The first computer keyboard was a far less intuitive control mechanism, with its mysterious function keys and its control-shift options.

I wrote my second book on a machine that looked and sounded a lot more up to date than the Imperial. Olivetti had commissioned Mario Bellini to shape what the company claimed was the first portable golf ball in the world, the Lexikon 82. He worked on it in 1973, and it went into production at the company's Glasgow factory in 1976. It looked great: Bellini gave it a sensuous, rounded form in injection-moulded ABS plastic. There was a two-tone cream version, mine however was a very dark anthracite grey, which came with a plastic golf ball picked out in vivid red. But at eleven kilogrammes it was too hefty to be really portable. Even though it came in a cool-looking moulded-plastic carrying case, moving it across the room felt like lugging an old cathode ray television set around.

The keyboard took some getting used to. The Imperial demanded considerable physical effort, with the full hand pressed down, fingers bouncing off one key to find the next, with the rhythm and force of running on the balls of your feet. It was a technique that took an effort to unlearn when I finally took to a laptop. With the Lexikon, touch one of its keys, no matter how gently, and it took off with startling speed, as if trying to escape, in a sudden detonation of energy. Whether from a defect in the design, or shortcomings in the quality-control standards in Glasgow, after ten minutes of continuous use the Lexikon became incapable of delivering a straight line of type.

It was the first time that I remember feeling a sense of hurt disappointment with a design that had failed to deliver. I had seen the Lexikon on the cover of *Design* magazine, moodily photographed as part of a story on the appeal of black for product design. This was the machine that was going to turn me into a writer, a fully equipped member of the modern world. The Lexikon was a machine that seemed to promise a direct line to the sophistication of contemporary Milan. It wasn't cheap. But I had to have it, because I knew it would be worth it.

As I fiddled the off-switch up and down in a vain attempt to encourage it to return to aligning its output on straight lines rather than crooked rambles across the page, I came to curse it. And the body, while it aspired to formal perfection, simply could not match the quality of the finish of the IBM Selectric. The IBM machine represented the rigorous resolution of every physical, mechanical and technical problem. It was an achievement of industrial culture of the highest quality. It had done away with not just the levers that depressed the keys, but also the carriage that moved the paper. IBM's golf ball bounced around like a fairground shooting-gallery pinball on an air jet, darting back and forth. The Lexikon was seductive to look at, but when you touched it, the allure dissipated. The Olivetti engineers delivered Bellini an intellectually slovenly half-solution to his formal brio. The Lexikon golf ball did not track the page, the typewriter still needed a carriage for the page to move back and forth. I put it back in its carrying case and hoisted it up on to a top shelf, where it quickly acquired a discouraging film of dust. The Lexikon had been my first serious love affair with Italian design, and it had ended unhappily. It has turned into a relic, but the layout of its keyboard followed that of all of its predecessors, and set the pattern for its successors too. Voice and handwriting recognition are still attempting to catch up with it. Either approach could one day finally kill off QWERTY, turning it from a universal portal back into the sign of a skill as specialized as shorthand.

R IS FOR RAMS

Looking at the charmless and misshapen electric tooth-brushes that carry the Braun logo today, or the questionable use that the latest Chinese licensees have made of the brand, it is hard to understand the impact that the company once had on how everyday things look. Braun in its golden age, the years between 1950 and 1975, defined a kind of high-minded materialism that retains a remarkably strong grip on the imagination, if not of every consumer, then at least on that of most designers. It was the celebration of the kind of simplicity that is not at all simple.

Braun, and Dieter Rams, the company's long-standing head of design, gave the middle classes guilt-free permission to acquire their television sets and their stereo systems, the definitive domestic status symbols of the 1960s, by presenting them as if they were austere, serious-minded pieces of equipment rather than using the more obvious means of attracting attention. Some companies gave their products cute names; Braun just used letters and numbers. It made for a product range that seemed so high-minded that it might have come from a Bauhaus classroom which, by some curious quirk of social history, had found its way into the shopping malls of Europe. It had the self-confidence to act as if one of its food mixers could be understood not as just another electronic appliance but as the antidote to all the clutter produced by the wave of new-found afflu-ence from the post-war years. Braun made consumer goods without a trace of the conventional artificial sweeteners of marketing, and without the benefit of much in the way of market research. For designers ever since, the language that Braun defined has been the starting point for any electronic appliance or domestic object that aspires to suggest a certain discreet and unthreatening modernity.

It's a language that was the result of the work of Rams and the Braun design studio, which he ran from an unassuming building on the suburban fringes of Frankfurt for almost thirty years. Rams transfigured the most banal and the most humble of everyday things into ideal forms. He made objects that were never in any colour you liked. They were black, or they were white, with infrequent primary-coloured exceptions. If he had had his way, the only musical accompaniment to a Braun television commercial would have been composed by Schoenberg. Rams didn't, of course, have his way, which resulted in one rather curious ad for an electric shaver that cut back and forth between a Porsche 911, with its tea-tray rear spoiler, ploughing through a grassy landscape, and a Micron Universal, its brushed-steel body embellished with black rubber dots, traversing the stubble of a human chin.

Rams made objects that hinted at some deeper meaning beyond their obvious purpose. Making toast, shaving or tuning a radio the Rams way was much like transubstantiation for his true believers. An electric razor from Braun seemed to offer the prospect of turning shaving from a time-consuming chore into a religious daily ritual. A Braun juicer made squeezing an orange into a painless version of the Japanese tea ceremony.

Rams's Teutonic devotion to order and sobriety could irritate as well as seduce. When the artist Richard

Hamilton first started tinkering with the Braun logo and attached a set of false teeth to the top of an electric toothbrush to create a work that he called *The Critic Laughs*, he was introducing a tinge of irony to his representation of the cult of good design. The Braun toaster had already been the subject of a series of Hamilton's screen prints, and an essay by the English critic Reyner Banham. These were not quite the unquestioning endorsements of timeless platonic form that we now expect of Hamilton's work.

Hamilton and Banham were conflicted about Braun. Their early attitudes to the Braun objects that they explored in their attempts to find significance in the consumerism that was changing the face of the world were those of the Independent Group. They wanted to celebrate throwaway pop culture all the way from Cadillacs to giant refrigerators. They were from the generation that had been through war and rationing, they endured baths limited to four inches of hot water, utility furniture and clothing coupons. They had had enough of restraint, and they weren't keen on objects that were going to last for ever when there might be something newer and better to come along shortly. Reyner Banham, who had a weakness for the more robust American approach to product design, complained in one of his articles about the essentially authoritarian nature of a Braun toaster that came with an instruction manual that demanded tolerances of plus or minus four millimetres in the thickness of the bread that it could handle.

But as Hamilton continued to work on projects that used Braun designs as their point of departure, he abandoned ambivalence. In a text written for an exhibition on Braun in Berlin, he suggested that the toaster had the same significance for his art that Mont Sainte-Victoire had had for Cézanne.

Rams tried to give the everyday a kind of dignity and a sensibility that was reflected in every detail of his working environment, which was controlled with unrelenting precision. Each model, pencil, prototype, sample and drawing board in his Frankfurt studio was placed carefully in its proper place. They were precisely aligned with a grid that guided everything from the position of the storage shelves – a Rams design, of course – to the size of the floor tiles. The only colour came from the orange pack of Ernte 23 cigarettes that was constantly in Rams's hands. The pack had the same effect as the occasional injection of colour that Rams introduced to the Braun palette. A lighter or a coffee maker might be finished in a colour stronger than his habitual monochrome, as Rams put it, 'like a vase of flowers in a room'.

Despite the antiseptic materials, the studio did not feel clinical. Rather, it had the atmosphere of the carpentry workshop that Rams still keeps at home, even now he has retired, to serve as a memory of the cabinetmaking apprenticeship he went through before starting his architectural studies. Sam Hecht, the British industrial designer, once suggested that everything Rams designed in the course of his entire career seemed as if it had been designed for one room. If there ever were such a place, this was it.

When 'Snow White's Coffin', the name that Braun's

competitors used to disparage the first-ever record player with a Perspex cover, was launched in 1956 under the official title of the SK4, Rams had no idea that what he had done would become the standard configuration for every hi-fi system that came after it for thirty years. It was a crucial project for the company founded by Max Braun after the First World War and newly under the control of his two sons, Artur and Erwin. The SK4 was Braun's leap out of the age of valves and into transistorized technology. A new visual language was needed to show how much things had changed.

In the pre-war years Braun had specialized in making radios in which the task of the designer was understood as domesticating technology to make it fit for the living room. The two younger Brauns had ambitious plans to modernize the company, and to make it a cultural force as well as a technical innovator. They hired the film-maker Fritz Eichler, who acted as a creative inspiration for the company, and Hans Gugelot, who before his untimely death led the industrial designers working for Braun. Gugelot himself had been a teacher at the Ulm School of Design, the embodiment of German post-war modernity, where he had been an assistant to Max Bill. Bill had studied at the Bauhaus, offering Braun a connection to the heritage that Rams consciously drew on. And he was a credible artist, as well as a designer.

Dieter Rams, still in his twenties, had only recently arrived at Braun when the SK4 was being designed. He had come from Otto Appel's architectural practice to work on designing showrooms for Braun. Appel had been an assistant to Albert Speer, working on his monstrous transformation of Berlin into the new Nazi capital city of Germania before the war. When Appel set up on his own, his practice had to rely on corporate modernism rather than National Socialism. He was the associate architect for Skidmore, Owings & Merrill's US government projects in West Germany. And it was this version of mid-century modernism that shaped Rams's view of design.

The SK4, Gugelot believed, had to break with the imagery of domestic furniture that had been used to house-train consumer electronics. But Gugelot's idea of a metal lid for the record player didn't work. The vibrations on the prototype were too distracting. Rams's contribution was to use Perspex instead. 'At first Gugelot said it was too flashy, too much about style, but he came around,' said Rams.

Shortly after Gugelot died Rams took on the leadership of the Braun design team. Of all of the designers involved with Braun over the next three decades, Rams was the most determined, and the most consistent spokesman for its very specific approach to design. For Rams, the point of design is not to sell more things, but to make the ones that you do sell better. It was not a popular attitude with marketing departments. Rams could be seen as a designer who has tried to resolve the irresolvable contradiction between design as a cultural programme and design as a commercial activity.

Even if Rams was unable to match Max Bill's lyrical range, it is clear that he was interested in how things look as well as in ergonomics, for all the emphasis that he places on logic and order. Rams took care to find the precise grade of clear plastic for the tuning panel on the front of his radiogram to show off the names of the stations. The backs of his radios were treated with as much precision as the front.

Meeting Rams in the mid-1980s felt something like encountering a sleeping legend, a giant lost in his Frankfurt Valhalla, awaiting the call to rescue another generation from the insidious dangers of postmodernism and decorative frills. The Braun that Rams had known, a moral guardian defending the values of West Germany at its peak, when an economic boom coincided with a sense of the responsibility that an enlightened capitalist economy has to the consumer, was about to expire. Braun was acquired first by Gillette and then by Proctor & Gamble, companies for whom such utopian values had little relevance. They simply wanted to sell Rams's successful products as hard as they could, and to drop the lost causes. Electric shavers and toothbrushes had a future, but making stereo systems and TV sets for the mass market was no longer possible in Europe. Rams left soon after.

By this time, his work seemed like a throwback: electronic calculators had become technologically redundant. Their circuit boards, batteries, keys and LEDs could all be accommodated in an object the size and thickness of a credit card. They would shortly be subsumed into a mobile phone. But instead Braun offered something much more substantial. The Braun ET44 that Rams designed with Dietrich Lubs was being sold not as a piece of electronics but as tactile sculpture. It was a calculator that seemed to offer the consolations of perfection in the radius of every curve, the sequence of buttons, in the logic of the control system, the polycarbonate wallet which the calculator came in, and the colour coordination. In a messy, complex and possibly meaningless world, the ET44 was a reassuring promise of a fragment of stability and meaning.

Proctor & Gamble has licensed all the Braun clock, radio and watch designs to a company that uses Chinese factories to make them, and which allows them to use the Braun logo on new products that they have designed themselves. The Braun vision had flickered into life again when the calculator interface on the first-generation iPhone paid deliberate and eloquent tribute to the ET44 with its yellow and brown buttons.

The last time I saw Rams was in London at the Design Museum's retrospective on his work. The museum created a space that evoked Rams's own living room. The floor was tiled with the very particular grid of white tiles that Rams has at home. On the wall was the reel-to-reel tape recorder next to the amplifier next to the loudspeaker that Rams designed for Braun, so heavy that the museum's technicians had to reinforce the wall specially. It was softly playing the Modern Jazz Quartet. The shelving system that Rams devised for Vitsoe lined the walls. There was a Braun TV set on the floor. On one level, nothing had changed since the 1960s. Rams's aesthetic was as relevant as it had ever been. More so in fact, because today there are the followers, if that is how one can describe Jonathan Ive, Jasper Morrison, Sam Hecht and Naoto Fukasawa, all designers who work in a language which clearly reflects the restricted colour palette and the care with which Rams approached his work.

Rams told me once that he had met the provocative and determinedly playful French designer Philippe Starck. 'Starck said, "Jonathan Ive, he has stolen everything from you for Apple."' Rams does not see it that way. For him Ive's appropriation of the calculator for the iphone was proof of the continuing relevance of his work.

Rams remains a formidable presence, as determined as a prophet. There are few designers in the present climate of moral relativism as prepared as Rams has been to put their names to a manifesto. Rams's world view is summed up by his idea of less but better, the most important of his ten principles, which he published for the first time in 2008. That is to say that visual and physical longevity gives us the alibi that we need to feel a little less guilty as consumers.

Rams appeals to a generation of designers who are nostalgic for the sense of purpose that came from the moral certainty of the 1960s, and the seriousness of the Ulm School. They are fascinated by the lingering appeal of the analogue age. We have yet to find a way to inject that sensibility into what design will be, rather than referring back to what design once was. But it is a reminder of the continuing power of material objects, and the continuing charm of refined simplicity in the way that they are designed.

IS FOR SLUM

A fear of slums was an essential part of the emotional background to the development of modern architecture. Both Friedrich Engels and the Salvation Army identified the slum as the most hideous outcome of the modern world. It was the breeding ground for sickness, degradation and crime.

Modernity was the means to eradicate slums and replace them with a utopian ideal of what the city ought to be. From Lord Rosebery, chair of the London County Council, to William Morris, much of the modern city was understood as a vicious monstrosity, to be treated as a diseased pathology, by surgical means.

'Slum' was a word that used to worry me. Jane Jacobs's book *The Life and Death of Great American Cities* shocked me when I first read it as an adolescent. She painted a picture of the honest virtue of healthy urban communities, and conveyed a vivid sense of the multiple threats that faced them. The physical fabric of the city, apparently so reassuringly solid, was revealed in Jacobs's urgent account as permanently on the edge of putrefaction. Apparently healthy urban tissue could be destroyed by even the most apparently trivial infection. It was as if the familiar streets around us were all in imminent danger of turning into urbanism's version of zombies: slums. A huge effort went into dealing with the threat that they were believed to represent. When they were not described in medical terms, the urban task forces, the development corporations and the area initiatives were presented as military operations. Before the war on drugs, there was the even more fundamental war on slums. The fallout from the unforeseen consequences was just as damaging. The city was regarded as in need of drastic action to save it from itself. Roads were driven through noxious urban tissue in the name of hygiene and sunlight. New homes with bathrooms and balconies and electricity replaced overcrowded tenements. And, as Jacobs revealed, many of these cures had results that were as bad, if not worse, than the disease they claimed to have cured. The city was presented as dangerous, threatening and out of control. There are still many observers who see it in these terms. Some of them seem to have developed a taste for the wild side of the city. Mike Davis, in *Planet of Slums* and a litany of similar books, has relished an apocalyptic interpretation of the fate of the city. More interesting is the idea that slums are the unique products of their environment: an Indian slum is different from a Chinese slum. And that slums can be places to learn from rather than to fear. The density and complexity of a slum offers lessons about what makes cities work, and also what doesn't. Closer observation of the rhythms of a slum reveals the creative, as well as the negative, aspects of urban life. A living city is not squeaky-clean, or hygienic; it's a messy but vital range of possibilities.

The classic slum that engages attention now is no longer in London's East End, where nineteenth-century reformers claimed to have discovered what they called the vicious poor, or New York's Hell's Kitchen. It is the shanty towns of Asia, Africa and Latin America that now attract the attention of reformers looking to draw attention to themselves. Responses to these places have followed a similar trajectory to their European predecessors: fascinated horror, followed by simple fascination.

As they blink into wakefulness, the perpetually jet-lagged have a way of starting each day with the same mixed feelings of doubt and certainty. They may never be entirely sure of where they are in the world, but they do know exactly which hotel chain they are dealing with. So it was for me one dislocated Sunday morning at the Hilton Towers. My surroundings, unmistakable as an international hotel though they were, at first sight could have been anywhere. The larger-than-average room was finished in several shades of the kind of cream paint that in my experience tended to be associated with Hilton more than, say, Hyatt. The desk by the window, the pair of sofas facing each other across a low table, the refrigerator stocked with excess calories, and bottled water that had been flown thousands of miles to get there, spoke of the very particular outcomes of the place-lessness that comes with the international corporate hospitality business, with its nuanced dance between reassuring familiarity and carefully measured doses of the exotic. The taps in the adjoining bathroom, with its lurid red marble floor, when turned, obediently and effortlessly delivered a steady stream of cool, clean water. While my brain negotiated all these generic signals of international hotel life, I began to realize that I could only be in one very particular place in the world. And it wasn't just the fact that when I arrived on the 2 am flight from Europe, room service had managed to deliver a dosa breakfast within ten minutes, and that I needed to remember when to take my malaria tablet. Through the window, I could see the hallucinogenic image of the University of Mumbai's Gothic towers, a tropical version of South Kensington formed in florid carved stone of quite unrelenting and hugely impressive ugliness, emerging through the dawn. Just as impressive was the clock tower that chimed the quarters, exactly like Big Ben.

I could see neon advertising signs, and office slabs faced in white marble, with anxious files of Ambassador cars waiting outside. For the Indian official class it was the only choice, just as it was forty years ago, when the original production line was shipped out from the Morris factory at Cowley, on Oxford's outskirts, after the model was judged irredeemably redundant for the British market.

This was a city that had changed enormously since I first went there thirty years previously. Then, it still had the musty, lingering smell of the 1940s about it. There were very few shops selling branded consumer goods, there were no shopping malls, no fast food, and not much advertising. What there was of it had been beautifully hand-painted in confident innocence.

Despite the faintly ramshackle air of much of the city, where the central law courts were roofed in corrugated iron, and their interiors recalled a legal system that would have been entirely familiar to Charles Dickens, with shelf upon shelf of mildewed briefs, you could see the tell-tale signs of sustained near-double-digit growth, for better or worse, everywhere. As you emerged from the hotel, which a year later was the scene of terrorist atrocities, a huge Gucci store eclipsed the silver and leatherware shops. Glossy Italian brands were driving out the bespoke shirtmakers. There were Japanese cars on the roads, and new office buildings. The backlit supersize posters showed airbrushed pale-skinned models. Knowing irony had infected the TV commercials. In one that promoted mobile phones, a hipster in sunglasses was seizing the microphone from a garlanded traditional politician in a Nehru hat and taking a picture of himself.

The construction cranes were busy turning the old mills, which gave the city its first burst of growth in the wake of the American Civil War, into gaudy shopping malls. The cows which were once allowed freely to graze the roads around the airport had disappeared. The densely packed city fabric cracked and fissured to make way for elevated roads that allowed the 10 per cent of its citizens with cars to float above its packed streets and move between the golf clubs and country clubs, the airport and the business districts that defined their Mumbai.

Half an hour after leaving the hotel, I was in the midst of a different city; one in which an entire extended family could expect to live in a single space no more than half the size of my bedroom at the hotel. Not just the family – the workforce, too. For the potters I was meeting, home and factory were the same thing.

The drive from Sir Dorab Tata Road, which divides Mumbai's hotel strip from the Arabian Sea, to 90 Foot Road, Dharavi's main drag, unpeeled the layers of the city's 300-year history. It started with Mumbai's most recent incarnation, the financial centre of India (and of much of Asia and the Arabian Gulf too), where the hotels are moored like giant luxury liners blazing light tethered at anchor. They were self-contained worlds floating in the dense urban fabric around them, full of gold and cut glass, international chefs and grand dinners, film stars and visiting academics, ecologists and carbon-footprint specialists, doctors and accountants, performing tirelessly for one another. This was the world that terrorism invaded in the brutal attack on the Taj Hotel and its neighbours in 2009.

Then there was the Victorian municipal city, its fretwork skyline erupting over the Maidan Oval and its balletic cricket players. The ground is still ringed by statues of nineteenth-century worthies, with Zoroastrians and Jains rendered in the manner of nonconformist Bradford cloth merchants, remembered for their good works for the poor in their day. Today they keep watch over pavement dwellers and double-deck buses. Next came the art deco tenements of the early years of the twentieth century, interspersed with Tudor-style villas.

Modern and utopian but, at the same time, hopelessly conflicted, India was represented by the deft internationalism of the country's veteran architect Charles Correa. Correa's towers presented an idea of a city that looked as if it should belong to all its citizens but which only its elite could afford.

As the road leaves the city centre, it winds through railway tracks and elevated roads from which you glimpse the huge illuminated cross above the Church of Christ the Saviour, past mosques and Hindu temples, past business parks that aspired to the condition of an edge city, as a chance to provide India's new business elite with a city that works.

The poor are never out of sight in Mumbai. They are in the city centre; they are clinging to the edges of the runway at the airport. They live on the fringes of the railways, on which scores of slum dwellers are killed every month.

Dharavi announces itself with abrupt suddenness; the road in is lined with densely packed shacks, their roofs piled high with the building materials that sustain their residents. At the entrance to the slum, where the stench of open drains is at its most extreme, past the electric pump workshop and the bicycle store, there is a shop selling gold, with a plate-glass window, white marble interior and big comfortable chairs covered in white vinyl for visitors to sit in. Despite the poverty outside the door, there were no security shutters, no visible armed guards, no security tags, no burglar alarms.

Life here stacks everything on top of everything else. The open kiln in which cotton waste was being burned to fire batches of clay pots might as well be in the backroom as the backyard of the slum dweller's home. There were people sitting on the backstep, keeping an eye on the stock, carrying huge loads on their heads, squeezing past you as they moved deeper and deeper into the slum.

This is what a place looks like when it has 300,000 people living packed into a single square kilometre. This is what it feels and tastes and smells like. It is, through the blue haze that hangs everywhere, like cigar smoke uncoiling in a Berlin bar after midnight, hauntingly but unsettlingly beautiful to look at. The repetitive earth-red forms of water jugs, destined for wholesale markets, merged into a single sculptural composition.

This is a slum that stands on land close to the city centre, surrounded by middle-class villas, with a net of railway lines that makes Mumbai India's city best served by public transport. It is land that could be, in fact is, enormously valuable. Beijing and Shanghai have similar issues to face. Slum clearance in India takes on an aspect familiar from the command and control activities of the Chinese authorities in their efforts to recast their cities. In India, too, the aim is to upgrade potentially valuable land by moving the densely packed slum dwellers to the city periphery. There are similar compensations: new accommodation to replace what they have lost; and similar problems. Maintenance costs will likely make it too expensive for many of the displaced to live in their new homes. They will be so far from their old neighbourhood that the victims of slum clearance will be cut off from everything that they depend on for survival.

The difference between China and India is that Britain's former colony countenances dissent. The potters were fighting the attempt to move them as part of a wider slum-clearance plan on the grounds that they have legal title to the land on which their shacks stand. They came here before independence and partition, and have British land grants that should in official eyes exclude their settlement from slum status. 'We have appealed to our Member of Parliament for help. We all voted for him, but he doesn't want to do anything,' they told us.

Within twenty-four hours I am back in London, where recycling is a lifestyle choice, not, as it is for Mumbai's ragpickers, a constant economic necessity. Like all Dharavi's Western visitors, I could step away from this world in which there is never an escape from the smoke and the dust, from the sheer press of people. But because there is running water at Dharavi for three hours a day, and there are second floors built on many of the houses, with gallows humour it can be described as a middle-class slum. For those who live there, education is not necessarily an escape route. The fourteen-year-old who translated his father's words into English told me that, when he has completed his education, his family would need him back in Dharavi as an extra pair of hands.

For Mumbai, with its six million slum dwellers, this is the way that the majority of its people live, though the slums occupy just 8 per cent of the city's area. For the shacks that are illegal and have no running water, or fixed latrines, it is worse. And for the hundreds of thousands who have nothing more than the pavement to live on, life is unimaginably harder than it is in Dharavi.

Mumbai takes justifiable pride in the way that its citizens pull together to cope with the flash floods that regularly leave areas of the city underwater, stranding motorists on the highways, cutting off large parts of the city. In the worst years, hundreds were drowned, but the slum dwellers took people in and fed them. They formed human chains to rescue drivers trapped in their cars on the highways that bisected their communities, they got blankets and emergency supplies distributed in a way that put First World

New Orleans to shame. But life, even on a good day, for many Mumbai dwellers looks pretty much like a permanent version of the Hurricane Katrina-torn city.

Life is certainly hard for the single men who come flooding in from the villages to escape the tyranny of the caste system, and to make the few rupees that they can send each month to feed families in the countryside, and who in Mumbai are the customers for some of the most extensive, and inventive, red-light districts in Asia. They sleep in beds rented by the hour. They wash in communal latrines. They rarely see their families.

India's slums are no place to become sentimental about the virtues of density and the kind of ecology that both come from extreme poverty. But in Suketu Mehta's fine portrait of Mumbai, *Maximum City*, you find an account of the place that they occupy in the wider city, and the kind of life that they make possible. It is not in their form that the squalor of a slum lies. The traditional graphic analysis of city fabric is the figure-ground drawing. In essence, this is a representation of the space between buildings. Put such a drawing of Dharavi side by side with one of Shinjuku, the Tokyo bar district with its narrow lanes and courtyards, and the black blocks sitting on white ground split apart by white cracks and pathways are apparently all but identical. Treated as an abstract pattern in this way, they might have been the product of a city planned by the pioneer of picturesque urbanism, Camillo Sitte. Yet one is a reflection of a world of plenty, the other of poverty. What were once Tokyo's slums have electricity, air conditioning and computers now. They have managed to decant some of their populations. The society that built them has been transformed by Japan's post-war affluence. Dharavi's plan is an abstraction of the realities of a precarious grip that often slips on what might be called the barest decencies of life. Is this a place and a way of life that proves the truth of the anger of Mike Davis in *Planet of Slums*?

A part of the conceptual apparatus that I have carried with me since I first began writing about cities is the comforting notion that, no matter how divided or deprived they are, cities are still, at one level, machines for turning the desperate into the not quite so desperate. They provide an essential first step in a process that will change their new inhabitants' lives for the better. Bit by bit they are places that can allow their inhabitants a range of possibilities that the villages from which so many came never can. But can one be quite so certain of that essentially positivist view, faced with the realities of life on the pavement?

That figure-ground comparison is a sanitized ana-lysis that hides the stench, and the fear. There are things about the lives of the slum dwellers that can seem comfort-ing or even heartening. Life in a Mumbai slum could be seen as being almost all right when compared with certain other possibilities. The slum is a place in which Jane Jacobs's street, protected under the constant gaze of hundreds of eyes, is an everyday reality. This is the polar opposite of the anomie and social isolation of a suburb in Phoenix. And it is nothing like a Brazilian *favela* or a Johannesburg shanty in terms of the daily level of violence. In terms of its ecological footprint, it does an amazingly good job, making up for the terrible mess that most of us westerners make of limiting our negative impact on the planet. That is why Dharavi has attracted the attention of such figures as the Prince of Wales. His visit to learn the virtues of grass-roots, bottom-up urbanism from the slums involved the construction, so it is alleged, of a special water closet should he have required one. And Kevin McCloud, British television's most successful architectural popularizer, returned from Dharavi overcome by what he had seen.

Focus on what slums can do well and it is possible to take comfort in the power of human ingenuity and collaboration to achieve remarkable things. Take Mumbai's armies of tiffin wallahs that each day pull off a feat of logistical complexity that would defeat the computer systems of a multinational, in order to collect the meals that are prepared across the city in domestic kitchens in every suburb and deliver them to the offices and workshops to feed hundreds of thousands of middle-class workers at their desks. With the intricate choreography of a ballet, covered colour-coded aluminium boxes of dahl, flat bread and cooked vegetables are picked up, taken on by stages to central collecting points, then distributed with extraordinary precision not just to the right building but to the right floor and the right person. Then, in the afternoon, the empties are collected up and returned by stages to the kitchens that will wash them and start filling them up again for the next day.

This is an object lesson in logistics that TNT could, and does, learn from, and it is all done without computers or bar codes. It is not just a convenience for the customers, it's a livelihood for the cooks and the delivery men. But, ingenious though it is, are its foot soldiers really accorded their due?

And, as *Maximum City*'s author so engagingly describes them, the strips of green overlooking the sea at the heart of Mumbai are the subject of a no less skilful and impressive industrially organized performance. During the day, these precious patches of turf are used by countless thousands of aspirant cricketing stars, practising, playing, perfecting in their neatly pressed cricket whites. No sooner than bad light stops play, armies of infinitely well-organized teams descend to transform the lawns into wedding pavilions, decked with glittering, mirror-studded representations of elephants, garlands of flowers, cushioned alcoves, displays of fireworks and wealth. By the following morning this instant city has disappeared, without damaging a blade of grass, and the cricket teams troop out again.

These are not just the social rituals that shape Mumbai life and make it so distinctive. They support an industry, and a supply chain; they provide incomes for all kinds of skilled craftsmen and training for a new generation.

There are other things to take from Mumbai, such as the sense that perhaps not all of our views of the world are as secure and fixed as we thought they were in the face of the daily realities of life in Dharavi: bribery, for example, and political corruption. Are they really such an unambiguously bad thing when they may function as the only way in which slum dwellers are going to get legal protection and running water, when it comes to election times and the need for local politicians to buy their votes?

And then there's democracy. India is not China. It believes in open and endless debate, a free press and the rule of law. These are things that are more secure in India's cities, than in its village heartland. And yet there are some things that China has achieved because it can avoid the tangles and twisted disputes of democracy.

And how comfortable can we be about this world where conventional crime is as reassuringly absent as it was in the small towns of the America of the 1950s, but where, as Suketu Mehta says, there is still the threat of the monster of intercommunal violence. 'And if that monster comes, it will be coming from the slums.'

Mumbai is part of the modern world even if there are aspects that look as if they have hardly changed in 200, or 1,000, years. There are terrible things being done in the name of modernization; slum clearance has resulted in some catastrophically grim housing blocks that would be unacceptable as prison accommodation in one of Stalin's gulags.

Greed and expediency is squandering the chance to make Mumbai a more liveable city, as its remarkable seafront setting demands. The old mills and the docks are looking for new uses now that they have become redundant. They could be used for communal good. So far, that is not happening. Mumbai is the Maximum City but, in India, a country whose Ghandian roots predispose it perhaps to a certain antipathy to cities, the big cities are still not free to shape their own futures: political power rests with the states and the central government in New Delhi.

Is there any real difference in our understanding, as supposedly objective observers, of the agonizing fault lines between the glittering, gold-plated, chaffeur-driven luxury of Mumbai's prosperous classes and the degradation all around it, and those who see it everyday and blithely ignore it?

Just because London is eleven hours in a Boeing away from Dharavi, and I can no longer see it or smell it, even as I feel the soot still in my hair from the potters' kilns, does not mean that I am any less a part of the same universe. Mumbai is, as one Metropolitan Police commander observed by his definition, one of the markers that define London's boundaries.

What if anything do I, and any of the other urbanists who come to see Dharavi in such numbers, have to offer such a city? Does our analysis really have any purpose? What kind of experts are we, when we belong to a society that is continually demolishing housing that far surpasses anything that Mumbai's slum dwellers could ever dream of, simply because nobody wants to live in it. Do we have any business being here at all? It's possible to take comfort from Suketu Mehta and his words that, if only because many of the next generation of Londoners are being born in Mumbai, it's important for this generation of Londoners to know as much about Mumbai as we can.

S
is
FOR
SOTTSASS

If modern design had its beginnings in Britain at around the time of the Industrial Revolution, with William Morris and Christopher Dresser, and was codified in Germany by the Bauhaus, it was Italy that redefined it in the 1960s. Modernity in the hands of the Germans was determined to be sober and austere. The Italians gave it a more seductive flavour, with tactile finishes, shiny plastic and saturated colours. We knew that Peter Behrens's electric kettle for AEG was important. So was the work that the Bauhaus team did. But it was bright-yellow adding machines in moulded plastic made by Olivetti and shiny lipstick-red plastic furniture made by Kartell that were the objects we actually wanted to own.

Italy was the last of the big European states to modernize itself and join the industrial economy, a process that was still taking place well into the 1950s. The transformation of the economy depended on a number of entrepreneurs, from Giovanni Agnelli to Adriano Olivetti, with dynastic, even nation-building, ambitions, and their work with an exceptional group of designers, including Giò Ponti, Achille Castiglioni, Vico Magistretti, Marco Zanuso, Joe Colombo, Ettore Sottsass and Mario Bellini. New factories and new technologies, coupled with what at first were low-wage costs, gave Italy the chance to find markets for its products, much in the way that China did half a century later. In 1972, New York's Museum of Modern Art marked the distinctive contribution of this group of designers with one of the most ambitious exhibitions on design that it had ever attempted, *Italy: the New Domestic Landscape*. It was the moment that saw Italy make the shift from fringe to centre stage. It was making the weather, as Japan was to do in fashion in the 1980s, and as we can confidently expect that China will do in the very near future.

In retrospect, though perhaps it did not look like it at the time, the two key designers represented in the MoMA exhibition were Mario Bellini and Ettore Sottsass. They both trained as architects, they both worked with their own studio within the Olivetti organization, and as independent consultants. While Bellini's work defined a certain glossy version of the Italian design language, Sottsass had a more complex position, working both within the industrial mainstream and outside it. Sottsass's long life reflected and illuminated the making of modern Italy.

He was born in Innsbruck in 1917, on the wrong side of the battlefront between Italy and Austro-Hungary that was to redefine both countries in the First World War. His parents spoke German as readily as Italian. Educated, like his father, as an architect, Sottsass worked with him and then in his own studio in Turin, before setting up in Milan to begin designing domestic objects, lighting, glassware and furniture destined to be made in tiny numbers.

As an architecture student at Turin Polytechnic, he was a busy set designer for the student theatre company, an accomplished artist, and a member of the Fascist student youth movement. He kept his membership card, along with almost everything that had served to measure his life through every phase. It is housed in a filing cabinet in the apartment in the Via Pontaccio in Milan where he once lived, but which he turned into his archive while he was still alive.

During the Second World War, Sottsass was a lieutenant in one of the elite Alpini regiments that Mussolini sent to invade Montenegro as part of Italian Fascism's inept attempt at imperialism. Sick leave kept him away from the barracks and stopped him from being dispatched to Albania to take part in the invasion of Greece along with the rest of the division. A few months later, he was even more fortunate to miss a troop train to the Soviet Union, to take part in a campaign from which very few Italians returned.

Sottsass began drawing when he was at primary school. He drew in exercise books and notepads, and on random scraps of paper. He drew on the back of recycled printer's offcuts, and on old stationery. He carefully filed all of them away, along with his exercise books, his passports, his photographic negatives, and even his father's school reports from his days as an architecture student in Vienna.

Sottsass's drawings from the war years in Montenegro reveal his overwhelming fascination with colour and tone. He used watercolours to record in exquisite detail the textile patterns that he saw in handwoven carpets. There is an even more remarkable drawing that he executed during the war in black ink, in which he patiently records in carefully chosen words the score or more of colours that were used in a peasant woman's shoulder bag. His diaries, written much later, record his experiences in that terrible war, with its futile bloodshed and its inevitable betrayals. Here were the Italians, invaders of the Adriatic coast opposite their own homes, many of whom found themselves siding with their own victims, against their former German allies. He describes the Serb and Montenegrin lovers he had, seemingly oblivious of what the consequences of being seen with an Italian officer in uniform would have been for them.

Half a century later, Sottsass was still preoccupied with colour in just as visceral a way as he had been as a young man in Montenegro during the war. James Irvine, an English designer who worked with him in his studio in Milan, remembers Sottsass describing a colour he wanted to use for a project as being like the colour of a dress that his first wife, Nanda Pivano, had worn for a party years before. Sottsass asked Irvine to go to her apartment to ask if she still had it, and if so to borrow it so they would have the reference they needed.

Interned in Yugoslavia by the Nazis when Italy capitulated, and faced with the choice of prison or collaboration, Sottsass joined the Monterosa division of the newly formed army of Mussolini's rump state, the Salò Republic. It was a decision that was to overshadow the early years of his post-war career. Long afterwards, he recalled being denounced as a fascist in the lobby of the Milan Triennale building, by another designer who had had the luxury of a less traumatic experience of war.

In the post-war period of Italian reconstruction, Sottsass found himself working on social housing projects, initially in partnership with his father, but also designing small domestic objects on his own. He moved from Turin to Milan, a city that was rapidly establishing itself as the Italian capital of design. Pivano was a literary translator, who gave her husband a perspective beyond the world of design, and Italy. She worked with Hemingway, and with the American beat poets, and much later translated Bret Easton Ellis. Sottsass photographed himself and Pivano in Cortina, in Venice and in Cuba. He went to New York with her, and for a brief period worked in the office of the leading American industrial designer George Nelson, giving Sottsass a transatlantic cachet that helped him secure the first of his commissions from Olivetti in 1959. Astonishingly, it was to give form to a mainframe computer, the first that Italy had ever built. With no previous experience of any kind in the world of data processing, Sottsass moved from working on decorative fruit baskets to a giant computer, which he sketched for the first time on the back of one of the layout sheets for *Industrial Design* magazine, the US publication he had worked on for Nelson. But it was perhaps no more of a leap than the shift taken by the Norwegian artist Jean Heiberg, who moved from learning to paint in Henri Matisse's studio to shaping the definitive form of the twentieth-century telephone for Siemens in Bakelite.

The Elea 9003 was the first, and almost the last, Italian-made mainframe computer. Mario Tchou led a team of engineers who devised an all-transistor machine for Olivetti that was intended to compete with the best American, British and French manufacturers. Sottsass's role was to give the Italian machine a distinctive identity. The name with which they christened the computer said a lot about how Olivetti saw itself. Elea was a Greek city state on the Italian mainland with its own school of pre-Socratic philosophy.

Sottsass made something of a breakthrough by conceiving of a computer as a collection of individually manageable parts, to be slotted together as needed to build the required capacity. He treated the computer as if it were a piece of portable furniture. It had no screen, and a capacity of less than one million alphanumeric characters, not enough to accommodate a complete Tolstoy novel. The Elea sprouted cables at high level rather than demanding a raised floor to conceal them as its competitors did. The arrangement made it easier to install, and it suggested that the Elea was an object rather than an integral part of the building in which it was housed.

'What should a computer look like?' Sottsass asked himself when he started work on the project. 'Not like a washing machine,' he wrote on a sheet of paper that is now preserved in the University of Parma's archives

The Elea was the size of a living room, but it was designed so that its operators, who tended it in air-conditioned sterility, were not made to feel as if they had been swallowed up by a machine. And to this sensitivity for the individual, Sottsass added a feeling for the emotional qualities of design. The keyboard for the Elea 9003 seemed to communicate that you were in touch with something important and momentous. This was the portal to the future, and Sottsass made it look the part by searching his subconscious memory for the visual clues suggested by sacred objects through the ages.

Equally significant as a landmark for Italian design was the Valentine, a portable typewriter designed by Sottsass with Perry King for Olivetti, an object that used a bright red plastic body, contrasted with two vivid splashes of orange on the twin ribbon spools, to make what had previously been understood as a mundane piece of business equipment into a personal possession. Everything about the design was asking us to understand Olivetti's products in a different way. Sottsass made the breakthrough of giving a product category associated with office routine a domestic, playful quality – through its moulded-plastic body and its vivid red colour scheme. The Valentine represented one end of Sottsass's approach. For more conventional office machines, such as the Tekne electric typewriter, he preferred a less expressive aesthetic vocabulary. 'When you have several hundred machines in an office, you don't want them all drawing attention to themselves as individual objects. They should work together in an architectural way,' he said.

For two decades, when it was still a family-run business, Sottsass remained closely associated with Olivetti and his studio-designed typewriters, office furniture, adding machines and accessories. They served to define the idea of modern office equipment for a while. But Olivetti was never able to fully adjust to the digital world; and this reluctance to adapt to change eventually destroyed the company. It had grown on the strength of the ability of its engineers to make mechanisms that drove adding machines, calculators and typewriters, skills that were rapidly becoming redundant.

Sottsass always maintained a presence beyond

Olivetti, in his own studio, exploring more personal ideas of what design might be. When, in the 1980s, the Memphis movement exploded the conventional idea of what passed for contemporary design, Sottsass, who was its guiding genius, had already qualified for his pension. But far from giving up, Sottsass was embarking on what turned out to be the most successful and creative period in a career that had already been exceptional.

A quarter of a century later, in 2007, Sottsass, a grave figure with the sad eyes of a bloodhound and a carefully tied pigtail, celebrated his ninetieth birthday, still active, still working with a studio in Milan, and still gently acerbic.

'Greatness' is the most overused word when it comes to describing success. But with Sottsass, it is nothing less than his due. It was Sottsass, and a few others, notably Achille Castiglioni, who showed how contemporary design could go beyond the utilitarian, or the cynically manipulative, and become a genuine form of cultural expression. But Sottsass was also able to make the most from contemporary production. It was this combination of a taste for poetry with the ability to work in the industrial mainstream that set Sottsass apart. He was ready to engage with the pragmatic everyday problems of working life in an office. But he was also absorbed by the expressive qualities of objects.

To move from the world of the Olivetti factory to the deliberately transgressive assault on conventional good taste of the Memphis movement that Sottsass founded might seem like a huge turnaround. But in fact there is a strong sense of consistency throughout Sottsass's output.

The spirit of his ceramics and glassware from the 1950s was still evident in the work coming out of the studio almost until the time of his death. And it is in this quality, as much as in Sottsass's ability to operate within an industrial world but not to be consumed by it, that his greatness lies. Sottsass saw too much of life to be deluded by the shiny optimism of a glossy surface. And yet he knew how to make something beautiful out of the sadness that comes of experience.

From the 1960s onward, Sottsass had a continuing interest in the counter-culture. He was in California at the time of Timothy Leary and Allen Ginsberg, and in India when the West began to look for alternatives to its own conventional materialistic values. He worked with Alessandro Mendini as art director for *Domus* magazine, steering it away from the complacency of Italian good taste, and together they crystallized this sensibility in design in the Studio Alchimia collections.

Later, Alchimia was eclipsed by Sottsass's own creation of the Memphis movement, with which he brought together a group of young Italians, principally Michele De Lucchi and Aldo Cibic, and an international group of postmodernists, including Michael Graves, Shiro Kuramata and Hans Hollein, in a move that made up in impact what it lacked in aesthetic consistency. Memphis looked like a fusion of high art with popular culture, a deliberate attack on conventional ideas of good taste. The name Memphis was variously explained by Sottsass as a reference to a Bob Dylan track, to Elvis, and to Ancient Egypt. Irony and a gently subversive approach to design was combined with a highly decorative approach to colour and pattern. The vivid colours and patterned laminates came partly from Sottsass's own imagination, and partly from his rediscovery of the innocence and optimism of the early days of Italian modernism in the 1950s, which by the 1980s was only to be found lingering in faded coffee bars in the suburbs of Milan. Even for those who were unmoved by its aesthetic vocabulary, Memphis had a conviction and excitement that could not be ignored.

Memphis was a joyous, un-bossy manifesto for design as an emotional expression. It was also an attempt to bite the hand that fed it by gently satirizing the manufacturing system. Design is, in the end, about making us want to buy more things, and Sottsass, at heart always deeply subversive, was highly ambivalent about that. He built a series of extraordinary houses, including one for his dealer, Ernest Mourmans, in Belgium. I remember a weekend there when I was editing *Domus*. Sottsass wanted to get it published. 'Why don't you ask Helmut Newton to take the photographs?' Newton was beyond the magazine's budget, but he came anyway, and the two men spent the time gently sparring for dominance in a house built around an aviary for Mourman's rare birds.

We live in a world which values the useless ahead of the useful, which celebrates art, untainted by the least hint of utility, above the ingenuity of design that is burdened by function, and creates a cultural hierarchy to match. It was perhaps the greatest achievement of Sottsass's long and remarkable career that he made this distinction irrelevant.

He was not interested in making objects that sell because they look pretty or seductive or precious. What he wanted to do was to find ways of giving everyday objects some sort of meaning. He wanted to show that they are not just banal clutter but are shaped by creative intelligence and an understanding both of how they are used and how they are made.

Throughout his life, Sottsass managed to pursue two parallel careers. At the same time that he was working on the mass-produced, trying to give some sense of dignity to the mundane, he was also creating ceramics and glass, and limited-edition furniture pieces that had the emotional intensity of art.

The design world has become fixated by youth, and by the merciless pursuit of the next big thing. But age had no effect on Sottsass. With the English designer Chris Redfern, he was still running an active office engaged in creative work right up until the end of his life in December 2007.

Sottsass, like his father, also called Ettore, saw himself first and foremost as an architect. Almost all Italian designers trained as architects in Sottsass's day, and too many of them want to go back to designing buildings, even though they are manifestly better off sticking to the scale of cutlery and chairs. Sottsass was an exception in that he was gifted as an architect, even though he remained outside the mainstream. He knew everybody, and worked everywhere. He built an apartment in the unlikely setting of the Albany in London for Jean Pigozzi, the celebrity photographer, collector and entrepreneur. At the other end of the scale he designed a golf resort for the People's Liberation Army in China.

Sottsass's generation cast a long shadow over Italy. Many of them lived and worked into their eighties. They left little room for the generation that followed them. Milan remained a global centre for design, but it was a city that depended more and more on designers from outside Italy.

T is for
Taste

Making sense of taste represents a certain challenge for intellectuals. They understand the subject in class terms. They understand, of course, that they themselves are a class, but mostly prefer not to talk directly about their personal tastes, and they certainly do not like the idea of being typecast by them.

German philosophers and sociologists and French structuralists, from Immanuel Kant to Pierre Bourdieu by way of Georg Simmel, have understood taste and fashion (which for them is almost the same thing) as the means by which class is signalled and defined. In the Kant-to-Simmel scheme of things, ruling classes set fashions and create tastes, while the rest of the pack struggle to catch up but can never quite manage it. By the time the socially disadvantaged get anywhere near them, the elite taste-setters have changed the rules and skipped ahead again.

Though his analysis of everyday objects, from toasters to ice-cream vans, made him a particularly acute observer of taste, Reyner Banham did not by and large discuss fashion directly. But in his choice of neckwear he maintained a running commentary on the changing significance of fashion. It was one of the ways in which he demonstrated his perception of himself as a truculent outsider. Despite his doctorate from the Courtauld Institute, he was keener to talk about his days as an engineering apprentice than he was about studying with Anthony Blunt and Nikolaus Pevsner. He started using Banham's middle name, rather than his first name, Peter, and he took to wearing a bolo tie.

In English usage, a bolo is a bootlace tie, a narrow strip of leather held in place by a silver clip, which had been popular with the Teddy-boy cult of working-class dandies in the 1950s. In America, the bolo tie is a manufactured tradition in the Western states with its roots going back no further than 1940. It is a form of neckwear more associated with conservative republican politicians than architectural historians. By adopting it, Banham was carefully signalling both that he knew a lot about the world of taste, and that he did not care to be part of it.

Adolf Loos had an equally detailed interest in fashion. He was a notably sharper dresser than Banham. He used the English tailoring that he had acquired on his way home from America as a way to mark himself out as subtly different from his Viennese rivals. 'Well dressed?' Loos once asked. 'Who doesn't want to be? What use is a brain if one doesn't have decent clothes to set it off?' He went so far as to design two of Vienna's more fashionable men's outfitters: for Knize, the store from whose Berlin branch Mies van der Rohe bought his suits, and for Goldman & Salatsch, among the earliest-known examples of what has become the near-universal phenomenon of the architect-designed fashion outlet.

Loos was an elegant controversialist in the columns that he wrote for two now-defunct Viennese newspapers: the *Neues Freie Presse* and the *Neues Wiener Tagblatt*. And perhaps his own interest in his personal appearance helped him come to a more nuanced understanding of taste than one that was simply class-based.

> What does it mean to be well dressed, it means
> to be correctly dressed; for fashion we use such
> words as beautiful, elegant, chic, smart or dashing.
> But that is not the main point at all. The point is to
> be dressed in such a manner as to attract as little
> attention as possible. A red tailcoat would attract
> attention worn in the ballroom, therefore a red
> tailcoat is not the modern style for the ballroom.
> A top hat would attract attention when ice-skating.
> Among the best people, to attract attention to
> oneself is considered vulgar. This principle, however,
> cannot be adhered to everywhere. With a coat that
> would be perfectly inconspicuous worn in Hyde
> Park, one would certainly attract attention to oneself
> in Peking or Zanzibar.

Curiously perhaps for an architect whose sophisticated and subtle building on the Michaelerplatz in Vienna attracted so much obloquy, Loos believed in discretion, in the architectural as well as the sartorial sense. Loos was not averse to attracting attention, if not to his clothes then to his intellectual position and to his architecture. He relished the controversy that his Michaelerplatz building attracted for its confrontational attitude to the Hapsburg imperial palace, and he relished even more the chance to defend it in public.

Writing from the vantage point of the start of the twentieth century, Georg Simmel appeared to see fashion as a fundamentally anti-democratic phenomenon, one that a genuinely egalitarian society would dispense with.

> Among the Kaffirs the class-system is very strongly developed, and as a result we find there a fairly rapid change of fashions, in spite of the fact that wearing-apparel and adornments are subject to certain legal restrictions. The Bushmen, on the other hand, who have developed no class-system, have no fashions whatsoever – no one has been able to discover among them any interest in changes in apparel and in finery.

There is not much evidence about the extent of field work carried out by Simmel to explore the dress sense of Southern Africa, or that of Florence, but that does not prevent him from concluding that:

> Occasionally these negative elements have consciously prevented the setting of a fashion even at the very heights of civilization. It is said that there was no ruling fashion in male attire in Florence about the year 1390 because everyone adopted a style of his own. Here the first element, the need of union, was absent; and without it, as we have seen, no fashion can arise. Conversely, the Venetian nobles are said to have set no fashion, for according to law they had to dress in black in order not to call the

attention of the lower classes to the smallness of their number. Here there were no fashions because the other element essential for their creation was lacking, a visible differentiation from the lower classes being purposely avoided.

The very character of fashion demands that it should be exercised at one time only by a portion of the given group, the great majority being merely on the road to adopting it. As soon as an example has been universally adopted, that is, as soon as anything that was originally done only by a few has really come to be practiced by all – as is the case in certain portions of our apparel and in various forms of social conduct – we no longer speak of fashion. As fashion spreads, it gradually goes to its doom.

The way in which the fortunes of Thomas Burberry, once a shopkeeper in Hampshire, then a Yorkshire-based garment maker, once associated with the British officer class and its trench coats, then with a working-class football cult, and lately a revitalized high-fashion label, has fluctuated over the last two decades might seem to prove Simmel right in that observation.

When British football teams started to play in Europe in the 1980s, their working-class followers, them-selves the products of a culture in which clothes were a passion, saw their Italian rivals wearing Lacoste and Fila. Their response was to acquire the same labels, or in a kind of nationalistic reflex to adopt the nearest domestic equivalent. And so, after the Mods and the Skinheads, was born the Casual tribe. And from out of the Casuals came even less fashionable working-class sub-cultures. They settled on Burberry, or what appeared to be Burberry, for their baseball caps, their scarves and their shorts. The beige/black-and-red Burberry pattern was pirated everywhere. Burberry had to address the problem, partly by dealing with counterfeiters and discounters, and partly by investing heavily in a more creative interpretation of Burberry's identity. Christopher Bailey made Burberryness a much subtler quality than the crass application of a pattern.

It's a process that doesn't entirely confirm Georg Simmel's views of fashion. Even at the height of Burberry's proletarian associations, there were self-identified fashion obsessives prepared to wear it precisely because they understood its complex significance. The signals transmitted by taste are not developed independently of each other. They migrate from one class to another in either direction. Some affluent middle-class schoolchildren in London will adopt the speech rhythms of the children of Caribbean migrants as a defence mechanism in order to blend in with their age group on the street, rather than the other way around. Others feel self-confident enough to believe they can maintain their status even while adopting the tastes and styles of other classes.

Taste is not always a process that describes the aspirations of the proletariat to look like their social superiors. Tattoos, tracksuits and an interest in football have all been adopted by the middle classes in the last three decades.

Ghetto youth in the US took to wearing their trousers very low, as a reflection of a look that most likely had its origins in the prisons where inmates' belts were removed. It made them look tough. It is a style that can now be seen to be adopted by public-school boys in Britain by way of Alexander McQueen.

Taste has been a continuing preoccupation of institutions that promote design. They do their best to present it not in terms of class, but suggest rather that it is a means of differentiating good from bad design. Henry Cole, the founder of the Victoria and Albert Museum, gathered together a display of what he considered to be 'bad design' as a demonstration of what not to do. Charles Dickens satirised it. And Cole had the grace to confess that is was the most popular exhibit in the museum. The Design Council in the 1950s was doing much the same as Cole, comparing the efficiency and simplicity of 'modern' fireplaces with the dust-gathering drawbacks of 'fussy' and 'decorative' alternatives. This did a lot to create the impression that Good Design was something inflicted on those that knew no better by their more enlightened social superiors, with predictably negative results. In the 1980s, 'Taste' was the subject of an exhibition at the Boilerhouse, the Design Museum's forerunner based at the V&A. In a text rendered in what looked like the director Stephen Bayley's own handwriting, it suggested that 'taste was one of the processes by which we make judgements about design'. Those items presented as in good taste were positioned on easels and plinths, others sat on top of dustbins.

As it turned out, the exhibition was in itself understood as making literal judgements about objects rather than being about the idea of taste. The architect Terry Farrell, on discovering that a model of his postmodern design for the TV-am HQ, with its playful egg-cup iconography, was being shown on a dustbin, snatched it back from the exhibition floor.

The first book that I wrote, *Cult Objects*, was a somewhat wide-eyed look at taste. 'Do you speak Burberry?' asked the cover, long before Christopher Bailey had turned the elderly raincoat manufacturer of the same name into the most successful fashion brand that Britain has ever had. What, it asked, makes a Morris Minor nicer to know than a Datsun? I never owned a Burberry, or drove a Golf, but looking back at *Cult Objects* now, I see that it was actually more confessional than analytical. It was an account not so much of taste as a phenomenon, but of my own tastes. It celebrated RayBans and Rolexes, Barbours, Filofaxes, the Omega Accutron (the first digital watch), Swiss Army penknives and Zippo cigarette lighters. I thought I was writing about the nature of objects; actually I was writing about a particular time, the early 1980s, and what they had done to me.

It's a collection of objects, and indeed a book, that conforms precisely to the process so perceptively and wittily charted by James Laver in 1937 in *Taste and Fashion*. Laver was a curator in the department of prints and drawings at the Victoria and Albert Museum who pursued a successful parallel career as a playwright. He had a much lighter touch than Simmel. Laver drew attention to the way that our attitudes change as we become more familiar with fashions.

Fashions too far ahead of their time are regarded as unacceptably transgressive, while fashion that is not past its time enough is regarded with scorn rather than outrage. But past this stage, the formerly transgressive, subsequently the dowdy, will come to be considered beautiful. Laver reckoned that it took ten years for the indecent to move through the shameless and the outré stages to become smart. One year later it would be considered dowdy, in ten years hideous. After the passing of a further century it would have become in turn ridiculous, amusing, quaint, charming and romantic.

Laver's premise still holds good, even if the time-scale that he envisaged has accelerated and telescoped.

U is for **UTZON**

I never met Jørn Utzon, but I did see him speak once. It was 1978. He was sixty years old, a slender, elegant and very tall man, and had come to London to collect the Royal Gold Medal for Architecture. In his speech, he suggested that if you truly wish to honour an architect, you commission him to design a building, you do not just give him a medal.

It took another ten years for me to actually see Sydney Opera House, the design that made him famous and which transformed the world's view not just of Sydney but of Australia too. Utzon never saw it completed. He left the country in 1966, nine years after winning the competition to build what turned out to be one of just a handful of genuinely iconic works of twentieth-century architecture, when the opera house's superstructure was only just beginning to take shape. Utzon did not go back.

He resigned from the project after a series of bitter rows with local politicians that were not primarily about money, though it was obviously an issue. As in the case of the Scottish Parliament in Edinburgh, politicians were accused of deliberately underestimating costs to get the project started by putting up a misleadingly optimistic budget, then squeezing the design team. Ultimately the conflict was about power. The real questions were: was this going to be an architect's building, or was it going to be a monument to New South Wales's minister for public works at the time? Or was it, as in fact happened, something for the city and for Australia?

At the same time, there were serious technical questions about the building that provoked the rupture. Before desktop computing had eliminated almost every limit that constricted structural engineering, Utzon was asking for a lot in trying to get his complex shells built in load-bearing concrete, while accommodating all that the brief called for. He had to cram a great deal into a restricted space; so much that the multiple auditoriums were never going to provide enough seats for a financially viable opera house.

And there was also the question of Utzon's own frame of mind. He began the project with the best advice that he could get, working with the enormously influential engineer Ove Arup. The relationship between the two Danes, warm at first, turned toxic. After Arup's death, the English critic Peter Murray was given access to his private papers. They suggest that the engineer repeatedly offered Utzon workable technical solutions, but because they did not reflect the purity of the architect's vision they were ignored. Throughout a particularly troubled period, Utzon failed even to acknowledge Arup's letters. Utzon seemed paralysed by the complexities facing him, quite unable to offer a clear way ahead. The fact that Arup refused to walk away from the project when Utzon resigned triggered a bitter and lasting break between them. To Utzon, Arup was being disloyal. For Arup, the responsibility was to the client to finish the job. Utzon lost the political game, and was finessed into resigning without ever fully understanding that he was taking an irrevocable step. He thought his resignation was a threat that he would never be expected to have to act on. When his bluff was called, Utzon left Australia permanently. He was replaced by a panel of local architects, who went on to complete the building. One of them had actually signed a petition that circulated in the New South Wales government architect's office pledging not to work on the project if Utzon was sacked.

For an architect there can be no fate worse than seeing a project that should have been the crowning achievement of his career taken away from him by what he saw as a cabal of uncomprehending philistines. It was not a question of budget overruns that allowed the politicians to oust Utzon. In fact the worst of these came long after Utzon had left Australia. What did for him in the end was a change of party in the New South Wales state government that coincided with disagreements – ostensibly about the cost and character of the proposed plywood-lined interior – fought out in the claustrophobically small world of local government in Sydney. And it left Utzon humiliatingly out of pocket, the victim of a punitive double-taxation regime, in debt to a combination of the Australian and the Danish tax authorities.

Utzon maintained a dignified silence about his treatment by Sydney. When the Queen finally opened the opera house in 1973, Utzon was invited, but was unavoidably elsewhere. When the Royal Australian Institute of Architects awarded him its gold medal, Utzon accepted, but he stayed away from the ceremony. When Utzon was asked to take part in designing a resort in Queensland, he agreed to take on the commission, but sent his two architect sons, Jan and Kim, to deal with the client instead. Sydney tried to make amends by awarding him the freedom of the city in 1998, but the Lord Mayor had to take the keys to Denmark to present them to him. For the building's twenty-fifth birthday that year, Utzon's daughter, Lin, went to Sydney and joined the state premier in launching the Utzon Foundation, a trust to award a £37,000 biennial prize for outstanding achievement in the arts – but Jørn Utzon himself never went back.

After Utzon's eightieth birthday, there was something of a reconciliation with Australia. A decision was taken to remodel the interiors of the opera house as much in the manner that Utzon had intended as possible. And his son Jan took part in the planning process in an attempt to deal with the acoustic problems of the auditorium and the difficulties caused by a critical lack of space behind the scenes. It was not an easy task. Utzon's grandson Jeppe, also an architect, has questioned whether it was in fact possible at this stage to fully realize the original vision.

Utzon survived the trauma of Sydney. He was able to design other important buildings, at least two of which – the Bagsvaerd Church in his native Denmark (1968–76), and the Kuwait National Assembly Building (designed from 1971 onwards, completed 1983 and rebuilt 1993) – must be counted masterpieces. Like Sydney, they seemed to stand outside the mainstream of twentieth-century modernism. All three have a sculptural purity that makes them truly compelling works of architecture. The house that Utzon built himself in Mallorca, overlooking the Mediterranean, in which he spent many years, was a domestically scaled summation of Utzon's architectural ideas, full of tactile qualities and reminders of architecture's roots in the fundamentals of light playing on stone.

Yet for an architect of Utzon's special talent, it was a modest output for such an extended career. And the Kuwait building, like Sydney, was fatally compromised. It was the unloved child of a short-lived move towards democratic government in Kuwait, abandoned by the ruling family, shelled by the Iraqis, and blandly restored by the American architects HOK after the Gulf War.

Could it have been any different for Utzon? On one level, there is a temptation to think that had the opera house gone more smoothly, then it could have opened the way to a career that might even have matched that of one of the twentieth-century's acknowledged architectural giants, Louis Kahn perhaps, or even Le Corbusier.

If Utzon had managed a sustained run of work exploring the essential themes that underpinned his greatest successes, he could genuinely have transformed the architectural landscape. But he didn't, and perhaps he never could have done. Utzon was profoundly out of sympathy with the idea that architecture could be practised as a corporate business, taking on multiple projects around the world. When Utzon won the opera house competition, he turned down an offer to design Louisiana, an art gallery just outside Copenhagen. It would have been the perfect commission, yet Utzon rejected it because he did not want to risk losing concentration on the opera house. There was something in Utzon's psychological make-up that seemed to make him find the idea of professional success too troubling to get to grips with. Certainly, Utzon's personal architectural language was a curious mix of influences and sources, from the sweeping curves of the yachts that his father specialized in designing to Mexico's man-made landscape of Monte Albán and other great pre-Colombian sites, from the medieval castles of the old Denmark of his homeland to the work of the European modern masters.

But Sydney Opera House is a truly singular building, one that changed Utzon's life, and probably the course of Australian history as well. The competition to design it was launched in 1956, the year that Melbourne, Sydney's great rival, was hosting the Olympics, at a time when Melbourne was still the unchallenged central focus of urban Australia. Melbourne was bigger, more famous, richer and more successful than its northern rival.

The opera house, financed by a specially constituted state lottery, managed to change all that. It was the landmark that signalled the start of a huge turnaround in perceptions of Australia in general and Sydney in particular. It was the project that more than any other allowed Australia to ditch the 'cultural cringe'. Architecturally that cringe is monumentalized in the National Museum of Australia in Canberra where, in a bitter architectural reference to Sydney, the designers incorporated a fragment of the opera house in the main entrance hall. According to the museum's architect: 'It's not the bit by Utzon, it's a fragment of the glass curtain that was designed after he had gone, to show how wrong Australia can get things.'

The opera house was the building that made Sydney Harbour escape from a tangle of industrial squalor and tram lines to become one of the greatest waterfront cities in the world. By the time of the 2000 Sydney Olympics, for-ty-four years after those held in Melbourne, the opera house was a familiar but still striking image in the television cover-age broadcast round the world. And it was Utzon who had made it possible.

Nothing quite like the Sydney Opera House design had been seen before. Utzon had, however, entered a compe-tition a decade earlier to design a replacement for London's Crystal Palace, and even though he was unsuccessful his submission did show that he offered the city the chance to build something just as extraordinary as the opera house. It was personal, sculptural and apparently quite outside the mainstream of architectural development at the time. The only work that seemed to relate to it was the soaring, sweep-ing concrete roofs designed by Eero Saarinen, one of the judges for the opera house competition. Saarinen adopted a similar approach to Utzon's for the TWA Terminal at New York's JFK airport.

The opera house belonged to an alternative pattern of modernity. And had Utzon had a different temperament, it might have been so much more than a historical one-off. But he didn't. That has not stopped the growth of an Utzon cult in Australia and beyond; a cult which presents him as a wronged genius. It's a cult that has played into the mania of the first years of the twenty-first century for icon build-ing, one that has thankfully subsided somewhat from its peak at the creation of Frank Gehry's Guggenheim building in Bilbao. Not uncoincidentally, Utzon was awarded the Pritzker Prize in 2003, a tribute from a jury that included

Frank Gehry. And, perhaps equally revealingly, Utzon, who was born in Copenhagen and studied architecture at the city's Royal Academy of Fine Arts, worked in the Helsinki office of Alvar Aalto, another champion of non-standard building types and curves.

Sydney and Bilbao seem to suggest a certain superficial similarity. Both are buildings whose inventiveness have served to make them the identifying landmark for their respective cities. They have both become a kind of urban logo. But in fact they represent very different sensibilities. Utzon's opera house is the product of a highly controlled and controlling approach to architecture, shaped by the belief that perfection is a possible option for design. Gehry's architecture is also capable of producing the most memorable and recognizable of forms and shapes. But Gehry is from California, not from Scandinavia, and his work is based on the acceptance of the random and the accidental. If Utzon could have learned how to do that, he would never have had to leave Australia.

V IS

FOR

VIENNA

What is now called the University of the Applied Arts was established in Vienna in 1867. It occupies a brick-and-terracotta palazzo built for the purpose on the city's Ringstrasse, not far from Otto Wagner's masterpiece, the Post Office Savings Bank, the Sparkasse, which was constructed forty years later. The bank, with its rooftop maidens cast from aluminium, garlands held high over their heads, its banking hall with milky glass-vaulted ceiling, and its distinctive chairs, their legs protected by chaste metal socks, was modernism's first monument. It is just across the street from the university, which used to be known as the Kunst-gewerbeschule. It was originally set up to train the artisans needed for the Austro-Hungarian economy, for manufacturers by appointment to what was known as *K. & K.*, or *Kaiserlich und Königlich*, the Imperial and Royal court of Vienna. Or, as the Viennese wits scatologically called it, *Kakania*. It became the place that helped to shape the intellectual climate which made the design of the bank possible.

The Kunstgewerbeschule was renamed the Hochschule für Angewandte Kunst, before turning into a university. When I arrived in 1993 as a guest professor, if you looked at its vaulted ceilings through half-closed eyes it was possible to believe that there was still a Hapsburg on the throne. Every term began with a dauntingly carnivorous professorial breakfast of cold meat, beer and pretzels. Ron Arad and I, as the two visitors from London, would find ourselves assaulted by cries of 'Grüss Gott!', or 'God greet you!' If only we had known enough to use the sardonic response of the protestant German north: 'Hoffentlich nicht so bald,' which is to say, 'Hopefully not too soon.'

Your salary could, if you asked, be paid into a numbered bank account that the tax authorities would never find. The bank card, if you chose a less surreptitious account, had a hologram of Beethoven, cupping his ear. Travelling expenses were a bit of an issue. The empire might just as well still have been there, because the Hochschule's accounts department had yet to acknowledge air travel as a possibility. The school would refund the cost of first-class train travel from London to Vienna, but not an economy air ticket.

But an even more striking insight into the Austrian way of doing things was provided by the letter in every professorial pigeonhole, addressed to us individually from an American law firm, about the action they were bringing against the current rector of the school who, it was claimed, had wrongly attributed a number of works to Joseph Beuys.

This was Vienna, the city in which Kurt Waldheim had occupied the presidential palace and denied that he had ever been a Nazi, despite photographic evidence to the contrary. The rector admitted nothing, never apologized, and did not resign.

Vienna was a complicated place to work in. It's the city in which my grandmother's brother went to study law as a Montenegrin subject of the Austro-Hungarian empire back in the last years of the nineteenth century. When I got there, the professorship made me a member of the Grüss Gotting class. But in the four years I spent commuting back and forth from London, I never felt comfortable in its embrace. The Vienna whose language I shared was the city of the underclass of taxi drivers and waiters from the Balkans, the migrants who spoke the Serbian or the Croatian that I could understand much more easily than the German of the surface world.

But Vienna also seemed a place in which it was important to spend some time. This was the city that around the start of the twentieth century produced Josef Hoffmann – one of the key figures in the Hochschule's history, and the Wiener Werkstätte – as well as Adolf Loos. It was the city that Otto Wagner reshaped into a modern metropolis. He designed its infrastructure, canalized its rivers and built its underground railway system, leaving a number of exquisite stations that were to set a model which Paris and London followed in their own idiom. Wagner gave form to new institutions, from newspapers to banks, and to new technologies, and he did it with radical new forms and radical new materials.

I had the idea for a while that it was possible to get closer to the heart of modernity as it applied to design in Vienna than anywhere else. It was here, not at the Bauhaus's outposts in Weimar or Dessau, that modernity as a militant aesthetic ideology was born. Barcelona and Glasgow produced particularly florid manifestations of art nouveau that had as much to do with nationalism as modernism. In Vienna modernity in its earliest incarnation achieved its fully developed realization. Much of it is still there, outwardly intact. Vienna was a metropolis then, not an outpost. You can still order a Martini in Loos's American Bar and, around the corner, find the enormous Lobmeyr showroom that sells the glasses Loos and Hoffmann designed for the company in 1910. You can still see the Steinhof, the vast city of the sick and the mentally ill that Otto Wagner planned, crowned by the extraordinary church he designed to console its inmates. You can visit the house that Ludwig Wittgenstein built for his sister. The implacable ruthlessness of its proportional logic is still clear, even if its interiors are cluttered with the evidence of its recent reincarnation as the Bulgarian Cultural Centre. And there are streets in which you can feel as though you are on the set of *The Third Man*.

I arrived in Vienna embracing the received wisdom that modernity was a representation of the idea of progress. What I had not understood then was that the radical qualities of Otto Wagner's work had some far from progressive associations in Vienna's recent history. Wagner got his chance to build from Karl Lueger, a mayor whose appointment Franz Josef I refused to confirm, despite his victory at the polls in three separate elections. The emperor believed that Lueger and the anti-Semitic policies of his Christian Social movement would damage the city and the empire.

Lueger finally took control of Vienna in 1897, and set about a modernizing agenda to address a population explosion. Municipal gas, water and electricity systems were introduced or upgraded. Vienna developed a social welfare policy and began beautifying its parks and civic spaces. It was Lueger, when he finally took office, who was behind the Post Office Savings Bank, and the Metro stations that Wagner built.

This was the same moment in time that Freud and Jung developed a new understanding of the mind, that Gustav Mahler was at the height of his powers, and when Klimt was active. Positivist readings of history attempt to associate creative leaps in all these fields with the idea of economic and social progress. But this flowering of Viennese culture took place in the last days of an imperial system that was on the edge of destruction. It was not long before Vienna's Jewish citizens, on whom so many of these achievements depended, would have to flee their homes or perish.

In Vienna modernity was in fact associated more with the end of a society than with the beginning of a new one. Vienna at the end of the twentieth century was a city that felt maimed by the loss of the group which had done so much to create its intellectual and creative life. Cultural life in the void they left had been defined by the darkness of the Actionists – artists such as Hermann Nitsch, who worked with blood and flesh in a sustained howl of anguish, and Wolf Prix's equally violent and troubled architecture. The remains of the first modernity may still physically be present. But the people who had called it into being are gone.

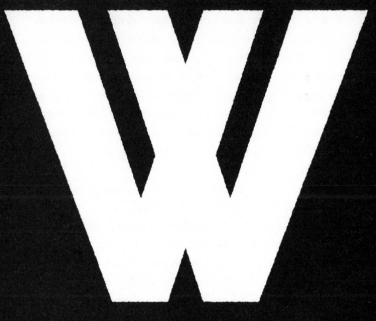

IS FOR WAR

The Design Museum acquired an AK-47, the notorious assault rifle developed in 1947 in the Soviet Union, for its permanent collection in 2012. It was a decision that attracted some hostile questions. Weapons do not form part of most museum design collections; a reflection perhaps of the continuing persistence of the concept of good and bad design. An assault rifle – that is, one designed to be used in combat at close quarters, with people trying to kill each other a maximum of 400 metres apart – may be robust, reliable, easy and economical to mass-produce. It may, by those definitions, represent functionalism of a high order. It is an object that has shaped history, which has appeared on the national flag of Mozambique, and represented considerable technical innovation. And there are not so many other industrially made objects that have been in continuous production since 1947. Evil or not, it's hard to deny that the AK-47 is a piece of successful design.

But if collections of design are intended to show examples of good design – as indeed most of them, at least originally, were – weapons of any description are excluded. Because of its lethal purpose, a brilliantly designed weapon cannot be described as 'good'. So there are no assault rifles in the collection of the Museum of Modern Art, in the Museum für Angewandte Kunst in Vienna, or in the Neue Sammlung in Munich. Exceptions are made for other objects that have military purposes: the Jeep, for example, and the helicopter. But guns are taboo, despite the early part that they played in the development of standardization, mass production and modular construction.

Weapons are not to be glorified, or made a fetish

of, but they can offer important insights into other objects. That is why the Design Museum acquired its AK-47. The weapon represents an argument about the nature of objects. To be significant, design does not have to be 'good' design in either of its two most commonly understood meanings: neither morally virtuous, nor fit for purpose.

The Spitfire is a rather less contentious piece of design, most likely because of its decisive role in the defence of democratic Britain against totalitarian aggression. It combined multiple technical innovations with a refined beauty in the way its wings were integrated with the body of the aircraft, making it immediately recognizable.

The paradox that any analysis of design has to deal with is that so many key developments in technology and design have depended on the accelerated investment that war brings with it. The development of the jet engine was brought forward by the Second World War. The fact that there is any kind of prophylactic against malaria is an outcome of the wars that Britain and America fought in the mosquito-infested jungles of South East Asia.

The internet is now a civilian system based on the planning for distributed military communications systems that could survive atomic warfare. Three-dimensional printing, or additive manufacturing, had some of its earliest deployment in the US navy, to provide emergency spare parts at sea for aircraft carriers.

At the end of his long life, Mikhail Kalashnikov himself began to feel a sense of guilt and doubt about the malign impact of his design. His priest suggested to him that there was no shame in creating a weapon to defend the motherland. What he did not say was that there is no clear division between military and non-military development. That is why the AK-47 can be read as a highly significant piece of industrial design, with multiple meanings.

is for

XEROX

Two of the world's better-known brands, both of them involved in one way or another with making or manipulating images, have their roots in the same obscure city in upstate New York. Both have a five-letter name. In each case, it begins and ends with the same letter. They have been enormously successful, and have had as important a part to play in the creation of some of the key artefacts in the history of industrial design as any designer. Their histories have many parallels, but it is the differences between them that are more revealing. One survived, the other didn't. It is the continuing longevity of some manufacturers that says as much about the rise and fall of others.

Neither Kodak nor Xerox, its slightly younger neighbour, still have the name that they were born with. Kodak was once called the Eastman Dry Plate Company; a name that came from its founder, George Eastman. Xerox began life fifteen years later in 1906 as the Haloid Photographic Company. Both companies spent their defining years in upstate New York, in Rochester, a city of less than 250,000 people that could be seen as the definitive location of the back of beyond. They have left behind the two dominant structures on Rochester's skyline. Kodak's Gothic skyscraper is the more imposing and distinctive of the two, and reflects the earlier peak in its fortunes. Xerox built its anaemic glass box much later, in the 1960s, and moved out of the state almost immediately afterwards.

Kodak, which eventually took to calling itself Eastman Kodak, is little more than a flickering afterglow of the swaggering corporate giant that it once was. Its ubiquitous yellow boxes and its envelopes, with their contrasting red logo designed to draw attention to its products, are fading from memory. After seeking protection from its creditors, its best asset now is its patent armoury. It offers its owners the chance to challenge more successful companies for alleged infringements of its intellectual property. This is more valuable than its ability to make or sell things; another manifestation of capitalism in its decadent phase, like the stock market trades that no longer use capital to invest in productive industry, but simply deploy it to bet against the fluctuations of the market index.

Kodak was once among the most successful and innovative businesses in the world, employing 140,000 people. It had a virtual monopoly on the manufacture and processing of film for decades, until Fuji from Japan was finally able to mount a serious challenge. When George Eastman introduced the first Kodak camera in 1900, he was setting a path that Steve Jobs and Apple would one day follow. He transformed the loading and exposure of film from a chemical experiment into a simple purchase. He invented photography for the masses. Eastman took processing exposed film, and printing of the result, out of the hands photographer. He turned photography from a special interest into a universal pastime, and Kodak was able to charge for both the service and the products it offered. 'Pull the cord, turn the key, press the button, and for another 100 pictures, we do the rest' was the sales pitch in the early days.

Kodak made its mark on hardware too by designing and manufacturing its own cameras. The box Brownie was one of the most characteristic objects of its time, going through successive facelifts to culminate in a die-cast, vaguely art deco form designed by Walter Dorwin Teague. Much later came the Instamatic, launched in 1963, with its compact rectangular format, its brushed metal and chrome case, and its cassette-format film for idiot-proof ease of loading. In car-styling terms, it was the shift away from tail fins, or from the Morris Minor, to the modernity of the Mini, which took place at exactly the same time.

I was too young to drive a car, but I was thrilled to get an Instamatic as a Christmas present the year that it was launched in Britain. It was the first self-consciously modern object that I had ever touched. For a while, it was perhaps the only such possession in a house in which, hot water for the bath came from an Ascot gas heater, and which had no refrigerator. It was joined a few years later by the mustard-yellow streamlined 1960s version of the Anglepoise desk lamp with its sculpted shade. Hanging from the spring-loaded arm was a little black-and-white triangle that carried the words 'Selected for the Design Centre'. I bought it myself with the money I got as a reward for passing all eight of my O levels. And shortly afterwards I acquired a Sony cassette tape player. It had a brushed aluminium body, with a racy-looking chamfered edge for the piano-key controls, and a businesslike needle displaying what might just as well have been frequency response as battery life. I knew it was important because all the other cassette players had plastic bodies and looked years behind in styling terms. All three objects were important to me, but it was Kodak's Instamatic that really made me understand what an object might be trying to say about itself.

Kodak was always ahead of the pack in those days, just as it had been a decade earlier when my two older brothers came back from America with samples of a phenomenon still entirely unknown in Britain: colour prints. When the first Instamatic 100 came out Sony was still at the bargain-basement stage; turning out cheesy lookalikes of original American and German products. Samsung was more interested in its insurance business than in making consumer electronics, as South Koreans patched up their country from the devastating war that had ended barely a decade earlier.

Despite the seductive nature of the Instamatic, the real money in photography for Kodak was in the processing, not the hardware. In the same way Gillette sells blades and gives its razors away, and mobile phone companies subsidize phones in order to sign up subscribers for its premium tariffs. The cameras may have looked different, and been slightly easier to use, but there was no substantial technological shift or change in the business model in seventy years.

Kodak moved beyond print film into colour transparencies, and then came up with a spin-off brand, Kodachrome. For a while it seemed like the definitive view of modernity, before it too was overtaken by the great digital revolution. Slide film opened up a new way of talking to groups of people that went a few steps beyond the magic-lantern lecture of the early days of the twentieth century. The invention of the carousel slide projector allowed for multi-screen projections of the kind pioneered by Charles and Ray Eames, and which foreshadowed PowerPoint as the presentational tool of choice. I have boxes and boxes of slides, mounted in little cardboard sleeves, each carrying the Kodak logo and a date stamp recording the month and year that they were processed: I have not looked at them in a quarter of a century. They belong to a world seemingly as far distant as gas lamps and pianola rolls and all the other countless victims of the mass extinctions of once promising technologies that never reached their full potential before the end of the analogue age.

At its peak, in 1997, just before sales of film fell off a cliff, the company was valued at $30 billion. Fifteen years later, Kodak was bankrupt. The company had seen digital photography coming. It built Apple's QuickTake, launched in 1994, which was one of the first digital cameras aimed at a general audience, even if the price when it first went on sale was $750. But when images are stored as random collections of pixels, rather than on silver and paper, the technical expertise in chemistry and the distribution system it had built up over decades were no longer relevant. There was very little that Kodak could offer Apple. Once digital photography took firm hold, Kodak's income collapsed, threatening the company's survival.

The end was shockingly rapid. In 2000, the US bought 950 million rolls of film, most of it from Kodak. Ten years later, the total was less than 100 million. Analogue camera sales, which peaked in 2000 at twenty million, are now too small to be a visible segment of the market. It had taken just seven years for digital cameras to go from zero to overtake analogue camera sales in 2003. To judge by its share price at the end of 2011 Kodak was worth just $265 million. At the beginning of 2012 its brand was described as worthless.

Despite having its roots in a closely related product category, Xerox has done much better over the years. It has maintained its grip by understanding what customers will pay for, not by focusing on the things that it already knows how to do. The technology of copying has played a crucial part in the evolution of industrial design. It was Raymond Loewy's restyling of the Gestetner duplicator that brought the seductive qualities of consumer objects to business machines for perhaps the first time. Having one in the 1930s was as much the mark of an ambitious company wanting to establish its forward-looking business as a citrus-coloured iMac was in the 1990s. The Xerox Corporation went further than simply re-skinning an object; it reinvented the process of copying.

In its days as Haloid, Xerox had grown slowly, specializing in photographic papers. Its entry into the copying market was to have an enormous impact on the way that offices work. Copying, filing and storing paper is the underpinning of every bureaucracy in the world: the source of the paper trail. Xerox came to dominate it gradually. Initially it secured the rights to the Photostat process, essentially a means of photographing documents, which it licensed to Kodak. Then Chester Carlson, an inventor, scientist and patent lawyer who had been hawking his idea of a copying system to all-comers, came to Haloid. It took the best part of twenty years' work to bring it to the market, but when the Xerox 914 was launched in 1959 it was a massive success. Previous copying methods used messy ink. The Xerox systems worked with electrically charged dry powder. They made modern bureaucracy possible, but they also provided a generation of radical students with the means to put across their political message, which is why the dictatorships in Latin America and the Warsaw Pact were so anxious to keep them under lock and key.

When the Xerox 914 turned into a runaway success the Haloid Company renamed itself after its new product, just as Eastman had done. After the copier, Xerox targeted the duplicating process: not quite as fast as printing, but cheaper and simpler. Now it is promoting itself as a publisher of technical manuals, and as a manager of call centres, rather than simply a supplier of photocopying machines. One day paper may no longer be involved, but Xerox plans to continue finding ways of doing the things that photocopying once did for its customers, whatever the media or the means.

Kodak did have products aimed at business, but most of its effort concentrated on the domestic consumer; Xerox dominated the workplace. One looked disaster in the eye and then blinked, the other moved its headquarters to a rather more welcoming environment and survived. Xerox moved its HQ to Connecticut, and set up a research centre at Palo Alto in California, which helped give it the perspective it needed to see beyond the things it already knew about making photocopiers, and to understand what new technologies might mean for them. Kodak went from unquestioned world leadership to oblivion as it found it impossible to adjust to the impact of digitalization. It was a business that made its money selling film, and it could not adjust quickly enough when nobody wanted to buy any.

Xerox had always invested heavily in research. It was working out how to connect its copying machines with copper telephone lines in the early 1960s. It focused not on copying but on information itself; on storing and transmitting it. Xerox's scientists put all the elements of the forerunner of the personal computer together, with a QWERTY keyboard, a cathode ray screen, the graphic user interface and the first usable mouse. Xerox was shrewd enough to understand that it had to see itself as a business rooted not in any one technology. It gave a number of remarkably gifted researchers the resources to pursue a whole range of far-sighted technologies, many of which it never made use of itself. In Walter Isaacson's biography of Steve Jobs, he recounts a confrontation between Jobs and Bill Gates in the 1980s when Microsoft launched Windows. For Jobs, the Windows click-and-point icons and mouse graphic user interface were nothing less than theft. 'You are ripping us off. I trusted you, and now you're stealing from us.' Gates kept his temper. 'Well, Steve, I think there's more than one way of looking at it. I think it's more like we both had this rich neighbour named Xerox, and I broke into his house to steal the TV set, and found out that you had already stolen it'.

The longevity and sheer ubiquity of Kodak and Xerox, both names which have involved a certain amount of artifice, demonstrate that not all fabricated identities are manipulative or pretentious.

Xerox, though it might sound like a random generation of vowels and consonants, actually has a plausible source. It comes from the Greek words for 'dry', *xeros*, and for 'writing', *graphia*, put together by Chester Carlson to name his process Xeroxography.

Kodak is a name that has its origins in George Eastman's passion for the letter k. It was the first letter of his mother's name. But as he wrote to the British patent office in 1888 when he filed the name Kodak, 'This is not a foreign name, or a word. It was constructed by me, to serve a definitive purpose. It has the following merits. It is short. It is not capable of mispronunciation. It does not resemble anything else in the art.'

Branding has been the snake oil of the post-industrial world. A complex network of businesses has been built on the idea of the value of the intangible, of a name, an identity, of an idea of what a business might be. Yet as Kodak and Xerox demonstrate so clearly, it is not the image of either name that is valuable, it is what it is able, somewhat more tangibly, to offer.

is for

You

Tube

Chad Hurley brought the skills that he had acquired as an undergraduate in the print-making class at Indiana University Pennsylvania in Philadelphia to his first major design. It was completed just a few months after he graduated in 1999. He drew a not-especially inspiring logo for a new online finance business, known as PayPal. He used an italic sans serif font rendered in blue on white. As a design student, he had been fascinated by the potential of the new hypertext HTML computer language and taught himself to write code. He did classes in art and technology, and in building three-dimensional models for the web. They gave him the creative equipment to become a very successful example of a new version of designer, one who dealt in the non-physical world as much as the physical one. Jonathan Ive, born ten years before Hurley, is old enough to have approached design from a physical point of view and was able to integrate it with the digital world. Hurley was born too late to have a professional engagement with the analogue. His first really significant piece of work wasn't PayPal's logo but its payment button, a one-click way of transferring money for safe keeping until the vendor's goods had reached the purchaser. It turned out to be particularly useful for acquiring eBay products. It was a device that worked so well in making eBay a success that less than three years after Hurley had designed it, eBay bought the whole company for $1.5 billion. It's a button that manifests itself as nothing more than a glowing image on a screen, but it represents a far more complex set of mechanical and formal issues than any door handle, keyboard or switch. And the

PayPal button was perhaps the most valuable switch ever made. Three years later, Hurley had designed something that was even more valuable. With two former colleagues from PayPal, Steve Chen and Jawed Karim, he produced a way of sharing videos. It could handle those created on mobile phones, which made it particularly attractive. It was called YouTube, and it was successful enough to be worth $1.65 billion to Google in 2006.

Back in the 1970s, the appearance of the first video cameras aimed at non-specialists was embraced by a generation of radicals as the means by which the grip of big media would be broken, giving ordinary people a chance to reflect their own lives and experiences. It was a vain hope. Crudely edited community video channels were never any kind of threat to the BBC. Set against Hollywood, they turned out to be anything but liberation, and were actually the sort of home movies that nobody wants to see.

At first sight YouTube looked like something entirely different. But within weeks of its launch there were some YouTube uploads that had been viewed by millions. Almost immediately, it had become a massively influential alternative to every TV network in the world. It was the medium in which music careers were launched, news was broken, terrorist threats were delivered, Holocaust deniers spread their venom, and kittens danced. This most likely was not what Hurley and his collaborators had in mind. There were a lot of myths around the foundation of YouTube that involved swapping dinner-party videos seamlessly, or locating live footage of Janet Jackson's famous wardrobe malfunction. Another version had it that YouTube would be some kind of dating site, popularity measured by likes.

The design problem that YouTube had to deal with was both technical – what once might have been called mechanical – and creative. How could the site handle all the different video formats? How would it deal with files that were too large to email, or for which it did not have a media player that worked? But it was also conceptual. Was YouTube going to be a site for people to post videos of the products that they wanted to sell on eBay? Was it a social medium, keeping people in touch with each other?

Hurley decided not to make it too specific . YouTube evolved into a medium that could be used for almost anything, rather than a specific language that could be used for only one form of transaction. Its function was closer to printing than it was to being an alphabet. And it arrived at a time when there was enough spare web capacity for a lot of content to be delivered inexpensively.

Chad told Bill Moggridge – pioneer designer in California's Silicon Valley and a former director of New York's Smithsonian Cooper-Hewitt, National Design Museum – that he did his best to make the YouTube website not look over-produced or corporate. And he gave it a name that suggested what it could be used for: a personal television network.

When YouTube was acquired by Google, it had less than 100 employees, a stark reminder that while technology was creating value, it wasn't doing much to create jobs. Kodak in its heyday had supported 140,000 highly skilled jobs.

YouTube's explosive success says a lot about the state of the world. It reflects just how rapid the pace of change has become. It took fifty years for the telephone to go from a prototype to market saturation, ten years for the fax machine to do the same, and just a matter of weeks for Apple's iPad to sell a million copies. It is a reflection of how much the practice of design has been transformed by the digital world. It is a demonstration of how quickly such developments can transform the way that we see the world, one that is brutally frank in its representation of success and failure. Every clip is measured. No talk, no post, nothing that I have done has ever clocked up more than 6,000 views. By the standards of YouTube, where millions of people see the same images in hours, that is less than invisible.

Every hour, months of content are uploaded to YouTube – so much material that nobody could ever see even a fraction of it in a single lifetime. It has created something analogous to the storerooms of a major museum, on a vast scale. When an institution has a collection of four or five million objects, it's impossible for any individual to make sense of it without the help of a catalogue. In its raw state it makes no sense, it has no meaning, there is no way of seeing or understanding it. There is no YouTube catalogue. YouTube makes sense of content through the relentless driver of popularity. It is the most-viewed clips that rise to the top of the search engines, and so reinforce their positions. It is a phenomenon that runs counter to the notional democracy of YouTube. If the images are not at the top of the tree, they become invisible, and the culture of YouTube is tilted irreversibly in directions that tend to reinforce existing tastes rather than challenge them.

IS FOR ZIP

One important way of thinking about design is to concentrate on the ordinary and the anonymous, as distinct from the artful and the self-conscious. It is to rebuke those who try to chart design through the biographies of celebrities, and a procession of attention-grabbing sculptural objects. It is an approach that has become the means to question one-dimensional readings of design that seek to present it as a form of self-expression, and instead to explore the reality of industrial production. Looking at anonymous design is a way to understand the contribution made by those who might not describe themselves as designers, but have nevertheless had a crucial impact on the world of things.

Anonymous design is a category that ranges from the mass-produced to the handcrafted. It is broad enough to have attracted the enthusiastic attention of both Victorian traditionalists and twentieth-century modernists. Japanese scissors, hand-stitched brogues from Jermyn Street, Georgian silver three-pronged forks, zip fasteners, aircraft propellers and paper clips are all objects that in their own ways can be considered as the product of anonymous design, even if they are actually the work of generations of individual craftsmen, or teams of engineers, all of whom have names, and many of whom feel a powerful personal connection with the objects for which they were responsible. These are objects unencumbered by obtrusive signatures, and by the arbitrary shape-making and the egotism that comes with them. When design is modest enough to allow itself to be anonymous, it is not being cynical or manipulative.

Yet the designer's signature, or what might be

called brand, has been an essential accompaniment to the development of design in its contemporary form. It is a phenomenon that has become more and more unappetizing just as it has become inescapable.

This is not a recent phenomenon. Josiah Wedgewood played his part in shaping the contemporary practice of design when he created a market for ceramic products that carried his company's brand. So did Christopher Dresser, one of the earliest designers to work as a consultant to multiple manufacturers, and to ask them for royalties for sales of his work.

Raymond Loewy, the first designer to appear on the cover of *Time* magazine, helped to turn design into a fairy-tale narrative free of complexities or subtleties. For the purposes of the fairy tale, the designer must become the all-encompassing genius, the heroic form-giver, ushering a new object into being through sheer force of personality. Loewy's career as an industrial designer began with the Gestetner duplicator in the 1930s. But to suggest that he designed it is to skip over a few key questions. All the things about the machine that allow it to do its job had been worked out before Loewy got involved. His role was no more, and no less, than to give the Gestetner a new skin. Selling the machine with a sleek, streamlined look, and just Loewy's name attached to it, rather than introducing the whole cast of contributors who made it possible, was a much simpler task than attempting to explain how the machine really came into existence.

Certainly there is no individual name linked to the paper clip. It is an object that belongs to the category of anonymous design. It is an ingenious and economical use of material to carry out a task. Such objects very often have complex histories. They are measured by multiple episodes of individual ingenuity rather than by single flashes of inspiration. A patent was issued in 1899 in the US to cover the copyright for a machine that could be used for making a paper clip. The clip itself, for which there is no patent, had existed long before the machine to make it.

The authorship of the zip has an equally complex story. Gideon Sundback, a Swedish-American inventor, filed a patent for the Hookless Fastener No. 2 with the US Patent Office in 1914. His work was a refinement of an idea for a fastener based on interlocking teeth that had been circulating among engineers for decades. Whitcomb Judson patented a design for a metal-clasp fastener in 1893, but it was difficult to make, and didn't work very well. Before Sundback, no one had managed to get the zip quite right. The hooks were either too weak to hold two surfaces together, or they wore out too soon to be useful.

Sundback designed a needle-like projection on the top of each nib, and put a dent in the corresponding position on the underside of the tooth, which held them all firmly in place. Even if one of the row of teeth came apart, the rest were still locked in. It was different enough from Judson's design for Sundback to get a patent.

The first customer for the new product, manufactured by the Hookless Fastener Company, was B. F. Goodrich, which started manufacturing rubber overshoes with a zip fastener in 1923. The zip turned putting the overshoes on and taking them off into a quick, single movement. Goodrich called it the Zip-er-Up, eventually contracting it to the Zipper, which in turn became the name of the fastener. And the Hookless Fastener Company renamed itself Talon at the same time.

In its first decade Hookless depended on Goodrich for most of its business. The zip was a relatively humble artefact, confined to footwear in its initial use. But by the 1930s, the zip had become an essential sign of modernity and it started to find customers everywhere. The zip was adopted by anyone in too much of a hurry to put up with the archaic customs of buttons. The distinctions of class and gender that buttons inevitably smuggle into almost any garment dependent on whether they are to the left or the right, precious metal, simple bone or cloth-covered, were made redundant by the zip. The workmanlike, no-nonsense, unfussy zip became the sign of the organized proletariat or those who wanted to be identified with it. Military uniforms started to adopt zips. The parka and the flying suit depended on them, as did the leather biker's jacket. The zip could be positioned diagonally like a lightening flash across the chest, as it appeared on Dan Dare's spacesuit, and added as a decorative flourish in entirely unnecessary places, such as the cuff in a belt-and-braces duplication.

Most highly charged in its symbolism is the use of the zip in place of fly buttons for trousers. Introduced after centuries of buttons, despite the risk of serious damage if incautiously raised, the zip came to be seen as a signal of shifting messages of sexual availability. The zip was celebrated by Erica Jong and deployed on *Sticky Fingers*, the Andy Warhol-designed Rolling Stones album cover.

Even if buttons are more demanding to deal with, they have survived. And with time, the zip has lost its functional associations with rational modernity. Paper clips, Japanese scissors, silver forks and zips are all objects that have supposedly eliminated superfluous excess. They are the products of a process of continuous refinement that have succeeded in achieving maximum economy of means by Darwinian evolution. The results of this process reflect the aesthetic preferences of modernism. It's a movement which always claimed to be allergic to style, but which paradoxically had the potential to become highly self-conscious about it. Marcel Breuer, for example, described his tubular steel furniture as 'styleless' and suggested that what motivated him was designing tools to equip people for daily life. But tubular steel for a while became a highly self-conscious sign of the aspirations of architects and designers, and in many cases of their clients' intentions to be taken as 'modern'.

Understanding the nature of an anonymous industrially made object has become a recurring preoccupation of design curators around the world. They bring together collections of paper clips and ballpoint pens, Post-it notes, clothes pegs and rubber gloves, and all the other humble masterpieces, as they are often called, chosen for their simplicity and fitness for purpose. Or, as in the case of the glove developed especially for shucking oysters, or the towel reduced to the size of a bar of soap by shrink-wrapping, for the ingenuity that goes into problem-solving for very specific tasks.

Putting such objects in museums can be traced to Bernard Rudofsky, an acerbic Austro-Hungarian-born critic and curator who moved to America. Rudofsky's best-known project was *Architecture without Architects*, an exhibition at the Museum of Modern Art in 1964. He brought together a wealth of material on what at the time was called vernacular building: waterwheels from Syria, mud fortresses from Libya, cave-dwellings and treehouses, which managed to address the demands of climate and function with a grace and a level of efficiency that eclipsed much of what conventional architectural practice is capable of. Rudofsky was fascinated by designs which, though conceived without the involvement of a professional architect, had aesthetic qualities that they could not match. He went further than looking at vernacular buildings and the nonchalant way that they dealt with such issues as climate control, which cause our energy-greedy era so much grief. With a gently mocking eye Rudofsky started questioning contemporary conventions about every aspect of daily life; he explored the underlying assumptions of how we eat, how we bathe and how we sit.

Anonymous design, or design without designers, might be understood in much the same way. We may not know who is responsible for the zip, in fact it may be impossible to be precise about assigning to it the name of any one designer. But there can be no doubt that the zip is one of many design innovations that defined the twentieth century. Some objects in this category are the product of the work of better-known individuals – the Tetra Pak, for example, developed by Ruben Rausing and Erik Wallenberg. Tetra Pak played a significant part in changing the way that a generation of Japanese growing up in the 1970s looked by making milk a part of the country's staple diet.

It was another piece of low-tech innovation, the sea container, that transformed not just the shipping industry but the docks that accommodated it, and the port cities that depended on them, and so the world. Shipping containers demanded bigger ships, and big open-air docks. As a result London's upstream docks closed, and within two decades were cleared to create the new financial district of Canary Wharf.

The ballpoint pen, or Biro, named for its inventor, is of course anything but anonymous, but it was the result of a simple but powerful insight into how to deliver an even line of ink in the most economical and efficient way.

By inviting us to examine objects that have become so familiar that they have disappeared from our conscious attention, we are being presented with a way to find what really drives design. It is an effective way to address the tension between the myth-making version of design and the reality of step-by-step refinements, between the cult of the individual genius and the way in which enterprises are driven by teams and groups.

There is no styling or egotism to a safety pin, or a paper clip; they are as simple and as universal as a reef knot. The comparison between the modesty of anonymous production and the brittle egotism of signature design is apparently about reclaiming design from superficial styling and celebrity. But for all the aura of sanctity that comes with the authenticity of the unselfconscious and the anonymous, the closer you look at the anonymous the more complex the question of what it actually represents becomes. Anonymity can be presented as a kind of automatic writing, the inevitable outcome of a practical approach to problem-solving; a kind of functionalism. But anonymous design is still the product of individuals, and individual decisions. And the zip retains its sense of design outside time. Velcro might be taking its place for some uses, but the zip, after more than a century, is still a small marvel.

Acknowledgements

This book began as a conventional dictionary. That turned out to be a category that was one of the first casualties of the digital explosion that has overtaken publishing. But Stefan McGrath, who had the idea of doing it in the first place, always encouraged a certain degree of subjectivity. With the support of my editor, Helen Conford, that subjectivity, or enthusiasm, is the starting point for this book. Much of this book is based on the places I have seen, and the people I have talked to over the years as an editor, first at *Blueprint*, then at *Domus*. When I was at the *Observer*, Jane Ferguson was a particularly encouraging editor, dispatching me to meet Nathaniel Kahn in California, and to write about returning to Belgrade, among many other things.

The *London Review of Books* gave me the chance to reflect on Léon Krier. Elena Foster got me thinking about the complex relationship between artists and architects. Johanna Agerman Ross of Disegno was responsible for my meeting Orhan Pamuk. Rolf Fehlbaum's elegant speech at the Boymans Museum in Rotterdam raised the issue of imperfection for me.

Debating the rights and wrongs of Ruskin with

Grayson Perry at Charleston (I lost, humiliatingly), made me re-read *The Seven Lamps of Architecture*. Ricky Burdett of the LSE's Urban Age project got me to Mumbai to see Dharavi. Ron Arad took me to see the museum he designed in Holon.

But above all the Design Museum where I have worked ever since I started writing this book has been the best possible vantage point from which to explore the contemporary world of architecture and design.